THROUGH THE UNKNOWN, REMEMBERED GATE

THROUGH THE UNKNOWN, REMEMBERED GATE

A Spiritual Journey

EMILY BENEDEK

SCHOCKEN BOOKS

New York

*While all of the incidents in this book are true, some of the
names and personal characteristics of the individuals
involved have been changed in order to protect their privacy.*

All rights reserved under International and Pan-American Copyright
Conventions. Published in the United States by Schocken Books,
a division of Random House, Inc., New York, and simultaneously in
Canada by Random House of Canada Limited, Toronto. Distributed
by Pantheon Books, a division of Random House, Inc., New York.

Schocken and colophon are registered trademarks of Random House, Inc.

Grateful acknowledgment is made to Harcourt, Inc. and Faber and
Faber Ltd. for permission to reprint excerpts from "Little Gidding"
from *Four Quartets* by T. S. Eliot. Copyright © 1942 by T. S. Eliot
and renewed 1970 by Esme Valerie Eliot. Rights outside the United
States in *Four Quartets* from *Collected Poems 1909–1962*, adminis-
tered by Faber and Faber Ltd., London. Reprinted by permission of
Harcourt, Inc. and Faber and Faber Ltd.

Library of Congress Cataloging-in-Publication Data

Benedek, Emily.
Through the unknown, remembered gate : a spiritual journey /
Emily Benedek.
p.   cm.
ISBN 0-8052-4138-8
1. Benedek, Emily—Religion.   2. Jews—United States—Return to
Orthodox Judaism.   3. Judaism—United States.   I. Title
E184.37 B46 2001   296.7'15'092—dc21   [B]   00-063571

www.schocken.com

Book design by Trina Stahl

Printed in the United States of America
First Edition
2   4   6   8   9   7   5   3   1

For
Hannah Shira and Noa Arielle

We shall not cease from exploration
And the end of all our exploring
Will be to arrive where we started
And know the place for the first time.
Through the unknown, remembered gate
When the last of the earth left to discover
Is that which was the beginning . . .

—T. S. Eliot, *Four Quartets*

Contents

∞

Preface · xi

One BLINDED · 3

Two WHAT IS A JEW? · 23

Three EXILE · 42

Four LEARNING TO SEE · 72

Five FIRST STEPS · 121

Six THE TRUE LIVES OF STORIES · 160

Seven HOME · 178

Eight DESIRE · 233

Nine CONGREGATION B'NAI JESHURUN · 239

Ten IF NOT NOW, WHEN? · 282

Eleven LETTERS FROM ISRAEL · 295

Twelve WHAT NEXT? · 314

Notes · 331

Acknowledgments · 334

Preface

✺

WHEN THE FUTURE Rebbe of Vishnitz was a young man, he was sent out from his village to wander for a few years. It was customary for spiritual aspirants to do this, to "see what was going on in golus" as Rabbi Shlomo Carlebach, who told this story, put it. One day during his journey, the young man, Mendel, came upon a house in the forest, in front of which a little girl danced. Mendel was struck by this unusual sight, a little girl all alone, dancing to her own music, and he approached her. The little girl saw him watching her, and after a time, she asked him if he would like something to eat. He said yes he would. And so the little girl went into her house and carried out a chair, and then she went back into the house and carried out a table, and she went back inside and brought out some food and drink. As he ate, the young man told her his name was Mendel, and she told him her name was Rivkelch and she was eight years old. They made a deep connection. Before Mendel left, Rivkeleh told him that whenever he should find himself near her house, she hoped he would come and see her so she could give him some food and drink. Over the next few years, he came to see her three times.

The young man returned to his village, and at the age of eighteen he became a rabbi. Ten years passed, and his reputation grew until he was known far and wide. But all was not well with Rivkeleh. When she was eighteen, she came down with a mysterious illness that left her unable to walk. Her parents called all the doctors they could, and none of them knew what was wrong with Rivkeleh. She became very despondent and she thought of her old friend Mendel, whom she understood was now the Rebbe of Vishnitz. Something told her that he might be able to help her, and she asked her parents if they would bring her to see him.

But the parents told her not to be silly—they had taken her to all the doctors, and none of them had been able to help. Why did she think the Vishnitzer could help her? Besides, he was an important man and very busy and had many other things to attend to.

When Rivkeleh was twenty, she was no better. Again, she asked her parents to take her to the Vishnitzer, and they said no, he couldn't help her, she might just as well get used to the way she was. And then she was twenty-five, then twenty-eight, and she begged her parents to take her to see the Rebbe of Vishnitz, but they refused.

Finally, she told them that if they didn't take her, she would throw herself down in the street and roll there. Well, of course, they couldn't allow a spectacle like that, so they put her in a wagon and began the trip to Vishnitz. All the while, they warned her that the rebbe had probably forgotten her, and further, he might not even be there, and if he was, he might not see her, because he would surely have many other people waiting for him.

Meanwhile, the rebbe told the students in his bais midrash, the study hall, that he was expecting a visit from someone very special. Before she arrived, he wanted them to cover every ledge with candles. He wanted them to light as many candles as would fit in the room. He wanted hundreds of candles on every surface.

Rivkeleh and her parents arrived at three o'clock in the morning, before the dawn, when it was still dark. The last part of the ride had been the most difficult for Rivkeleh. Her parents had been particularly hard on her, and she was in a very low state. She worried that she would take up too much room on the floor, that Mendel might not see her or remember her. But when they approached the bais midrash, the first thing they saw was that the court was ablaze with light. And as soon as they carried Rivkeleh inside, a Chassid ran over and whispered to her, "The rebbe is waiting for you."

Rivkeleh was put down on the floor, where she lay flat as a board. When the rebbe arrived, he walked over and said, "Rivkeleh, did you think I could forget you? I have not forgotten you for one day of my life." And he lay down beside her, flat on the floor. And Rivkeleh's soul returned to her. Then the Vishnitzer said: "You helped me before when I was hungry, when I needed you, and now I need you again. And what I need is for you to get up from the floor and walk over to the table of food and bring it to me. I need you to bring me some food. Please, Rivkeleh, get up from the floor and bring me some food again."

And so Rivkeleh, who had once danced life into the young man and animated his lonely heart, saw that he needed her again. And she picked herself up from the floor and walked to the table. She carried over a chair, and then she carried over the table. And then she brought him nourishment, so that he could eat and drink.

THROUGH THE UNKNOWN, REMEMBERED GATE

Chapter One

⚶

BLINDED

THE HORIZON STRETCHES before me, yellow and flat and dry, marked off by run-down cafés, garages, small warehouses. I brake at the intersection that marks the halfway point of my shortcut between Lemmon Avenue and Harry Hines Boulevard. Above me, the traffic light hangs absurdly high; it twists in the breeze, baleful, an omniscient red eye, looking out for trouble.

When the light changes, I continue past Judge Roy Bean's Saloon and Sowell's Liquors, inching my car over the railroad tracks. I check left and right; not only do roads meet here from five directions, but the intersection is also complicated by the raised cicatrix of the railroad tracks. As I pass, I catch sight of a train engine on one of the tracks to my left. It appears to be slowly entering the intersection at an oblique angle. I start, but when I look again, I see it is parked, and remains parked, in back of an oddly out of place Chinese take-out restaurant. As I proceed, I have a funny sensation in my eyes, as if the sky ahead of me had hiccuped, the air had given way.

I take a sharp left and continue past cheap, one-story offices, a sales lot for truck cabs, a neighborhood of shabby bungalows. Most of the city of Dallas seems immune to zoning of any kind, so gas stations bump up against housing complexes, offices are sandwiched between truck lots. Although Dallas has its share of luxurious and beautiful neighborhoods, many areas lack the slightest aesthetic note.

I am headed in the direction of Parkland Hospital, one of two spots in Dallas toward which all roads point, and which still evokes the same images it did when its name and façade were burned into the public consciousness twenty-eight years ago. The other spot, not too far away, the heart of downtown, is the Texas Book Depository, from whose sixth-floor window Lee Harvey Oswald shot President John F. Kennedy.

Just before Parkland Hospital, as I pass Majors Scientific Bookstore and roll down the slope past a 7-Eleven onto Harry Hines Boulevard, it happens again, a wrinkle, a tremble in my eyes, a crumpling of space.

THE NEXT MORNING, I wake up and I cannot see. I run my hands over the woven bedspread, slide my legs open and closed like scissors. The sheets are not twisted around me, nor am I sweaty. There is no sign of a nighttime struggle. Rather, the bed is perfectly neat, as if I had hardly moved.

I feel strangely calm. The adrenaline of panic concentrates me, makes my muscles smooth and coordinated, allows me to think clearly. I close my right eye and look straight ahead with my left. The image is clear. I see my host Nancy's collection of mercury glass on the built-in bookshelves that flank the fireplace. I see odd vases, door-knobs, reflecting globes of mirrored, luminous silver glass. I see two ivy topiaries on either side of the mantelpiece.

I move my eye left and right and up and down, and it moves where I direct it. I then close my left eye and look with my right. I can see out of that eye, too. Again, I open both together, and all I can see is a great blur. I look back to the mercury glass, and I realize I am see-ing two of everything. I shut my eyes again. I feel sleepy, as if a spell had taken hold of me in the night.

I can see the sunlight, which pours through the windows, on the inside of my lids. I have the thought that when I open my eyes again, the blurring will be gone. I don't concentrate on clear sight, though. I don't try to wish it into existence. In a strange way, alarming though it is, the clouding feels comfortable. I am tired of trying to under-stand my life; I am weary. I open my eyes again. I mentally walk around the blur, feel my way through it, as I look from the mantel to the windows and toward the living room. I feel removed from the scene, separated by a membrane of unreality. My experience in Dal-las in the nine months since I arrived has been so bizarre, so tortured and incomprehensible, that waking up unable to see seems to make perverse sense.

I sit up in bed and swing my legs around to the floor. I stand and realize I feel a bit shaky, so I shut one eye to create a clear image and head for the bathroom. I flick on the light and walk right up to the sink and look in the mirror. I have four eyes, two noses, and two mouths. I shut one eye and look at my face. There are no strange rashes or awful distortions. My complexion is clear, my face relaxed. I look at my left eye. It looks normal, light brown, luminous, rising to a light green around the edge of the iris. I close my left eye and examine my right eye the same way, and it too looks familiar and fine.

THE WAITING ROOM of the outpatient clinic at Parkland Hospital has stackable, upholstered chairs in bright colors. Magazines like *Horse and Rider* and *Popular Mechanics* are scattered on tables. I sit down with a copy of the *New Yorker* that I have brought from home and a yellow legal pad, which I lean against my chest. I cross my legs and set my bag beside me. It occurs to me that with my posture and this pad I am saying, "I am taking notes. Don't try any funny business." I am not at all sure what kind of doctors I'll find in Dallas.

A middle-aged farm couple is sitting opposite me. The man is thin, with watery blue eyes, and an attitude in his body of trust, trust for the authority of the doctors who will come out and treat him. His wife's gray meringue of hair does not move, even when she leans over to pick up the magazine that has slipped from her lap.

Within a few minutes, I am ushered into an examination room and asked to sit in what looks like a white dentist's chair. The room is clean and brand-new. I settle in with my magazine until I am joined by a young doctor who appears thin, pinched, and very white. He has mousy brown hair. He asks me to read eye charts. He peers into my eyes and asks me to roll them this way and that. He leaves, quickly returns with another doctor, a short woman with curly, shoulder-length hair and spectacles. I want to like her, because she seems competent and serious. She hands me a card, which shows she is a neuroophthalmologist and is board-certified in ophthalmology as well as neurology.

I tell her I have double vision, though I can see fine if I look out of only one eye. She sees that when I look to the right, my right eye seems to give up before reaching its farthest point. "Cannot bury sclera into right lateral epicanthic fold," I watch her write on her paper. She asks me if I have any other symptoms. All I can think of is that I have had a stiff neck for a few weeks, something I get when I am tense. "Soft meningeal symptoms," she adds.

She fits me with different lenses that measure the extent to which I cannot look to the right. She gives me a shot of an enzyme called edrophonium to see if I am suffering from an immune system disorder called myasthenia gravis, the disease from which Aristotle Onassis suffered that required him to tape up his eyelids with Band-Aids. My belly shakes as the drug passes through me, but it has no effect on the double vision. This, she tells me, means I do not have myasthenia gravis. I'm not sure if I am relieved or not. There is a lot of bustling and measuring, but no one says much to me.

After more tests, she writes down "right sixth nerve paresis" and explains that the muscle that pulls my right eye to the outside, away from my nose, is called the right lateral rectus muscle. It is fired by the sixth nerve, a long, narrow filament that travels from the brain stem all the way around the outside of the skull to the eye. There is one on each side, serving each eye. The sixth nerve on my right side, she explains to me, is not firing properly, and it is making my right eye just a tiny bit slower than my left. She does not know why the nerve is misfiring and preventing the two eyes from tracking together, the cause of my double vision. Before I leave, Dr. Zimmerman says she would like me to get a magnetic-resonance-imaging scan, an MRI, to see if there is any abnormality in my brain. The thought of a tumor had occurred to me. For a moment, I brighten. A heaviness lifts at the thought that there might be an explanation for the catastrophes that have befallen me since my arrival in Dallas. Perhaps a brain tumor would explain why my relationship with my boyfriend, Craig, collapsed, or why my job as a television news reporter and producer was falling apart.

When the neuroophthalmologist finishes her exam, I walk out of the clinic office holding a card on which is written the date and time of my appointment for an MRI scan. Before I leave the building, I stop at a pharmacy on the first floor and buy a black eye patch, as Dr. Zimmerman has suggested. "Remember to change it from eye to eye," she tells me, "so both will get exercised." I laugh to myself. I will look eccentric, won't I, eye patch on one eye or the other, changed at will, as if it were some bizarre fashion accessory?

TWO DAYS LATER, my friend Nancy drives me to the MRI, ice clinking in the smoky green glass of diet soda she holds in her right hand, cigarette burning in her left, gold bracelets falling prettily around her Rolex watch. We are in her BMW sedan, which is as heavy as a tank, and hard to maneuver even without the Pepsi glass and ice cubes. Nancy is a beauty. I met Nancy at a gym in Highland Park. She looked to me like she belonged on Nantucket, and I told her so. It turned out she loved Nantucket, and her garden was full of Nantucket hydrangeas.

Now, six months later, she is no longer working out. She is in the middle of a divorce from her husband of twenty years, a man with whom she has two sons. He has left her for one of her friends, a lawyer who works in his office and is herself married to another man. Many of the women I have met in Dallas are embroiled in painful, humiliating relationships. One of them, Tammy, a former Oklahoma beauty queen and Oklahoma U. student, married a hefty, rich lawyer who wears custom-made suits and $1,500 English shoes. Tammy wants a baby, but her husband would rather eat than have sex. Instead, the couple bought a miniature dog named Dunhill that

Tammy carries around in her handbag. When Dunhill finds his tiny feet on an Oriental rug, he gets an uncontrollable urge to pee. Tammy is suicidal and taking Prozac.

The slag of Dallas is dragging Nancy down, pulling her with it into the mire of emptiness, materialism, puffed-up dreams gone sour. She sees all this, and even articulates it, but she is not strong enough to free herself from it. After Craig and I broke up, she very kindly offered me a room in her house, and I accepted.

The medical office with the MRI machine is at the end of a freshly graded road carved out of a remnant of woods in downtown Dallas, just beyond Sonny Bryan's Smokehouse barbecue. We roll up the curving road, past brand-new medical buildings, and park before a one-story office. Nancy throws her cigarette on the ground before we step in, but I am already saturated with cigarette smoke. I wonder momentarily if my eye has gone haywire from a couple of weeks of secondhand smoke.

After I check in, I am asked to take off my clothes in a changing room off the main corridor. With whitewashed oak walls and white cotton curtains at the stall doors, it looks like a nice public swimming pool or a health club. Nancy is making dirty jokes about the paper gown I am putting on, and I'm getting punchy. I pad out in a hospital johnny and disposable slippers and walk toward the MRI machine. I am instructed to lie down on a sliding chamber that looks like an enormous outstretched tongue. A quiet, dutiful young man explains that the tongue will be redrawn back into the mouth of the machine, and I will hear a loud thumping. I am not to move, scratch my nose, wiggle, or stretch, or I'll blur the $1,000 picture that is being taken. I can't believe how lucky I am that my new health insurance became effective the very day my eye got blurry.

It isn't so bad inside the box. I do not feel claustrophobic. I keep myself distracted and calm by thinking of gardens I have loved and visited in person and in my mind. When I get out, Nancy smiles at me. I look toward the man who is reading the screens. I can tell from his expression that something is wrong.

"You didn't see any extraordinarily huge tumors did you?" I ask. I realize I have phrased my question in such a way as to give him an out.

"We're not allowed to interpret the pictures," the man says. I look at his name tag and see he is a radiologist in training.

"But, no," he adds, "I didn't see any extraordinarily large tumors."

"Come on," says Nancy, diet drink raised high, right hand digging into her large Louis Vuitton bag. "What you need is a cigarette. The doctors have it all wrong about cigarettes. Cigarettes make you healthy." I laugh, in spite of myself. I have fallen so deeply into the absurd, I take one and light up.

UNTIL DR. ZIMMERMAN looks at the scan and calls me back, I have a window of peace, a temporary reprieve. For a few more hours at least, I remain free of the news that may turn my life upside down. There is nothing I can do to avert my fate. I think about the many times I have felt caught between the ongoing present and the future, measuring the hours or minutes before an exam or a speech, a track meet or a swim race, filling them with mental games, preparations. But now, there is nothing to do, nothing to prepare for.

I am standing in the living room, looking out into the leaves of a huge pin oak when the telephone rings.

Dr. Zimmerman gets right to the point. "The brain scan was not normal."

"Yes," I hear myself say. In my head, it seems as if I am listening to an engine starting, turning over, getting ready to race—to race away. I reach for a pen and begin to take notes.

"I have received the radiologist's report," she says, all business. "The MRI revealed extensive lesions in the white matter of your brain. These types of lesions suggest an idiopathic demyelinating disease."

Then she pauses, gives me a moment to speak.

"What is the white matter?" I ask. She explains it is the fatty material surrounding the nerves, like the plastic coating of an extension cord. The marks on the MRI indicate inflammation of the material that protects my nerves from short-circuiting.

"And what is a demyelinating disease?"

"It causes the breakdown of the myelin, the white matter. This can lead to problems with sensation or motor control."

"I have never heard of demyelinating disease," I say. "Is there any more familiar name for this?"

She hesitates, then she says, "Multiple sclerosis is one form."

"Multiple sclerosis!" I say. I know very little about it, but the word conjures images of wheelchairs and phonathons. That's impossible, I think. There is absolutely no relation in my mind between that word and myself.

She says, "It is an autoimmune disease, like arthritis or lupus. The immune system attacks the white matter, perceiving it as the enemy."

At this point, I am struggling just to keep track of what she is saying.

"And what does 'idiopathic' mean?" I ask.

"It means," she says, "that the cause is unknown."

I feel an almost uncontrollable desire to run backward as fast as I can, to rewind the tape of my life of the past year. I think of a story by Delmore Schwartz called "In Dreams Begin Responsibilities" in which the main character is viewing a film of his parents' courtship. In the middle of the movie—or the dream—he stands up and shouts at the characters on the screen before him, urging them not to go ahead, not to get married, not to step into the future he knows will cause terrible misery for all concerned.

I feel like screaming at myself to jump off the film that is rolling before me. Surely I have found my way onto the wrong strip of celluloid. Just let me slip off and turn back home, back to New York, and this nightmare will disappear. No more flea infestations, no more painful memories of Craig, no more small-town TV politics and back-stabbings, no more bizarre illnesses only other people — strangers — can get.

"There is one other diagnosis that is possible, however," Dr. Zimmerman adds. "And that is Lyme disease." She asks me if I have been in the woods recently. I have indeed. A couple of months ago, just after Craig told me he would be moving out, we drove to Tyler, Texas, to see the city's famed azalea gardens. We hiked off into the woods at one point, and Craig had touched my arm suggestively. "It wouldn't mean anything," he quickly said, noticing the question on my face. "You know I get turned on when I'm in the woods." At that point, nothing would have surprised me about him, and I walked away. It would have been too fitting if I had been bitten by a diseased tick on that day.

Dr. Zimmerman asks me if I noticed any red bite on a leg or arm, any bull's-eye rash. No, I tell her, I don't remember noticing anything like this.

"Lyme disease has been documented in Texas. In its advanced stages, it can mimic demyelinating diseases. I'd like to schedule you to come in tomorrow so we can run some blood tests."

I place the phone back into its cradle. I look around the room and realize there is nothing familiar around me. I am in a stranger's house, and I have lived among strangers for the past five years. I am alone in a world I seem no longer able to master. I lower my face into my hands, and I cry. I am scared for myself. In one moment, all the expectations I held, a long life of writing and learning and exploration, possibly a husband and children, may have been smashed. In their place is the possibility of a long horizon of interruptions, struggles, afflictions. How could it be I have a body like a piece of electronic equipment that does not work, but suddenly shorts itself out? How could my body fail me in such a way?

I call my father.

I weep again as I tell him the news. But he listens calmly, and I am grateful for that. He is a physicist who studies medical matters and he does not give much weight to the possible diagnoses offered by Dr. Zimmerman and tells me that diagnosing disease can be a tricky thing and a fine art. He gives me the name of a former student of his, an M.D.-Ph.D., who is now a neurologist at the University of Pennsylvania and who might help to interpret the test results. My father trains students to be medical researchers. Many of them earn simultaneous advanced medical and scientific degrees. This is what my father hoped I would do, and I began Harvard as a physics major. The idea crosses my mind that my current predicament is punishment for what seems now to have been a feckless decision to become a writer instead.

After I put down the phone, I get up from the chair and walk to the piano. I sit down on the bench and play a few measures of the ragtime I used to know, then stop and stare at the blur of white and black keys. I feel the smooth, heavy ivories under my fingers, and I stop for a moment, absorbed by their rich sensuality. I am aware of the thick pile of the Chinese carpet under my feet. I feel my three middle toes stretched over the cold brass piano pedal. I feel the air against my skin and realize I may not depend on clear sight as much as I think I do. I feel my senses changing, waking up, listening in a new way. I wonder if my hearing will perk up to countervail the loss of my vision. I think that in some circumstances I can use touch to make up for the lack of depth perception in looking out of one eye. I think how adaptable the body is. If one muscle fails to work, there may be another one that can be taught to take up the slack.

I stand up and walk back into my room. I put on my glasses. I have taped a piece of glossy magazine paper over my right lens so that I can read without squeezing my eye closed. I sit down in an arm chair, turn on the radio, and adjust the dial. I hit on an Aerosmith tune, "Dream On," that I used to love in high school. After listening to a few lines, I begin to sing along with the music. I stand up and swing my hips over my feet, then move into a little dance. I follow with my hands and my arms, cutting small paisley shapes in the air. I step, I snap my fingers, I sing.

OVER THE NEXT FEW DAYS, my right eye gets worse. I notice that when I look straight ahead into the mirror, it has started to wander toward my nose, like some fractured Cubist face. I am horrified at the thought of looking cross-eyed. Eyes out of control suggest to me thoughts or souls out of control, and I think—wrongly?—that people with such eyes are idiots or criminals. I realize that I can keep my eyes pointed in the same direction if I look slightly to my left, a position where the right lateral rectus muscle plays a smaller role.

My mother calls me. She tells me that she knows a woman who has multiple sclerosis. She is in her sixties. "It's not so bad," she says. "She walks with a cane, but she gets around." I cringe at her words. I cannot even think of this now. My mother wants to know if I'd like her to read aloud what *The Principles of Medicine* says about the disease. No, I say. But she is determined. She begins to read. When she speaks the words "possible loss of bladder control" into the receiver, I hang up.

I call my father's former student. He tells me that the objects seen on the MRI are "UBOs," or unidentified bright objects. In fact, they are water, and indicate discrete locations of inflammation. I ask why, if I have several of these spots, I have only one symptom, and he tells me the brain has a lot of extra capacity, many underused neurons. This fact calms me somewhat.

He goes on to say there are several types of demyelinating diseases. No one understands why the immune system attacks the myelin; one theory maintains that there is an as-yet-unidentified virus that resides in the myelin and stimulates the immune system to attack. But no such bug has ever been found. The disease takes two forms: exacerbating-remitting, which is more common and in which symptoms come and go, and chronic-progressive, in which symptoms persist and worsen. The disease is more common in women, and more common in Americans born north of the Mason-Dixon line. There are treatments for relieving the symptoms, but there is no cure.

I drive back over to Southwestern Medical Center to the library. I find the neurology stacks, and I work my way through the shelf. I read and look at pictures of diseased brains. After three hours, I gather up the books that are spread around me on the floor and replace them on the shelves. I walk over to an easy chair and sit down.

I open my right eye, which I have held closed to read and navigate my way around the library. I look into the blur, and then follow it as I look at the stacks of books, the sturdy wooden tables, and the medical students hunched over them. Retreating behind the fog is again comfortable, as if I were removed from everything in view. Again, I have an odd feeling of familiarity. I have no idea why this should be, but a disease that can come and go, can leave me blind or paralyzed and then release me back to normality on its own whim, seems not entirely unfamiliar, not alien, somehow, to my mental fabric. At some primitive level, it makes sense to me that at a moment's notice I could lose something as mundane and yet as crucial as the movement of an eye.

As I sort through the clouds of my thoughts, I hear the voice of a child prattling somewhere among the stacks. That cheery babble seems delightfully out of place here in the medical school library. After a few minutes, I see a young man leaning on a rolling cart of books, pushing it slowly down the aisle. He is studying a volume that lies open atop the cart. Then I see that a little girl is riding along on top of the cart, like a book herself. I look again, trying to figure out this scene, and I gather this man, possibly a graduate student trying to get some reading done, is not reshelving books but, rather, trying to get some pages digested while also trying to entertain his little daughter. The game of pushing the cart is their compromise.

I realize I have never felt so alone in my whole life.

A FEW DAYS after my blood tests, Dr. Zimmerman calls. "I have good news," she says. "Your Lyme titer was positive."

Before I can register the rush of excitement I feel, she tells me that the antibody titers are notoriously unreliable. However, she says, the lab technicians repeated the test, and came back with a second, even more positive, result. She wants me to take a course of intravenous antibiotic treatment.

I talk to my father again, and with cool, uncomforting logic he tells me that as a matter of science, a repeat test that comes back with better numbers to confirm a hoped-for result is suspect. I make more telephone calls to Lyme experts and to neurologists. The East Coast Lyme specialists are doubtful that the disease has made its way to Texas. However, I come across a cover article in *Texas Medicine* that announces its presence in Texas, and describes what seems to match my symptoms and test results precisely: "a syndrome that suggests multiple sclerosis, accompanied in some cases by hypodense areas compatible with demyelination seen on magnetic resonance imaging, has been reported." Lyme disease is hard to identify and even harder to treat, I learn, but at least there is something to try. Dr. Zimmerman says that even if it turns out that *Borrelia burgdorferi*, the bacteria that causes Lyme disease, is not present in my nervous system, the antibiotic treatment will not hurt me. Further, if there is a chance that I have been infected, it would be imprudent of her not to recommend antibiotics.

Later that evening, I call my father back. I tell him what I have learned, and I outline my thinking on the matter, and he says, "It's good to hear your bright, quick mind." I burst into tears. And judging from the strained silence I hear over the line, so does he.

Against his advice, I decide to go ahead and take the antibiotics.

I am admitted to the Zale Lipshy University Hospital, and begin to receive Rocephin. A line is inserted in a vein on the back of my hand, and a large plastic bag hanging from an IV pole drips one gram of medicine into my arm every twelve hours. After a few days, Dr. Zimmerman finds a home health care company that will provide me with the supplies to give myself the Rocephin at home. I can no longer stay with Nancy, as her son, in whose room I was staying, is back from camp. Another friend of mine, Wendy Zellner, the bureau chief of *Business Week* magazine, offers me a room in her house while she is away on vacation. I water her flowers, feed her cat, and enjoy her sunny, pleasant garden. Because by this time almost all the veins in my hands have collapsed, a plastic tube, called a pic line, is inserted into a vein in my arm and run up almost to my heart. Twice a day, I attach this line, which is stoppered with a valve near my wrist, a Heparin Lock, to a bottle of Rocephin. As it drips in, I feel I can taste a metallic, alcoholic flavor, which the nurse tells me can happen with a pic line. A week or so into the antibiotic treatment, I get another symptom. A patch of my skin, a perfect square, from my breast to my pelvis, and from the center of my abdomen to the center of my back, like half a corset, becomes slightly numb. When I touch that area with my fingers, it feels different, duller, though not completely without feeling. On occasion, a touch to the skin feels sandpapery. This is called a radiculopathy, I learn, a symptom, among other illnesses, of advanced Lyme disease.

I DEVELOPED DOUBLE VISION on August 1. I was admitted to the hospital on August 21. On August 27, I was discharged and able to drive with both eyes open. On September 2, I experienced a radiculopathy on my torso. On September 11, I completed my Rocephin regimen, and the pic line was removed from my arm.

On September 12, my eyesight was back to normal. On examination on September 18, I had perfect vision—(20/15)—and Dr. Zimmerman could not detect or elicit double vision. The radiculopathy had almost disappeared.

Although I can see perfectly again, because of my imprecise diagnosis—of diseases that vary significantly from patient to patient—I do not know if or when the double vision or other symptoms may recur, and if or when they do, whether they will again disappear. I know only one thing for sure: I don't believe my nightmare has been meaningless. The symptoms were too appropriate for the state of existential dread in which I found myself that year in Texas. This ill-ness—whatever its medical diagnosis—with all its uncertainties and its grim threat of blindness or paralysis or worse, seemed a perfectly apt manifestation of the complete contingency I had felt in Dallas, a disconnection, literally, of my consciousness, or my spirit, from my body and from the physical world.

I believe there is a key. I feel the cause of my illness was a deep psychic confusion, a rupture from myself. I believe that the cause of this illness was inside myself, in my psyche and in my soul.

I believe this because even as I experienced the worst of my mys-terious neurological symptoms—strange beepings and buzzings and numbnesses—I felt in me a joy and a resilience I did not know I had. When I got the news over the telephone that the MRI had revealed an abnormality in my central nervous system, I wept, yes. But then I began to dance. I danced and I sang to myself, propelled by a sense of hope that mystified me, and does still.

I think many times of those moments. Why, in the depth of my fear, at a time of complete helplessness, had I begun to sing? To what can I attribute the wonder that felt like a summons toward something infinitely and profoundly engaging? I believe that in naked fear, stripped of all defenses, literally blinded, I had a moment of true sight, of true insight. I saw something pulsing at the center of my being, something out of view of the blood tests and brain scans, something larger than nerves, immune systems, spirochetes, neurons.

I saw, I believe, my first inklings of the divine.

TWO WEEKS LATER, I open the telephone book to the letter "J." I am not looking for salvation, or even a place to pray. I don't know what I'm looking for yet. This is what I tell myself: I have found a new apartment and I need to write some freelance pieces to pay the rent, and the thought occurs to me that I might write about Jews.

Under "Jewish" there are four listings: Jewish Community Center, Jewish Family Service, Jewish Federation of Greater Dallas, Jews for Jesus. I call the Federation and learn that there are 40,000 Jews in Dallas and seven synagogues. I call the Community Center and learn that it offers adult education classes, athletic facilities, after-school activities for kids, and hosts an annual book fair. I have never been to a Jewish Community Center. I don't think the Boston suburb in which I grew up had one, and during the four years I lived in New York after graduation from college, it never occurred to me to learn about Judaism.

I request a catalogue of classes. It arrives in the mail in two days, and flipping through it, I am filled with the same intense excitement I felt when I opened the Harvard course catalogue. On every page is an invitation to view a new part of the world. Reading the Harvard catalogue from cover to cover every semester, I felt as though I was searching for a vital clue, some answer that would change everything. I feel the same excitement now. I write out a check for $35 and enroll in two classes, one on Martin Buber's translation of Psalms and another on Jewish mysticism.

THE APPOINTED CLASSROOM at the Jewish Community Center is full. About fifty people are seated around four long tables that run the perimeter of the room. At one end, under a clock, is a portable blackboard in a wooden frame. Across the room hangs a set of long-horns. I glance up at the clock and see it is one minute before the scheduled start of the class on mysticism, yet there is no sign of a teacher.

I begin to feel irritated by the increasing volume of the friendly chatter around me. I look at the clock again, and it is two minutes past the hour. People seem to know each other; I overhear talk of other classes, family news, synagogue gossip. After scanning the front of the room again, I see that a man has entered the door and quietly taken a seat at the head of the class. He is of medium height and build and wears his hair in a corona of shiny white curls. He is dressed in jeans and a denim vest. He scrunches up his eyes and surveys the room.

The din continues. After another two minutes observing this man look over the class in studied disinterest, I begin to feel tense. I feel he is testing us and we are failing. I fix my attention on him as I try silently to will the rest of the class into order. No one else seems to notice. I find myself stifling an impulse to scream when, at exactly five minutes past the hour, everyone stops talking, as if responding to some shared but inaudible bell.

Without a word, as if he had been expecting this reaction all along, the man pulls an embroidered yarmulke out of his pocket, and with an unselfconscious flourish, attaches it to his hair with a bobby pin. He places his hands over the cloth and pulls it down, fixing it in place. He folds his hands together before him, bows his head, and begins to utter words I don't understand. "Baruch atah adonai, eloheinu melech ha-olam . . ." he says, and I recognize the first line of Hebrew blessings that is familiar to me from my childhood.

"Blessed art thou, O Lord our God, King of the Universe," is how my father translated it, reading from the prayer book he kept in the corner cabinet of our dining room. He read the prayer and we made a blessing over the wine and the challah. In the prayers I remembered, though, the opening was followed by such words as "who bringeth forth the fruit of the vine" or "who grants us the privilege of kindling the Chanukah lights." But the words this man speaks are different. I listen carefully, trying to understand them. The only word I recognize is "Torah." I realize then that he has thanked God for granting us the privilege of studying Torah.

Tears rush to my eyes. In an automatic effort to conceal my emotions, I fight them back. What has moved me so much, I wonder, and as I wonder this, another wave of tears comes.

"My name is Scholem Groesberg," the man says. He speaks in a Brooklyn accent so broad and so familiar that it instantly turns my tears into a huge smile. "I am the rabbi of a small congregation in Irving, Texas. I welcome you, one and all, to the study of Torah."

After class, I approach Rabbi Groesberg and timidly ask him if his synagogue is open to outsiders for Shabbat services.

"You are welcome!" he says.

"I have never been to a Sabbath service," I tell him. "All are welcome," he repeats.

The following Saturday, I find myself driving to the far edge of Dallas, past car lots full of eighteen-wheeler cabs and lube shops and barbecue joints. The neighborhood is so improbable that I keep glancing down at the address I have written on a scrap of paper. Finally, I come to a near-abandoned strip mall that is practically in the shadow of Texas Stadium, home of the Dallas Cowboys. A tattered sign for a driver's license bureau, since closed, hangs crookedly in the parking lot. A sporting goods store, its stock spare, sells uniforms, basketballs, trophies at a discount. The rest of the shops are dark. As I park, I see an elderly man, a yarmulke planted on his thinning hair, a cane in his right hand, tap his way toward a small storefront. I get out of the car and follow him. He leads me toward a glass door. The words CONGREGATION BETH EMUNAH are painted on its upper pane in white letters.

I pull open the door and step inside.

Chapter Two

❧

WHAT IS A JEW?

ELLA BEDONIE is a full-blooded Navajo Indian, a few years older than I am, with Asian eyes and mahogany lips. One day in 1986, when I was about to depart from her house to attend a Navajo religious ceremony, she asked me a question.

"What is a Jew?"

I turned and looked at her. A smile played around her mouth, perhaps in response to the expression of surprise on my face. I said nothing. I had no idea what to say. My eyes drifted up the wall of her kitchen to a bunch of stirring sticks. The Navajos say if you hang the sticks in your house, they will keep away hunger, because hunger perceives them as arrows that will kill it. Near the sticks was a thick bunch of prairie grass tied into a traditional Navajo hairbrush. I looked over the feathers, the beaded skin pouch, and the massive eagle wing used as a fan in peyote ceremonies. I knew these things. I knew her holy things and why she hung them in her home.

"What is a Jew?"

There was a hint of good-natured challenge in Ella's question. After all, I had long been probing her religious beliefs for a book I was writing, yet what did she know of mine? I think she was truly curious and had no idea that the question tacking left and right in my mind was not exactly the one she had posed, but rather, what did *I* know of my *own* religion?

The superficial answer was, Not very much. Although I had boundless interest in understanding Ella's heritage and customs, I seemed to have little curiosity about understanding my own. In the late fall of 1985, I had abandoned my life in New York City to move to Flagstaff, Arizona, to bury myself in the worlds of the Navajo and Hopi Indians, who were engaged in conflicts with one another and the government about their land and their futures. Only after I'd finished my book did I come to understand that I did indeed have a strong religious inclination, but it was so unfocused, and my religious knowledge so primitive, that I needed the charge of writing the stories of the Navajos and Hopis before I even knew the terms with which to explore my own.

The Navajos are a deeply spiritual people. They do not set aside Saturdays or Sundays to tend to religious obligations, but heed them full-time. Their relation to the gods is so fundamental that they have no word for "religion." Signs of the divine are perceived in illness, in lightning strikes, in the swelling and drying up of springs. Gods are not abstract ideas—they are presences. When Ella's mother, Bessie, picks a plant to make dye for her wool, she offers a prayer back to Mother Earth in thanks. Bessie believes that at the spots around her home where she makes these offerings, the gods hear her and come to know her. The Navajos have a personal conception of humans' role in the cosmos. The religious historian Mircea Eliade has put it this way in *The Sacred and the Profane:*

> What we find as soon as we place ourselves in the perspective of religious man of the archaic societies is that *the world exists because it was created by the gods,* and that the existence of the world itself "means" something, "wants to say" something, that the world is neither mute nor opaque, that it is not an inert thing without purpose or significance. For religious man, the cosmos "lives" and "speaks." The mere life of the cosmos is proof of its sanctity, since the cosmos was created by the gods and the gods show themselves to men through cosmic life.

Nonreligious people feel uneasy hearing talk of sacred objects and moments, as I first did when I arrived in the Southwest. Such talk was thoroughly alien to the scientific, rational world where I was reared and educated. But I was curious: How would it feel to believe the world "means something"? How would it feel to be known by one's gods? This curiosity was one reason that I was standing in Ella's house, that I had been drawn back to the reservation to write a book after completing an article about a land dispute between the Navajo and Hopi tribes for *Newsweek* magazine. I had sensed the presence of the divine among these people, though the significance of this perception was still unclear to me. And I sensed that this presence of the divine changed everything: our relations with one another and with ourselves.

Certain moments lodged vividly in my memory. When I saw Bessie rise one morning, slip her hand into a cotton sack of cornmeal, and step outside into the icy dawn to offer a blessing to the rising sun, upon which—as if on Phoebus Apollo's chariot—she believed the gods rode each morning to survey creation, I observed a gravity and an absorption in her face that lingered in me for weeks. I noticed the same reverence in Ella when she spoke of what her parents had taught her in her childhood about weaving and planting. At those times, Ella's voice would invariably lower and her eyes would change, as if she were no longer looking out but rather looking inside herself. These moments produced in her, and in me, a memorable, rich stillness.

It never occurred to me that I could find that reverence in my own tradition. I hardly knew what that tradition was. I didn't think these experiences were something I could have or seek on my own.

After my book, *The Wind Won't Know Me: A History of the Navajo–Hopi Land Dispute*, was published in 1992, Ella Bedonie asked me if I would come back and write another book, this one about her father's life. She wanted a record of the old ways, so her grandchildren, who would not grow up on the reservation, could learn about their great-grandparents. I agreed. The new book, *Beyond the Four Corners of the World*, evolved into a story of Ella's own life, beginning with her childhood in the ancient world of planting, sheepherding, and religious observance, and following her to government boarding school and then to a college education and the white world. The story of her difficult journey into modernity was intertwined with the narratives of her mother and father and grandparents—stories she had recorded and translated herself—the echoes of her past, the North Stars of her life. I understood how loud were those echoes, how steadfast the guiding stars.

I wrote the book because she had asked me to—not an everyday occurrence for a white writer. But later I came to understand that the writing had a much deeper significance for me. I realized that by making a compendium of her stories, a reliquary if you will, I was fashioning a collection to substitute for that which I myself did not have. What were the stories of my own mother and grandmother? I hadn't heard them. I lived in a family devoid of women's stories, of devout stories, of stories of devotion of all kinds.

Perhaps my predecessors' decision not to pass down their memories was an understandable reaction to the poverty and persecution their own forebears had suffered as Jews in Eastern Europe. Perhaps they wanted so desperately to fit in, to be American, that they left behind the stories of their foreign pasts without second thoughts. There were of course stories of the new world: businesses begun, marriages made, children born and sent to elite colleges, advanced degrees won. America offered a new start that they were happy to embrace. But of the past, the immigrant period, the period before that, there was very little.

Ella's forebears had also faced relocations, killings, and deprivations, yet they clung vigorously to their tradition. They had every interest in preserving memories of the old days because they have not yet found their destinies in the present. Ella understood how much her forebears' stories informed her own, and she knew the poverty she would feel without them.

Who are we without the stories of those who came before? We need to hear their voices before we can hear our own. Only through others can we see ourselves. I was writing Ella's stories, I realize, because I could not write my own.

IN 1990 ELLA MOVED AWAY from the reservation, accepting the government's offer of a new house in a white neighborhood in Flagstaff, Arizona. Ella relocated reluctantly and under great pres sure. She had had grave apprehensions about leaving the place that held her childhood memories, the place in which her own umbilical cord was buried. In fact, she had fought off the government's attempts to relocate her for fifteen years. But financial and housing pressures finally convinced her to go.

Almost immediately after the move, however, she recognized she'd made a terrible mistake. Her eldest son dropped out of school, joined a gang, and then disappeared after a gang-related fight. Ella felt she was responsible. The Navajo gods made absolutely clear the punishment for selling the land. "If you sell your mother, the earth," she had been taught, "the Holy People will take a five-fingered human from you." Soon after, Ella was diagnosed with breast cancer. The curse, it seemed for a time, might come true.

The modern ways were clearly failing her. After a lumpectomy and a course of radiation treatment, Ella decided to move back home. She and her husband, Dennis, rented out their new, modern house with the two-car garage and returned to the reservation. When the doctors suggested a mastectomy, Bessie objected and took Ella's medical care into her own hands. She orchestrated a course of treatment with Navajo anticancer herbs and traditional curing ceremonies.

After a year, the medical doctors were surprised to find Ella free of cancer. A few months later, after rounds and rounds of traditional Navajo religious ceremonies, her eldest son returned home. He went on to finish high school and begin college. There seemed a moral in her suffering. She should not so easily abandon her world; she should not disobey her gods.

It was just at this time that I had moved to Dallas, where I suffered an upset, disorientation, and confusion which in its own way paralleled that which Ella and her family had experienced after moving to Flagstaff. One year after my eye spun out of control, I got a new book contract to write the story of Ella's life. In a strange twist of fate, over the next two years, my own life seemed to mirror the drama I was recording about Ella—first a disorientation so unnerving and profound as to bring on grave physical illness, then a climb toward redemption through an investigation of the past, which for me was inextricably entwined with a curiosity about the divine. As I wrote of Ella's rededication to her tradition, I was beginning to search out my own. As I wrote of her steps away from catastrophe, I was picking my own way out as well.

I COME FROM A FAMILY of converts. We are not converts *to* Judaism—all of my great-grandparents, grandparents, and parents were born and lived as Jews. And nor are we exactly converts *from* it: No Jewish-Buddhists here or Jews for Jesus, though my great-aunt Esther confesses to being an admirer of Christian Science. I come from a family of converts *to* America. This didn't happen right away, of course. As in the vast majority of American Jewish families, religious practice, if not our Jewish identity, trickled out of the family generation by generation.

Although in my family we celebrated Passover and Chanukah and occasionally lit the Sabbath candles and blessed the challah, my sister and I received no formal religious education. Bible stories were not a part of our otherwise copious reading. I never saw my mother attend synagogue, and my father brought us to High Holiday services only when we were very young.

My sister and I were raised as New Englanders: hard-working, politically liberal, ecology-minded, serious of purpose. In our house, the classics had replaced my distant forebears' Torah. *Scientific American* and the *New York Review of Books* were the equivalent of our rabbinical commentaries. We were not WASPs exactly, but we were surrounded by them, and their ways were often ours. My sister and I attended private school during our junior high school years, and we were part of classes full of Cabots and Codmans and Averys. I rode and showed horses for several years, an activity I loved, and one my mother felt would keep me safely removed from other, less wholesome interests in my adolescent years. Our clothes were Yankee practical, our furniture tasteful Early American; recipes for our food came from *The New York Times* cookbook with an occasional detour into Julia Child.

My forebears embraced and loved America because it gave them what they could not find elsewhere: the opportunity to reach their potential, to study, to work, to live free of persecution and encumbrance, to succeed. And my family had certainly earned its right to feel American. My maternal great-grandfather, Joseph Silbert, arrived in the United States in the late nineteenth century from Lithuania and earned his way through Harvard Medical School by selling flowers in front of the Provident Bank in Boston. For a poor immigrant this seems an almost impossible leap up in the world and one I can scarcely imagine myself achieving. In 1891 he married his first cousin, Clara Minnie, and fathered four children. Joseph was known not to charge his poorest patients, even on occasion, when he made house calls, leaving money behind for medicine and food. Perhaps his empathy stemmed from a secret he carefully hid from his patients: he himself was ill with an enlarged heart. In 1908, at the age of forty-three, after climbing four flights of steps to treat his brother stricken with the flu, he had a heart attack and died.

But even my great-grandfather's premature death, leaving his widow with four children under the age of sixteen, did not deter the family from its embrace of America. Clara Minnie, harnessing the furious energy characteristic of the Jewish immigrants of the period, bought and sold coal until eventually she made enough money to acquire an apartment building, and in time she was able to send all her children, including a daughter, to Harvard. The eldest child, my grandfather Coleman, attended Harvard College and Harvard Law School, and tutored students to help his siblings go to school. The second son, Newman, also attended Harvard College and Harvard Law School, and a daughter, Frieda, graduated with high honors from Radcliffe; after marrying and having a child, she returned to Harvard and earned a Ph.D. in economics. The fourth child, Myron, attended Harvard College and Harvard Business School. Considering that there were quotas for Jews at Harvard at this time, the family educational record seems an almost unfathomable accomplishment.

The Silberts' integration into Boston's middle-class life was so effective that by the next generation, Coleman's son, my uncle Earl, followed the same route any blueblood Boston Brahmin might: Exeter, Harvard, and Harvard Law School. Earl J. Silbert held several positions in the Department of Justice, including United States Attorney for the District of Columbia. As principal assistant U.S. attorney, he helped prosecute a bungled burglary of the Democratic National Committee's headquarters in the Watergate complex on June 17, 1972. Not only had my grandfather's family embraced American history, but the family had begun to take its place in American history.

My mother, Josephine, named after her still painfully mourned grandfather Joseph, was beautiful and smart. She studied French at her own mother's alma mater, Wellesley College, and earned a master's degree in teaching at Harvard. She taught for one year at the Brearley School in New York before returning home to marry my father, an assistant professor of physics at Harvard. I myself continued the family legacy by attending Harvard College. The year I graduated, my grandfather wrote to then President Derek Bok to inform him with great pride that the fourth generation of his family of immigrant Jews had just produced its first Harvard grad. There would be four more graduates among us: two of my mother's sister Miriam's children, and her brother Earl's two daughters. (My sister, unimpressed by Cambridge ties, happily embarked for California to attend Stanford.)

The members of my grandfather's family were bookish, religious, and intensely devoted to one another, a connection that came out of those early years when they struggled to survive without their father. Family bonds were so intense that two of the three sons never married, and my grandfather himself didn't marry until he was thirty-nine years old. The two who had children, Coleman and Frieda, each named their firstborn for the revered father Joseph.

Clara Minnie and Joseph were both religious Jews who observed the rules of kashrut and attended Orthodox shul. Clara Minnie even embraced the idea of life after death, because when she knew her end was near, she told her children she was joyful at the prospect of being reunited with her beloved husband, Joseph. Apparently her children joked with her that she might want to prepare herself for the possibility that their father might not recognize her right away, as it had been almost forty years since they last had met.

Although my grandfather, Coleman, inherited his parents' devoutness—he walked to shul, studied Talmud throughout his life, and fasted on Yom Kippur until his death at eighty-seven—curiously, this tradition did not pass down to us. I have no memories of my grandparents involved in religious activities aside from the yearly seders.

No one helped me understand the Silberts' successful transition from being impoverished immigrants to becoming solid members of Boston's privileged class. I didn't know what my grandfather or my grandmother felt about Judaism or its ancient ritual practice. What did they believe, what gave their lives real meaning, where did they learn their sense of morality, what did they hold on to in times of fear or desperation? What did they think about their origins, their heritage, their connection to this ancient, complex people? To me, all this remained a mystery.

COLEMAN MARRIED a woman from a very different kind of family. The Rosenbergs settled in Boston a generation earlier, were not as academically accomplished, and financially were far better off. Though Lillian Rosenberg's father Julius arrived in this country from Lithuania penniless like Joseph Silbert, and, like him, started out in America as a peddler, he followed a different route. He didn't sell flowers to put himself through medical school; instead he went from being a boy in knickers, peddling scissors, needles, and pins with his father in New Hampshire to becoming a millionaire.

Julius's father, Mordechai, was born into a family of cantors in a small Lithuanian town. Mordechai's first rebellion was to decide to become a rabbi instead of a cantor, and while attending yeshiva in Vilna, he lived with a family in Smargonne, a nearby town. At some point in his studies, he encountered the writings of Moses Mendelssohn, the eighteenth-century German writer and philosopher who opposed segregation of the Jews, translated the Pentateuch into German, and advocated cultural exchange between Jews and non-Jews. Mendelssohn's ideas provided the philosophical underpinnings for Reform Judaism in Germany. When Mordechai began yeshiva, in the 1860s, emancipation of the Jews in Western Europe was nominally secure, though repression of the Jews in Eastern Europe persisted. The appeal of Mendelssohn's ideas proved greater than the pull of tradition, and Mordechai abandoned the yeshiva and married a young woman, Kate, the daughter of the family in

Smargonne with whom he had boarded. He worked and raised a family but became convinced the family would never prosper in Lithuania. His eldest son, Sam, was deaf, and the family decided to leave Lithuania before he was drafted into the czar's army.

In the late 1880s Mordechai, soon "Martin," arrived in the United States with his youngest son, Julius, my great-grandfather, and the two moved in with relatives in New York. After a day Martin decided he couldn't abide the city, and father and son set out for Concord, New Hampshire, where his brother-in-law had settled. Martin tied a pack on his back and, accompanied by the twelve-year-old boy, trudged up and down the length of New Hampshire, sleeping in barns and selling small household goods to the farm ladies but also— in what must have been a private joke for the former Mordechai— small statues of Jesus and Mary.

The farm women, wives of Canadian immigrants, were too poor to pay for the goods in cash, so they offered scraps of cotton fabric in trade. Martin and Julius carried the waste material to New Hampshire's paper mills, which paid cash for the rags that they used in the manufacture of high-quality paper. Eventually, Martin was able to buy a horse and wagon to haul the fabric remnants. He soon prospered and was able to bring over the rest of his family.

Eventually, Martin stopped peddling and, with his brother, Willie, and sons, Sam and Julius, set up a shop to which other peddlers brought their fabric scraps. At the time, cotton waste was valuable, both for the manufacture of paper and because it could be rewoven for clothing. My great-grandfather Julius became the selling agent for the family business, traveling to England and France to sell the cotton "shoddy." On the walls of the family shop were photos of the Hamburg–America Line, on whose commercial operation, the Red Line, the bales were loaded. My great-aunt, Esther, was brought up in such comfort that she imagined her father owned the entire fleet of ocean liners. Not quite; but by the beginning of the First World War, Rosenberg Brothers were the largest cotton waste dealers in all of New England.

Julius helped found and served as president of a Reform congregation that enlisted as members the leading Jews of Chelsea, Massachusetts; later he joined Temple Israel, a larger and better established Reform congregation. Like his father before him, he rejected Orthodox practice. He always loved music, though, and in a nod to his family's cantorial past, enjoyed listening to the Temple Israel choir.

When Lillian Rosenberg, a member of the third generation of a family that had embraced Reformism, married Coleman Silbert, whose mother maintained a kosher home and attended Orthodox shul, a deal had to be struck. The couple agreed to have successive wedding ceremonies: after the main one at Temple Israel, Clara Minnie Silbert secreted the bride and groom off to another room of the Somerset Hotel to be married—a second time, the bride's side of the family would maintain—by an Orthodox rabbi.

Although my grandmother Lillian retained her membership at Temple Israel, she agreed to keep a kosher home. Lillian loved "her Temple" and remained a devoted member of its congregation until her mid-80s, when she became too infirm to attend services. Her life revolved around Temple Israel: it formed the center of her religious, civic, and community life. My mother and her siblings were confirmed in the Temple's Sunday School, where my mother learned to read and write Hebrew. Temple Israel had become a powerful bastion of successful Jews who were making their way in Boston. Even my grandfather, a member of the Orthodox Kehilleth Israel, joined Temple Israel toward the end of his life.

Although Temple Israel became a large and influential congrega tion, it didn't have the legs to carry Judaism into the next generation, at least in my direct family. The prayers that the Rosenberg cantors chanted for generations had, by the time they reached my sister and me, faded to a few dull tones. While I loved school and generally adored my teachers, I remember the Beth El Temple Center Sunday School, for the brief months we attended, as exasperatingly empty, unenlightening, and dry. Yet even in my highly assimilated New England childhood, there were paradoxical moments of religious seeking and searching. One year, when I was twelve years old, my friend, Laura Perlo, and I took private Hebrew lessons. A red-haired Radcliffe student, who lived in the house in which the movie *Love Story* had been filmed, came over to our house every week, and we unfolded a card table in the family room and set it before the large windows that looked into the backyard. Laura, Karen, and I sat at the table, No. 2 pencils sharpened, practicing writing Hebrew letters in a notebook with specially drawn lines.

At the start of our classes, the teacher asked us for our Hebrew names. I didn't have one as far as I knew. The teacher gave me the name Ilana, which she said meant "oak tree." The lessons ended as mysteriously as they had begun, but we did learn to read and write the alphabet, and we learned the tune with which to light the Chanukah candles. That, along with the occasional Friday night candlelighting and yearly Passover seder, was the sum total of our religious education.

MY FATHER'S PARENTS had been no less eager to become American than my mother's. However, they came from a different country, Hungary, at a later time, after World War I, and to a different city, New York, than Mordechai Rosenberg and Joseph Silbert. The differences made their adjustment both easier and harder. They left

Europe for the same reasons, however. My father remembers hearing his parents repeat, over and over, with other relatives, the phrase, "There was no hope there."

The Benedeks established less solid geographical roots than had the Silberts and Rosenbergs. My father's parents never owned property; instead, they lived in rented apartments in New York City, Long Island, and then Miami Beach. Part of my grandfather's family settled in California, and some relatives moved to Israel. The name Benedek itself also offers a puzzle about the family's origins. It is a common Hungarian name for Christians as well as Jews. Perhaps the name was chosen as a Hungarian translation of the Hebrew Baruch, or "blessing" (benediction). But another theory has it that the family was originally Sephardic and were taken in by Benedictine monks as scribes after their expulsion from Spain. Whatever the truth may be, there was a sense of wanderlust in the Benedek family that was not evident in the directed, settled Silberts. I believe this less-clear sense of belonging came down directly to me.

My father's grandfather, Jacob Benedek, was a shoemaker and a religious Jew from the town of Nagyvarad (Big City), located in a disputed territory of the Carpathian Mountains still claimed by both Hungary and Rumania. He and his wife, Rosa, departed with their daughters, Margaret and Inka, on the White Star Line vessel *Olympic* from their town. They sailed through Cherbourg, France, and landed in New York on October 10, 1923. They moved into a house in Astoria, Long Island, which their son, Alex, my grandfather, and his sister, Clara, had found for them. Alex and Clara had been sent ahead, as was the custom of immigrant families, to set up a beachhead. Jacob and Rosa were rigorously Orthodox and maintained a kosher home. After Rosa died, Jacob moved in with Margaret and insisted that she too keep a kosher kitchen.

Alex wanted to become a chemist, and as soon as he arrived, he enrolled at City College with other ambitious Jewish immigrants and children of immigrants. With no one to support him or sponsor his studies, however, he was soon forced to find work. His first job was painting fuse boxes in a factory. Alex was a handsome man with a thick shock of black straight hair, strong, arched eyebrows, and a ready smile. In 1927 he married a sensitive auburn-haired Hungarian beauty named Viola Rethy, who had come to the United States to study music at Juilliard. Viola was from a wealthier family from the city of Debrecen, a city in Transylvania on the border of Hungary and Rumania. Her departure from an at least economically comfortable life was motivated by a difficult relationship with her mother, who had divorced Viola's father when Viola was very young and married a dentist who was Catholic. The mother, Maria, converted to Catholicism herself and made it clear to young Viola that she was not welcome in this newly defined family. Maria was violent and cruel to her daughter, and Viola nursed the dream of finding her real father, who had already moved to the United States.

Viola had an intense and difficult personality. She had traveled with her mother and stepfather on troop transport trains during World War I—presumably because her stepfather had been inducted as a medic—and the sight of the grievously wounded soldiers on their way back from the front had traumatized her. She told me that she remembered pogroms in nearby towns in Hungary. Her general misery—or bravery—was great enough to motivate her, when she had just turned seventeen, to embark for America alone. No one knows if anyone met her at the dock, or how she survived for the first few months. But sometime after her arrival, she looked up her biological father, who was living in the Bronx. Apparently he was quite surprised and not entirely happy to see his daughter; it is possible that his new wife and children were not even aware of Viola's existence.

Years later, after she had her own family, she was reconciled with her father and remained on good terms with him and his new family. Although the idea of family was very important to my paternal grandmother, perhaps because of her own difficult childhood, she seemed incapable of taking steps or making decisions that would have established stronger family ties in her own life or that of the children she eventually had. One thing was very clear to Viola: she wanted her two sons to be American, and she was convinced that a prerequisite was superior language skills. She did not teach them to speak Hungarian and she endeavored to erase the marvelous accent from her own speech, practicing elocution before a mirror. Viola had a lovely singing voice and was a gifted pianist. She adored her Knabe baby grand piano, which she kept covered in winter with a rug decorated with a romantic scene of nymphs dancing in a forest. I think this was the image she had of herself, the musical sprite in a medieval forest, dancing in rapturous innocence, seeking freedom—and perhaps internal peace—in this dance.

Whether it was because he had married too soon, or his parents and two other sisters arrived from Hungary before he was ready, Alex never completed his education at City College. Rather, he found work in the garment trades and eventually started up a small business making lace collars, cuffs, and other appliquéd and embroidered work for women's and children's clothing. My paternal grandfather's climb toward economic comfort was not quick or helped along by elite college degrees. The Depression hit just after the birth of his second child, and business didn't really pick up until the Second World War began. The shop eventually prospered, however, and in the mid-1950s, when it was twenty-five years old, it employed three dozen people, eventually providing Viola and Alex with a comfortable income and allowing them to pay their own sons' ways through college and graduate schools.

The dreams of academic success abandoned by Alex and Viola were fulfilled by my father. He earned a Ph. D. in physics, became a professor of physics, and is a member of the National Academy of Sciences.

I believe my father found refuge in physics. Whereas his family life had been chaotic, full of conflict and emotional scenes, physics offered the satisfaction of pure order, of problems whose solutions conformed to immutable laws. Interestingly enough, within the paradigm of his search for order through physics, he chose to look at phenomena that deviated from the norm—that behaved at first glance in unpredictable ways.

A student of my father's once said of him that although his job was to find mathematical equations that made sense of complex systems, like finding the equation of a curve, what he was truly interested in was explaining the behavior of the points that did *not* fit on the line. This was certainly my father: he always showed us the importance of going our own way and he gave us a sense of entitlement to live a life of the mind.

Because I had no other model, my father became my image of a Jewish man: scholarly, professorial, interested in a wide range of intellectual and artistic pursuits. He collected art and assembled a huge library of classics, most of which he read. He was devoted to his students, who were smart and worked hard, and he seemed quite democratic about whom he admired. He didn't favor Jewish students or even particularly notice who was Jewish or not. What mattered was the quality of their mind and their work ethic. He wanted to concentrate as much time and effort as he could on his research, on the real exploration of nature and physics, and he did his best to stay away from administrative duties. To me he was a model of fidelity and devotion to creative intellectual endeavors. He wanted to make discoveries that would serve the public good.

Unlike the Silberts, the Benedeks had an unselfconscious Jewish identity. There was no conflict about what synagogue to join, or the attractions of Reformism. My father's father, Alex, was comfortable in shul and knew all the prayers by heart. He read Hebrew well and led the family seders. His mother lighted Shabbos candles, waving her hands before her eyes in the old-world custom. Alex didn't wrap tefillin, though his father Jacob did so every morning. What my father remembers particularly about his father is that he loved to sing Jewish songs. In shul, during the Passover seder, or when he was horsing around with the kids—he sang songs. Jewish songs. And he and my grandmother helped found a synagogue near their apartment in the Bronx, called the Kingsbridge Center of Israel. As a young boy, my father studied at a small cheder that met in a storefront in the neighborhood.

It is of course profoundly interesting to me that forebears on both sides helped to found congregations—and yet my sister and I were brought up with hardly a trace of ritual practice. Occasionally, my mother lit candles on Friday nights and now and then my father would retrieve the prayer book from the dining-room cabinet and make the blessings over the bread and wine, reading steadily and clearly. He did not sing the prayers, as his father did. The Friday night ceremony was not illuminated by any discussion of the Sabbath or the weekly Torah portion. At some point, the candlelighting disappeared and our Friday night meals were no longer distinguished from the meals we had during the rest of the week.

What is a Jew? Ella Bedonie asked. It was a question I could not answer for her because it was a question I first had to answer for myself.

Chapter Three

❧

EXILE

THE GLASS DOOR of Beth Emunah squeaks closed behind me. I step forward into a reception area that contains a green sofa on which two small boys are jumping and screaming gleefully. The walls are hung with drawings of rabbis and scenes of ancient Israel. I continue down a hallway toward what appears to be a sanctuary, and pass, on my left, a room with a long table set with food. On my right are a couple of small classrooms.

At the end of the hall, I enter a good-sized room with a green rug and molded plastic chairs and an aisle down the middle. In front is a homemade walnut-stained pine ark, flanked by flags of the United States and Israel and illuminated on top with a flame-shaped orange electric bulb. In front of the Ark is a table covered with a green print fabric, on top of which is a podium on which hangs a plastic sign that reads SHALOM. Before it, on the ground, is an arrangement of white silk flowers.

The rug is spotted and the ceiling tiles broken and water-stained. But the walls are freshly painted and hung with copies of scroll fragments. Men and women with platters of food in their hands are walking to what appears to be a kitchen in an area behind the Ark.

I see Rabbi Groesberg at the front of the sanctuary plugging in speakers for a sound system. When he turns, I see he is holding an electric guitar. I wave, and he nods. He smiles and walks over to me.

"Shabbat shalom," he says, putting out his hand.

"Shabbat shalom."

"Have any trouble finding us?" he asks with a big smile.

"Not at all."

"This is Beatrice," he says, introducing me to a woman in her seventies who's about four-and-a-half feet tall, decked out in colorful dress, matching hat, and spike heels. "Beatrice is our Sunshine Committee."

"That means I welcome new people," Beatrice says in a whiskey soprano. She flashes me a smile of perfectly even teeth. "Welcome. You can sit wherever you'd like." So I sit. The ceiling may be stained, the rug may be old, but the place feels homey, lived in, cared for, valued. An elderly man with glasses and curly hair introduces himself to me as Irving Zalfas. I shake his hand. He introduces me to his wife, Phyllis, and speaks with a broad New York accent. They tell me they moved out here many years ago. Irving was a baggage handler for an airline. He plays in a softball league and loves to go country dancing, which Phyllis lets him do by himself. They have raised two sons here. Am I married? they want to know.

In a few moments, Rabbi Groesberg is joined by a jovial-looking man with light blue eyes, Phil Baum, the president of the shul, who carries an acoustic guitar. They take their places at the front of the room and begin to play. Rabbi Groesberg rocks his hips back and forth as he plays his guitar, a sight that nearly causes me to fall off my chair in surprise. I look at Phil Baum, who is smiling, his eyes sparkling. Beatrice is shaking a tambourine.

The music starts in me a cascade of memories and emotions. I struggle to catch a musical phrase that seems familiar, then lose it as it resolves into something else, or fades away. At some points, I think I know the tunes and I hum along. Others are completely strange. When they strike up "Heiveinu Shalom Aleichem," I begin to feel dizzy. I remember hearing my father sing this song. When could it have been? I remember his happy, resonant voice and its enthusiasm at the end of the song, "Heiveinu shalom, shalom, shalom aleichem! Hey!" and the fist he raised in the air to punctuate the end of the line. I mouth the words but do not sing; I am overpowered by a feeling of great sadness at the memory of this lost, happy time.

After the warm-up songs, the rabbi walks to the podium and turns to the service, which is written out in Hebrew and transliteration in the booklets. Because I know the Hebrew letters, I can slowly, slowly sound my way along. I revert to the transliteration when things move too fast. Since I am not familiar with these tunes either, I hum bits and pieces a fraction of a beat behind.

I hear the cantor before I see him. He has a nasal, tremulous voice. When he begins to chant, I turn to look and I see a dark-bearded man who is wearing a dark suit and black hat. He appears to be in his late thirties and he sings with such energy his body shakes from the effort. I struggle to read the Hebrew I learned as a child. I find the ornate Oriental lines of the alphabet suddenly so beautiful they are almost painful to look at. For the first time in months, images register clearly on my brain; not only because my eyes are recently back to normal, but also because I am surrounded by likenesses, sounds, and emotions that seem to have resonance inside me. As the prayers go on, I have a vague sensation of my father standing beside me, as he did a long time ago when I accompanied him a few times to synagogue. And I have the strange sense of hearing his voice intoning the words beside me.

I watch the rabbi and two other men make preparations for the Torah service. The men, draped in their prayer shawls, performing their designated duties, have an air of gravitas about them, and I flush with feelings that seem so far away from my existence now, and yet so well known: they are tending to something they know and love.

We put away the booklets and pick up the large books, which, I see, contain the Torah, the Five Books of Moses. When I open this book, which the cantor here calls a Chumash, I glance over the pages of Hebrew characters and feel overwhelmed. They seem to swim on the pages before me, then gather in shapes as if they were reaching toward me. I find them immensely beautiful, sure, sophisticated, austere, true. The letters draw me inside the pages.

The Torah service begins. Phyllis Zalfas lifts the scroll, which is covered in a handmade quilted cover of yellow, light blue, and white, out of the Ark, and carries it over her right shoulder in a procession around the humble room. The small round woman with bad teeth and thinning hair is transformed by her wide, proud smile and the bright glow in her eyes. The congregants, some elderly, a few on crutches, step with determination toward the Torah, to touch it with the corner of their prayer shawls or their prayer books, which they then bring to their mouths for a kiss. I am surprised by the sudden feeling of reverence in this room, by the inescapable fact that this scroll, this book of stories, has aroused such powerful feelings in these people.

The Torah is undressed and unrolled on the front table. How strangely anthropomorphic this ceremony is, I think. The scroll is bedecked in a dress and paraded like a queen around the room as we all stand in honor of it and kiss it, then it is laid flat and undressed like a baby.

Several men in prayer shawls hover about it then; one checks that it is unrolled to the right spot, another brings over a silver pointer and a card catalogue. The room becomes still as the cantor takes his position before the Torah and begins to sing, moving the pointer across the words, his voice forced with intensity. As he chants, I follow along in the English, devouring the words and the commentary. When the reading is over, the scroll is lifted and dressed again, and again brought back among the people. Again, they kiss it, as though they are sending a family member away on a trip whose outcome is uncertain, unknown. The most astonishingly mournful song I have ever heard is sung when the Torah is put away, out of sight until the next Sabbath. When the curtain is pulled over the Ark as the final act of the service, I feel, for a moment, bereft.

I look around at the poor, humble people sitting in this tiny room, but suddenly I don't see them. Instead, I see men and women in robes and sandals in Temple times. I see my ancestors sitting on wooden benches in Lithuania, in Hungary. I see Jews studying and thinking in little rooms in Boston, in New York, any place they can find a table and a light and some quiet. They read the same words then that we read now, words I know from somewhere, in my bones, deep in my unconscious.

I think: This is how my people, the Jews, have survived over thousands of years, in little rooms like this, all over the world. It wasn't through political demonstrations or books written about them by outsiders, like my book about the Navajos; the Jews survived because they cleaved to their Torah and their God. This is what my people loved and continue to love. This is the desire that moves their lives forward.

These people—we people—worship an abstract God who reveals himself in a book! We are devoted to words and ideas. I am filled with a feeling of shameless, weak-kneed gratitude. I feel deeply at home, as though my bones could relax for the first time.

As my forebears had done before me, I had picked myself up from home and moved to a strange land.

I didn't leave to save my life or to improve the lives of my children and grandchildren. I didn't leave to escape anti-Semitism; instead, I encountered it for the first time. I left to enact a rite of passage that was possible only because of the sacrifices and hard work of my ancestors. I wanted to prove myself, to see if I could be a writer. I hoped that by writing the story of two Indian tribes struggling to hold on to their lives and ways in the face of a hostile and changing world, I might influence Congress to conceive of a better conclusion to their long, complicated battle with each other and with the federal government.

I did not then see the parallels between the story I was writing and the one my forebears had lived. Nor did I have an inkling of why I was so deeply interested in the Navajo and Hopi Indians, whose lives were devoted to fulfilling arcane religious obligations. My life was certainly not concerned, as far as I knew, with matters of religion or spiritual longing. I just thought I'd stumbled onto a good story and had had the great good fortune of getting a contract to write a book about it. I thought I was being ambitious, embarking on a grand writer's adventure.

I didn't see that I had set up a journey that in a way mirrored—in reverse—that of my forebears. They had left a land friendless to them, a desert, to find a new home. I set myself adrift from home to enter a strange land, literally a desert, and a self-imposed exile from all that was familiar. They sought a life in which they could achieve a measure of comfort; I sought imbalance and discomfort. My forebears were intensely aware of being Jewish; in fact, they were never allowed to forget their Jewishness and they were hated for it. I chose to leave the comfortable home that they had struggled to establish for themselves and their children to write about another small tribe that was—amazingly enough—determined to retain its identity separate from the culture that surrounded it. Given an invitation to disappear into the melting pot, the Navajos refused. They knew that assimilation would lead to an eternity of despair. Trying to help them express those beliefs to an uncomprehending government, I was working to achieve for the Navajos the opposite of what my family of immigrants had achieved here: the right to remain separate and unique, though I did not think of it that way at the time.

I spent a year in Flagstaff, following several families for my book while contributing updates to *Newsweek* about the ongoing battle. Then I moved to Phoenix to concentrate on the governmental maneuverings and gain some distance from the people I had been observing. When I finished, I was convinced that every effort had to be made to allow the Navajos and Hopis to retain their own culture and religion while at the same time allowing them to take their places— at their own pace—in the modern world. The more successful families were those who still maintained traditional ways but also interacted with the white world. Many—but not all—Indian families who converted to Christianity suffered family breakdown and alcoholism. The successful ones, it seemed to me, straddled two worlds.

To earn money to supplement my book advance, I covered politics and banking for a magazine in Phoenix that was owned by the liberal *St. Petersburg Times* of Florida. There, I began a romantic relationship with a bright, good-looking young writer named Craig.

Three years later, after finishing my book, I moved with Craig to Dallas, where he had taken a job with the *Wall Street Journal*.

In one sense, the journey on which I had set out from New York ended there. In another, it had just begun.

ONE OF THE FIRST QUESTIONS Craig asked me was "Are Jews white people?"

I blushed with embarrassment, though I'm not sure whether it was for Craig or myself. Since he was the first person I had met in Arizona who talked about books, I was prepared to set it aside as a curious lapse. He told me he had grown up in Kansas City, Kansas, on the wrong side of the county line, and he had never met a Jewish person before.

It didn't occur to me that this question was anti-Semitic. Instead, I thought it was merely ignorant and I put it out of my mind, as other aspects of Craig seemed more recognizable and attractive. He spoke passionately of writers like Andre Dubus and James Salter. He told me he had studied fiction writing with Reynolds Price in college and had worked for the *Wall Street Journal* just after graduating. He had had a difficult childhood as one of four sons of an alcoholic meat cutter. He was like a Damon Runyon character, sensitive and intelligent but unworldly. He was also handsome, like a pretty Sonny Liston.

He presented himself with a heavy dose of self-deprecating humor. He was the rube whose etiquette was always wrong, who walked into a party with a piece of toilet paper still pressed onto a shaving cut. I didn't give a second thought to the fact that Craig was Catholic, a former altar boy, and from a family that held fundamentalist, blue-collar Catholic beliefs. The attraction was immediate, even before I saw a portrait of Geronimo hanging over his desk. The intensity of our attraction for each other seemed to be in direct proportion to our differences and was heightened by the contrast with our bland surroundings. We talked for hours while walking in the neighborhoods near our office during breaks from work, taking rests on a bench in a shopping mall. Before Arizona, I had never really seen a shopping mall. They were only just arriving in the Boston area when I was in college, and there were none as far as I knew in Manhattan. In Phoenix, malls found their natural home. Around us there were heavy women in polyester pantsuits, men with tattoos, blue-haired midwestern retirees—people whose stories, admittedly, I did not know but who struck me as alien, far away.

I fell in love with Craig on a mall bench beside a container of impatiens. It was a sunny Wednesday in April. Craig offered me his hand, palm up. His fingers were long and graceful. It was a fragile, tentative gesture for such a place. I slid my hand onto his, and he pulled me toward him. He was urgent and full of desire. I was lonely and unsure of my progress on the huge project I had undertaken. He had an intensity I hadn't experienced since I'd left New York, and I found it—and him—irresistible.

CRAIG KNEW A LOT about Catholicism and had read widely about the historical Jesus, and I was interested in hearing him offer literary and historical analyses of religious figures. I don't remember him speaking of his faith. I remember getting in a heated argument with him about religious hypocrisy. I felt that someone who preaches X and does Y is no better than his actions. Craig disagreed. He thought that intention was more important than action. Over and over, he said, "You can't blame the church for the failures of some of its priests." I kept thinking: what is it about the structure of the church that leads to those failures?

He was interested in learning about Judaism, but unfortunately, I couldn't tell him very much beyond the fact that actions speak louder than words for Jews. "Is there a concept of heaven and hell in Judaism?" he asked me, and I said I didn't think so. He was unbelieving. "What motivates people to do the right thing," he asked, "if there is no eternal system of punishment and reward?" I was dumbfounded. It never occurred to me that one needed either the hope of reward or the fear of punishment to do the right thing.

There was one tiny piece of Judaism that I did know, thanks to the Hebrew lessons we had taken as children, and that was the tune for the blessing made over the Chanukah candles. I had even brought a menorah along with me to Arizona. So the first Chanukah after I met Craig, I drove to a local Jewish gift store and bought candles. The first night of the holiday, I placed the menorah on a table, stuck two candles in it, struck a match, and lit the leader. I launched into the tune for the blessing and touched the leader to the wick of the first candle, then put the leader back in its place. I sang a second blessing for the first night, the Shehechiyanu, and when I finished, I looked up at Craig, who gave a half smile and murmured, "That's it?"

I agreed to accompany him to a Christmas mass at Phoenix's St. Mary's Basilica. I felt uncomfortable as soon as I entered the baroque, statue-filled sanctuary. I watched as Craig kneeled and crossed himself at the end of the aisle. We sat in the back and my mind began to wander, but I snapped to attention as soon as the sermon began and one of the first words out of the priest's mouth was "Israel."

The priest told the story of a man at Lod Airport who was carrying wooden religious figures of Jesus Christ. The Israeli security guards, the priest explained, were concerned that something might be hidden inside the statues, and insisted on taking them apart. A thin line of sweat broke out on my forehead, as I anticipated the priest was about to make a comment that would make me uncomfortable.

The priest continued: "The security guards told the man that they were very sorry, but there might be explosives in the goods. But what the security guards didn't realize was that the figures were explosive, but not for the reasons they feared. They were explosive because of the message they carried to the world."

That was it. End of sermon. I breathed a sigh of relief that nothing worse had come out and watched Craig receive communion and return to his seat with his hands crossed in front of his chest. I remember thinking how much he looked like his mother in that posture. We left promptly.

Although Catholicism was completely alien to me, in style as well as theology, I simply pushed our religious differences out of my mind, as if they had no consequences. I used the same kind of willful ignorance to put aside the fact that our family backgrounds were so different as to make the prospect of a long-term relationship problematic. Craig's family had been meat cutters for generations, and their particular brand of Catholicism discouraged them from striving for a better way of life. Craig explained that great pressure was put on anyone who got the idea of leaving "KCK." They were met with the area's equivalent of excommunication: "So you think you're better than us?"

Craig's father had been so affected by this philosophy that he never accepted a management job in the meat department of any supermarket. Instead, even at age sixty, he would report to the union every week or every few months, whenever his last temporary job was over, to get his new freelance assignment. Craig's father was quite inventive about getting back at his perceived oppressors, however. When I visited the family one year at Christmas, he told me how he had taken care of an uppity customer who explained a bit too much about how he wanted the beef prepared for his steak tartare: Craig's father prepared him, instead, a package of ground pork.

Although Craig had successfully created his own world and life—giving up drinking himself at age twenty-two, going to college, becoming a journalist, and moving to another state—he remained loyal to his family and the memories of his youth that led him to resent my privileged background. For my part, although I tried my best to act comfortable with his family, I felt quite out of place.

When one brother used the term "Jew me down" in my presence, Craig apologized profusely, explaining they had grown up hearing that term, but had never understood that it referred to Jewish people. His mortification seemed so complete that, again, I chalked it up to their parochial upbringing.

It was a holiday meal that aroused in me such profound feelings of alienation that I couldn't set them aside. The shrimp boil I could understand as a holiday custom, and besides, I certainly didn't keep kosher. But one night I was presented with a plate of sauerkraut on top of which sat two boiled pork vertebrae, the spinal cord still tangling between the bones. Though Craig's mother had looked at me just before we sat down to the meal, saying, it seemed apologetically, "This is our 'soul food,'" I sat before my plate, pushing the meat around with my fork, feeling instinctively that this was a hostile act, and an anti-Semitic one at that. I felt conspicuously Jewish, in a way that was unfamiliar and unwelcome. Craig's father was a meat cutter who had access to any kind of meat at a discount. The choice of pig vertebrae had to have had its reasons.

Still, again, I convinced myself that although his parents might harbor lingering if unconscious anti-Semitism, Craig did not, could not.

Our move to Texas began auspiciously enough. We found a large, sunny apartment on a tree-lined block in Oak Lawn, near downtown. The apartment had 1930s stained-glass windows in the large living room, clean oak flooring in the dining room, and a master suite with the largest bathroom I had ever seen. The house had a perfect study for me, a sunny room with built-in bookshelves and French doors. The front yard was landscaped with miniature white roses, lollipop-shaped ficus trees, and redbud. When we arrived, we found in the refrigerator a basket of fruit and cheese and a bottle of spring water with a welcome note from the girls in the upstairs apartment of the two-family house.

Soon after arriving, I interviewed for a job at the main paper in town, the *Dallas Morning News*. I met with the editor-in-chief and a few senior editors, and began writing freelance stories, one of which turned into an investigative report about a local diet doctor who routinely prescribed Prozac for the patients at his weight-loss clinic. The investigative report ran on the paper's front page, and was noticed by the head of WFAA-TV news, an ABC affiliate. One of the station's anchors had been trying to get the same story but had failed, and I was hired to produce stories for the station's investigative reporter.

However, right from the beginning, I had a sense that things weren't quite right in Dallas. To start with, Craig had arrived ahead of me to begin work, and had taken a dozen of my plants along in his pickup truck. When I arrived two weeks later and pulled up to his temporary lodgings, I saw some unusual orange coloring on my beloved plants. At first I thought they might be a strange new flowering, and I wondered if the humid climate of Dallas had awakened in the plants some genetic possibility that had lain dormant in the desert of Phoenix. But when I got close, I saw the yellow starbursts were not flowers at all, but rather scorch marks. Craig must have parked his truck in the sun, and the plants had got burned.

I was so dispirited by this finding that I couldn't mention it to

Craig for weeks. When I did, he said, "I told you I didn't want to bring them." What this meant to me was that Craig, who had been ambivalent about my accompanying him to Dallas, was trying to pull away. Just as I hadn't wanted to look at the anti-Semitism in his family, I didn't want to look away from the trouble in our relationship, which was at least in part related to our different backgrounds. It was my feeling that when we met, Craig had been fascinated by me because I had what he envied: an Ivy League education and a book contract from Knopf. But as our relationship continued, it seemed to me that he was trying to prove to himself—and to me—that I was no better than he was.

Craig was a very good writer and reader. Once he read aloud to me a James Salter story and then analyzed its structure to show how the author had achieved his effect. I was mesmerized; his strength as a writer, I would learn, was also structure. He could put a story together so that there was not a single sentence out of place. He sat in front of a blank computer screen for days, working out the structure in his mind. The moment it all became clear, he'd write the article in one sitting.

I didn't think that way. I wrote my way toward an idea or an emotion, hoping the order that emerged would be strong enough to hold. I couldn't then think in structures. I wanted to learn about structure from him, in writing, and I guess, in life. For my part, I harbored the fantasy of helping Craig become a more polished version of himself, an effort he didn't completely discourage. This dynamic, of course, was not the healthiest one on which to build a relationship. In its worst moments, it devolved into repetitive arguments over whose childhood was preferable, creating a metaconversation between us that led me to feel increasingly estranged from him and eventually from myself.

Dallas itself increased my sense of alienation. Although people were very friendly superficially, it seemed as if they were unavailable for much more than that. The girls upstairs, for example, who left the welcome basket in our refrigerator, never showed the slightest interest in getting together after we moved in. I wondered for a long time what could have possessed them to make such a thoughtful gesture if they had had no hopes of neighborly relations. It was my first hint that what took place above ground in Dallas was not always representative of what was going on underneath.

I MET WITH BYRON HARRIS, the investigative reporter at WFAA for whom I would be hired to work, at midnight toward the end of December in a strip mall in North Dallas. Byron was reporting a story about the owner of a restaurant who complained he was being squeezed out of business by the porn shops and dirty-book stores that were proliferating around him. We hung around in the freezing cold for a few hours as his photographer took pictures of the goings-on in the mall and Byron interviewed the restaurateur.

Byron gave me a lift back to the station in the early morning, and as we drove down Inwood Road in his posh white Lexus, slaloming around potholes, passing acres of car lots and cheap apartment complexes, I asked him why he had asked the owner so few questions about the nuts and bolts of the story: the zoning that actually forbade so many such businesses together, why the police didn't enforce it, and so on. Byron made several throat-clearing noises and then said, "In TV, you ask the question 'How does it make you feel?' You want emotion, drama. Also, you have to remember, for a package like this, you've got three minutes or less."

"You don't think like a TV producer, Emily," he added after a moment. "Why do you want to get into this business anyway?"

Because it is there, I thought. Because I like to rise to every challenge.

What I said was, "If the attention span of the American public is three minutes, then I guess I'd better learn how to tell a story in three minutes."

The next day, Marty Haag, the vice president for news for Belo Corp., which owns both the leading local television station WFAA and the *Dallas Morning News,* asked me down to the office "just so I can connect a name and a face."

I got a manicure for the occasion, a haircut, and a few extra blond highlights. I wore a blue silk Anne Klein jacket and short skirt. I put on high heels and a pair of shiny gold earrings.

"So," he said, "you graduated from Harvard, and you used to work for *Newsweek?*"

Yes.

"I'd like to ask you, though you don't have to answer," he said, "how did you get the diet-doctor story?" He didn't look at me, but off at one of the three television screens running silently on one wall of his office.

I told him I hadn't done anything unusual, I had just been dogged and relentless.

"Our reporter didn't have the time we'd have liked to give her to do the story." Haag looked off through the glass front of his office out at the newsroom. "She's had more and more anchoring duties, and these kept her from spending as much time on the story as she wanted." He paused. "You're too smart to lose to the newspaper. I'd like you to be a producer for Byron. You'll help prepare his investigative reports, with the idea that, eventually, you'll become a reporter yourself. What's important to me is finding somebody who can explain complicated subjects to the public. I'm not that concerned with the cosmetic thing."

I thanked him and left.

Later in the day, I called Byron. I told him Marty wanted me to start on January 4. Then I asked, "What does Marty mean by 'the cosmetic thing'?"

"Oh, that's something you'll have to get used to," Byron said. "Marty will never say this to you, but you're not beautiful. And they want beautiful people on television. All the focus groups tell them that people want to watch beautiful reporters."

I stopped hearing him somewhere along in here.

"You have to get used to that in this business," continued Byron. "You have to pay some attention to how you look and then forget about it."

I was thinking of all the faces I'd seen on TV in Dallas, and couldn't for the life of me imagine I was less attractive than all of them.

"But don't let it bother you. Marty has been telling me for years that I'm too ugly for television."

I ARRIVED FOR MY FIRST DAY of work at nine in the morning.

"Do you know what Q-ratings are?" Byron asked me. I shook my head. No. "It's a rating based on an audience's response to your face on TV. The management decides how much air time to give you based on your Q-rating. That's what happened to Phyllis here. Her Q-rating dropped, so she was given the option of having her salary cut by two-thirds, or getting another job. She moved to Detroit."

I remembered seeing this stunning woman anchor the news. Apparently, her career was sent into a tailspin after her husband committed suicide. She lost weight and looked haggard. That made her Q-numbers tank.

"She got shafted here," said Byron. "This was her desk. It's yours now."

Byron walked around the office with his left hand shoved into his trouser pocket and his right stroking his chin. Rounding corners, he sighed deeply. When he was startled by someone passing close by, he looked up through his graduated bifocals as if at a car that had jumped over the median strip.

When he returned from one of his trots around the office, I asked him what I should do. I had visions of sinking into the carcass of a story like a pathologist on a dead man and coming up with the small specimen, the unlikely clue that revealed the cause of death. I was wired and ready to work, hungry for big stories and ready to spend whatever time and ingenuity it took to get them.

"Gee, well, I don't really know what you should do. Why don't you get a cup of coffee while I make some calls."

OVER THE NEXT WEEK OR SO, I learned that Byron had never worked with anyone before. He did not seem to know how or where to begin. At times, he suggested I write a lead-in to a piece, which I would do. Then it would disappear into his briefcase, and I'd never see it again. Naturally, I was convinced that it was so dreadful that he couldn't bear to bring it up. I was sure, though, that if we talked about it, talked about what needed improving, I'd learn fast.

I tagged along with him as he gathered material for possible stories. He gave me piles of clippings he had cut out of the newspapers, so I could learn about his interests. Then he asked me to file them.

I tried making myself useful. I tried to be ingenious, working contacts in Washington to get secret reports for him. Nothing I did seemed to please him. He seemed excessively paranoid; though he had been a star reporter at the station for years, he spoke as if he could lose his job at any minute. One day, a source mistakenly called me on his line rather than my own. I heard him say, angrily, "Emily Benedek works *for* me. She works *for* me."

On January 15, 1991, the Gulf War began with an attack by Allied forces on Baghdad. For the next three days, WFAA was in a turmoil, with reporters running out to cover prayer vigils, peace demonstrations, support group meetings. The local coverage aired when the networks took breaks. The war galvanized Byron. He did pieces on Iraqi airpower, vulnerable oil fields, terrorism. Finally, he found a task for me: he wanted me to drive to Toys "R" Us to buy some plastic planes for him to use in a demonstration of how American missiles are guided by lasers to their targets. For fifteen minutes, I examined all the planes, trying to figure out which would best suit his needs. This was the most challenging task I'd had yet at WFAA, and I wanted to get it right.

When I got home from work and told Craig what I had done that day, he said, "You have a Harvard education so you can buy planes at Toys 'R' Us?"

What upset me most about this conversation was that Craig was being kind to me. The previous week, he had said, "I don't think we should be living as man and wife if this relationship isn't going anywhere."

"Is it not going anywhere?" I asked. He didn't answer.

It seemed he was disturbed that his parents had not objected to the fact we were living together. "Living in sin" was the term he expected them to use, though we had both turned thirty. Their acceptance of this arrangement, paradoxically, unnerved him.

What he said was, "I want my children brought up as Catholics. I want them to go to parochial school."

I didn't know if he was provoking me, or whether he really meant this. One day in Phoenix, I had awakened to find a wooden statue of Jesus, arms outstretched, on Craig's bedside table. I asked Craig what the statue was doing beside our bed. He told me angrily that it was a present from Reynolds Price, that it was made of olive wood and had been purchased in Jerusalem. I told him that I couldn't live with that figure in the house. Craig told me I was intolerant and disrespectful of his religious feelings.

I thought about what he said and felt remorseful. I was very interested when he spoke to me about religion, even his own feelings about the Catholic Church. But seeing a figure of Jesus in my house unnerved me. And I knew I would never bring up a child as a Catholic.

Despite our numerous conflicts, I could not bring myself to leave Craig. The prospect of ending this relationship filled me with a great fear. I remembered that for years after breaking up with my college boyfriend, I tried to remake myself. I tried to expunge the parts I thought had given him trouble. It was a painful, self-lacerating time and I dreaded it happening again.

MY TROUBLES WITH CRAIG only made me more anxious to make a mark at work, accomplish something that I could proudly take with me back East. It was already February, and my book, which I had sent off to my editor in September, was not yet in production. Though it had been accepted and paid for, the experience didn't feel real to me. The book didn't yet exist, because no one had read it. I already felt ashamed that I had taken so long to finish it and still had nothing to show for my long absence from New York, making me even more anxious that the job at WFAA work out.

Soon after my experience at Toys "R" Us, I went to see Marty

Haag. As soon as I stepped into his office, he said, "You're here because you're bored and we're not giving you enough to do."

"Yes," I said.

"What do you want to do?"

"I'd like to be a reporter," I said. "I am a reporter. But I know I still have a lot to learn. Is there some kind of weekend show that no one watches on which I can learn how to report for TV?"

"I'll call the producer in."

I was surprised that Marty said yes, and so quickly. He walked out of the office and returned a few minutes later with a serious-looking, very young woman. He introduced her to me as the producer of *Weekend Journal*, a show that aired Sunday afternoons at twelve-thirty and which dealt with a single issue each week, using material that had already been gathered by the daily staff. The producer, Angelique, seemed excited at the prospect of having a reporter for her show. It seemed the deal was done. I thanked Marty and told him I was very grateful for the opportunity to do some substantive work.

Byron and I avoided each other for a few days. He seemed relieved to be back to his own routine. Marty told me Byron thought I was "in a bit of a hurry."

"That's why you hired me, wasn't it?" I replied, hurt by the rebuke. "To be aggressive, and help the station get stories it couldn't otherwise get?"

A few days later, Byron took me aside and told me I was making a mistake working for *Weekend Journal*. He said Angelique knew nothing about writing and wouldn't be able to help me. This comment made me feel panicky again. Why was he saying this? At least *Weekend Journal* and Angelique offered me work, real work, and the chance to learn. I tried to put his comments out of my mind, and I set to work interviewing scholars and Muslim clerical leaders. Two weeks later, I finished my first script, titled "Holy War," in which I endeavored to explain what a jihad was, and what the West represented to Islam. John McCaa, *Weekend Journal's* anchor, read it and told me he thought it was very good. He gave it to Marty, who read it and, passing me in the hall, said, "I read your script. Very good script."

I spent a day at Audience Research & Development, a local company that coaches anchors and television reporters across the country. My teacher, Fran, ran me through a half day of drills, most of which involved my sitting at an anchor desk and reading from a TelePrompTer. She told me I had a monotonous voice, like Susan Stamberg of NPR. She said I sounded like an eastern intellectual.

"That's so bad?" I asked.

"Here in the South, dear, you have to be perky. You have to keep their attention. You have to make them like you."

I PRACTICED READING my script several times alone in a tiny taping booth, hand cupped over my ear so I could hear the modulation of my voice, reading aloud to myself until the words no longer made any sense. When I thought I was ready, I dubbed the tape. Then Don Smith, the chief tape editor, a highly skilled and patient man, made the pictures I had chosen fit the words. After the piece was put together, Marty looked it over, pointed out a couple of places where I could have spoken faster, then said, "Your voice is not hard to listen to—to put it in the negative."

A couple of days after the story aired, Ilene, the station's assistant news director, walked up to me with a huge pile of literature on an environmentalist coming to talk to the Salesmanship Club, a local service organization, about saving ancient trees. The club also sponsored a camp for troubled boys in East Texas, where part of the children's therapy consisted of living in nature. She asked me to prepare a three-minute piece on the camp for Friday.

I reddened with excitement. I couldn't believe this was happening. Ilene was treating me like a regular reporter, giving me an assignment for a story to go on a regular news show. This was it. I was making it. The air seemed to move differently. I felt I could breathe again.

I arranged a date to go to the camp. I found a good photographer, and I devoured the material Ilene had given me. Within a few hours, however, the interview was mysteriously canceled. There would be no story on the camp for troubled youth. I was disappointed and puzzled, but I turned instead to my other assignments for *Weekend Journal*. I continued to learn about the etiquette of the TV newsroom and the nuts and bolts of TV reporting, though the pieces I was doing, at fourteen or fifteen minutes, were unusually long for regular TV. The photographers let me know that they hated extended interviews: "Get your sound bites and get out," they told me. I fairly quickly learned to do that, and in so doing, I honed my storytelling skills.

I was starting to settle into work, make friends, and socialize with some of the reporters. I learned how to put on makeup for television and I bought some appropriate clothes. My third piece called on me to run a panel discussion on air, and I was surprised and delighted when one of the weathermen, after seeing me tape an introduction on a studio monitor, called out, "Hey, you look good on television!"

Then, quite out of the blue, one Monday, Angelique told me that *Weekend Journal* was going on hiatus for three months, to be replaced by a syndicated football show the station had purchased. Since she was a permanent employee, they'd reassign her temporarily to another job. She said she'd try to get me put on the permanent payroll.

But that was not to be. "You are working too many hours for contract labor," Marty Haag told me, "and the front office is starting to ask questions about what you are doing here." He told me there were no part-time slots open for a reporter, and the only way he could see me staying was if John Miller, the news director, could use me. I was shocked at the speed with which the promise of my new job had crescendoed and then disappeared.

But Miller and I struck a deal. "OK," he told me. "I want you to choose a few stories, and we'll try to put together a good combination of reporter, photographer, and editor. I want you to do stories that everyone looks at and remembers." He said he was sorry it didn't work out with Byron, because Belo Corp. liked the idea of having more investigative pieces, and Byron had the stature and track record to make the company executives think the money was worth spending. But if I could come up with a few "dynamite" pieces that made people sit up and take notice, then that might persuade them to find some money for me.

Over the next few days, I put together a list of several story ideas and met with reporters. Quite a few were enthusiastic about getting producing help for stories. John McCaa, the *Weekend Journal* anchor, told me he had several specials coming up, for which he needed help. But then he said, "The work you did on the pieces for Angelique was very good. Are you sure you want to go to the other side of the camera and become a producer?"

I looked at him and couldn't answer.

"What do you want to do?" he asked.

Maybe it was because I knew McCaa better, or because he was an African-American and had seen hardship in his life, but this question sounded very different coming from him than it had from the others, from Haag and Miller.

What did I want to do? It seemed the furthest thing from my mind. I was just focused on hanging on, keeping a job at WFAA, not getting the boot.

Had I been able to see myself clearly, I might have wondered why that was. And I might have asked myself how it was that someone who had spent four years writing about an arcane Indian dispute was trying to be on TV in Dallas, where the audience wanted someone pretty and perky.

I went home and a deep weariness descended over me. That afternoon, I planned to drive to Neiman's to return the clothes I had just bought. I'd have no need of them behind the camera, and on my new pay schedule, I wouldn't be able to afford them.

A FEW DAYS LATER, I was lying on the corduroy couch in my study, the afternoon light starting to weaken outside. I had just awakened from a dream in which I was wearing the diamond-and-ruby ring that Craig had given me a year earlier. I accidentally snagged it on something, and the ring fell apart, the stones clattering to the floor, revealing it to be cheap and insubstantial.

I heard the front door open and a rustling in the front vestibule.

"Hello?" I asked, raising my head. I peered around the door and got a glimpse of a swirling skirt and hesitant steps. Then Craig's voice, high, uneasy.

"Hi."

I lay back down as he entered the room. I felt deeply exhausted.

"I'm here to show the apartment to somebody," he said. We had agreed to break up, but neither of us had decided who would move out of the apartment.

"OK," I said, still sleepy in the afternoon sun, sinking into the pillows of the couch. I realized someone was standing by the front door and not coming in.

"Is someone here?" I asked.

"Ah, well, yes, it's Sondra, from work." I stood up and saw a young woman with full, flowery skirt, standing awkwardly at the front door.

"Come in," I said, not quite awake.

"I thought I'd show her the apartment," said Craig.

"Yeah, OK, sure."

I lay back down. The afternoon heat made me quite drowsy. I heard voices in the back of the house, then rustling back at the front door.

"We were going to get some pizza," said Craig. "Do you want to come along?" He seemed friendly. I had no idea why I said yes.

I drove my own car and he drove Sondra in his pickup truck. At the pizzeria, Sondra and Craig sat next to each other across from me. I thought it was interesting the seating had worked out this way. Sondra had not yet looked me in the face. She swept her dark, straight hair up in her hands and let it fall away from its part. I remembered Craig telling a story about someone in his office, a reporter, who had worked her way to the *Journal* from a poor Mexican-American family, who got a piece of bread stuck in her hair during a lunch meeting. He got red in the face, laughing about it, his smile forced, almost a snarl. He had expressed such exaggerated aggravation at this mannerism of hers and the fact of the bread in her hair, that I had wondered about it. Now suddenly the whole picture became clear. It made perfect sense that Craig would feel contempt for the woman he lusted after. It seemed pretty clear they were on the verge of beginning an affair.

"You two aren't thinking of living in that apartment together, are you?" I asked suddenly. It was rude, and I knew it.

"Oh, no," said Craig.

"Oh, no," said the girl. "I already have an apartment."

"Ah," I said, taking a sip of iced tea, bile rising. "So, why did you want to see the place?"

"Oh, just to see it, in case, you know, I had a friend who was looking."

I looked up at Craig. I hadn't figured that someone else was involved. He looked away. Then I understood what I should have understood at the beginning, what I should have gathered from the sight of the flowery skirt billowing in the afternoon breeze, by the feet that stepped uncertainly, as if hesitant to enter. But I hadn't been able to read it on Craig's face. Was he that good at lying? I remembered one of the first things he had told me: "I sometimes have trouble with the truth."

The next day I awoke with a twitch under my eye. It lasted for ten days. At first, I thought it was fury.

I LOOK FORWARD EVERY WEEK to attending services on Saturday morning. I wake up early, pull on a dress, and drive off, excited. It is many weeks before I am no longer overwhelmed by sense impressions during the service and I actually begin to pick out its structure. I begin to learn the prayers by heart. But then I have questions. When was the prayer book as we know it put together? Are certain prayers older than others? Do all Jews follow the same service?

Since we don't use a real prayer book, but a condensed version of the service that the rabbi has reproduced in the booklets, I don't actually see all the Hebrew words, only bits and pieces. When I have questions, I ask the rabbi during Kiddush. As I have more and more questions, I call him during the week. The *Beth Emunah Light*, the little newsletter we get in the mail, includes a phone number for the "Rabbi's Study."

I am completely charmed to see the word "study" used here in Dallas. My father had a study, into which he retired after dinner every evening to work on lectures or papers. Whom have I met since I left New York, besides myself, who has a study?

The rabbi's blue eyes are jovial, and his white hair forms a wreath of curls around his face. His toothy smile breaks open easily. He gestures with his hands as he speaks, turns his wrist, waves the air in gestures that look like the ones my father makes. Rabbi Groesberg is full of life and curiosity and humor and, though he is in his seventies, his manner is childlike. He has liberal and interesting interpretations of Judaism. He says that on the Sabbath he doesn't subscribe to complete prohibitions against driving or turning on lights. He feels that if you have worked all week with your hands, on the Sabbath you should use your mind. If you use your mind all week, on the Sabbath, you should be physical.

Every Saturday, he gives a short sermon. It is always well organized and structured, and when he finishes, the congregation asks a few polite questions and discusses what he says. I realize over time that the rabbi gives no ground, brooks no disagreement. After reaching a conclusion about a point, he never wavers from it.

The cantor is a very different fellow, whose black hat and suit reflect the influence of his rabbinical training at an Orthodox seminary. His name is Frank Joseph. When we are first introduced, I don't understand a word he says. I am afraid he has a speech impediment, but when his sister chimes in, speaking the same way, I realize they both have extremely thick Texas accents, real back-country twangs. I can't believe my ears. They tell me they grew up in Corsicana with two older brothers and an older sister, where their father was the rabbi of the Orthodox—and later, after the town's population diminished, also the Reform—shul.

During the war, their father Ernest and his family had escaped from Germany and made it to Shanghai, where they lived in a camp for Jewish refugees run by the Japanese, who were then occupying parts of China. Students and teachers from the famous Mir Yeshivah, which had decamped from Poland during World War II, first to Lithuania and then to Shanghai on visas written by Chiune Sugihara, the Japanese consul general to Lithuania, organized a makeshift yeshivah there to educate the children. Ernest learned at the yeshivah and survived because his own father gave most of his food to his wife and children, starving himself into lasting ill health as a consequence. After the war, the family came to America, and Ernest found a job in Texas.

Frank Joseph proves himself to be an exceedingly generous and selfless person. In fact, he postponed his earlier rabbinic training to care for his infirm and beloved grandmother until her death. He gives me books, and sometimes, in answer to a question I have, handwritten pages of explication. He earns a living tutoring bar and bat mitzvah candidates and as a traveling Torah reader for various Dallas synagogues. He is also a radio deejay, running a program of Jewish music on a local station.

I call my father to tell him about attending services at Beth Emunah. I don't tell him that I thought I sensed his presence beside me at times in the service. Rather, I tell him about the warm feel of the place. I tell him the stories of the rabbi and the Joseph family. I talk about the sweet blackberry wine for the Kiddush, the taste of the first bite of sweet challah on my tongue, its edge dipped in coarse-ground salt. I talk about the herring and the chopped egg.

And I tell him about the lady who came to the synagogue who had a wonderful Hungarian singsong that reminded me instantly of my grandmother Viola. This woman was tiny, with neat brown hair and a bright red suit. She told us that when the Nazis arrived in Hungary in 1942, she was mistakenly rounded up with a group of Jewish children who were being marched to the border. She was a married woman, but she twisted off her ring and hid it in her dress. She grasped the hand of the little girl beside her and walked on. At some point during their march, a Hungarian militiaman escorting the children caught sight of her and began to stare. She tried to avoid his gaze, but finally he stepped from his position, walked toward her, and said, "You look just like my sister. You will never return from this walk. Go, now, and run into the woods." The woman said that with her little partner's hand still in hers, she broke from the file and ran. The girls were taken in by peasant families and hidden until the end of the war.

I tell my father I asked her, "Did you ever try to find that man after the war, to thank him?"

I explain that the woman turned to me with a brilliant smile, her face illuminated, and said, "I would never have found him, don't you see? He was an angel. An angel from God."

MY FATHER BEGINS to attend services on Saturday mornings at Harvard Hillel.

A month or so later, my mother tells me she has started reading a Jewish newspaper in Boston and she has decided to take a Talmud class in Brookline. Both seem to be inspired by my new explorations.

Around this time, my sister and her husband buy a new house in Winchester, a Boston suburb. I ask her if the town has a synagogue. "No," she says. I hear defiance in her voice. "Does that bother you?" I ask, and she begins to cry.

Chapter Four

∞

LEARNING TO SEE

THE MIDRASH SAYS that one way to get close to God is to get close to a good person.

I found that good person.

He is not a rabbi, though he is a dedicated scholar, wise and kind. He appreciates Talmudic analysis and, in a manner of speaking, has devoted his life to it. Like Maimonides, he is an independent thinker and also a medical doctor. I imagine he believes in God, though I never asked him, and if I had, he might not have answered.

This good person is a psychoanalyst. My return to the religion of my forebears was nurtured in the office of a doctor whose profession was once believed to be a primary antagonist of religious belief. Further, my religious reconnection was encouraged by a man who is not a Jew, and whose scholarly and religious interests embrace the New

Testament. Strange as it may seem, my curiosity about Judaism was sparked by a Christian psychoanalyst; I am quite sure I would not have begun to go to synagogue had I not been in analysis with Dr. Andresen.

With Dr. Andresen, I experienced the enigma of revelation in language. He reinforced my belief in the power of words and the gravity of meaning, both of which had been pummeled by my experiences in Dallas and elsewhere in my life. Without the inspired care he offered, it is doubtful I would have felt the deep gratitude and weak-kneed joy I did later at certain words of the prayers, at certain moments of the liturgy.

Dr. Andresen used no tricks: he was a master both of interpretation and silence, and he knew the right time for each. His interpretations never included lingo or technical terms such as "Oedipal conflict" or "resistance" or "projection," though because of my intellectual interest in the subject matter, he did offer observations about psychoanalysis, Freud, and the workings of the mind. His words to me were usually enigmatic; I think this was because their purpose was to encourage me to think and probe independently of him or any fixed dogma about human behavior. He told stories about his experiences observing and helping others in distress, and he often made specific allusions to literature, mentioning the works of such writers as Charles Dickens, Gerard Manley Hopkins, Joseph Conrad, and T. S. Eliot. To my great surprise, he also referred to the Bible.

I found Dr. Andresen by calling the chairman of the psychiatry department at the University of Texas medical school a few weeks before Craig left. I was afraid of the dark brooding into which I was sinking, and I was afraid of mourning Craig dangerously, as I had mourned lovers before. I felt I hadn't the capacity to ride out a similar reaction again

The chairman, a psychoanalyst himself, gave me only one name, whom he was quite sure would be the man for me. Jeffry J. Andresen, M.D., was a graduate of the University of Pennsylvania Medical School who had been a psychiatry resident at Harvard's premier teaching facility, the Massachusetts Mental Health Center, and a teaching fellow at the Harvard Medical School. A psychoanalyst and academic in North Carolina for many years, he had just arrived in Texas as a professor of psychiatry and he was, the chairman assured me, literary and very smart.

THIS IS HOW IT BEGINS. Standing in an empty editing booth at WFAA, the door closed behind me, I pick up the telephone and dial. The phone is answered by a man with the gentlest voice I have ever heard. I ask if I might make an appointment to see him.

"All right," he says and pauses. I hear the pages of a book turning, and then he proposes a date.

I can hardly answer. I am counting off the days until then in my head, and I wonder if I will be able to make it.

"Oh, my," I say, "that's a long time."

"Will that be too long?" he asks. The fact of his asking seems so kind, it is as if he had offered me his hand. I decide that the sound of his voice will help me get through. "I'll be OK," I say.

"Well, all right then," he says, softly, almost tentatively, and he gives me directions to his office at the medical school.

THE ROOM INTO WHICH Dr. Andresen leads me is decorated in simple, modern taste, vaguely Scandinavian, filled with light and a half-dozen brilliantly blooming African violets. There is a bamboo daybed that serves as a couch, which I don't use, and two matching barrel-shaped chairs upholstered in blue that tip and roll and swivel. These chairs face each other. The one in which Dr. Andresen sits is placed between his desk and the head of the couch. The one in which I sit is across the room, in front of the door and a wall of bookcases. On a wicker table beside Dr. Andresen's chair, the pink flowers of an oxalis stretch up delicately from their purple leaves. More than a dozen diplomas and certificates hang on the wall beside him.

Dr. Andresen is somewhat taller than six feet, and, I guess, in his late forties. He has neatly trimmed dark hair, a high brow, fine, straight nose, and eyes that are both fiercely intelligent and kind. He dresses casually, in corduroy pants, button-down shirts, academic ties. He looks fit, and his posture and bearing exude a strong receptiveness, as if his body were capable of drawing pain away from others and holding it within himself. I wonder if he is an athlete. I have noticed that people who compete in sports develop a knowledge of their own bodies and internal capacities that is often reflected in a physical calm. Later, I discovered he shares this idea; he told me that he knew within ten seconds whether or not his medical residents had played competitive sports. "Athletes live in the ease of studied relations with their bodies," he told me, "and they've been formed in relations with coaches, so they expect wholehearted collaborations with teachers in demanding work. They don't look as if they are about to whine."

The room welcomes the emptying of my memory. It seems to be a space that is friendly to strivings like my own.

I AM SURE I am quite disagreeable when I first arrive. I am agitated and fearful. I have no idea why my world is crashing down around me; it seems that I am working as hard as I can, and yet I am failing at everything. I feel like Captain Ahab at the wheel of the *Pequod*, aware of little save the necessity of keeping the mutinous ship on course.

I begin by telling Dr. Andresen I believe I must be doing something wrong, or a whole system of things wrong. I believe there must be a key, an organizing principle to my errors. That is why I am here, to root out the bad spot and expose it to light.

What did I do wrong at WFAA? What happened there? Why is Craig leaving, and why is my book still unpublished? I feel pressed for time, and am painfully aware of days and months and years passing. I have already wasted six months in Dallas. In the blink of an eye, it will be a year. I must get back East, I must get my life back on track. How can I have squandered my promise in this way? How is it that I find myself lost in such a place?

These are the kinds of things I tell him, all in a rush, an urgent exhalation of words and worries. Then, more calmly, I assemble lists of observations about myself that I believe strike at some elemental truths: "I don't work well in organizations. I usually become convinced at one moment or another that the person who is supposed to watch out for me will betray me." . . . "I am hateful. Craig is leaving because I killed something between us." . . . "I can't seem to learn the rules like everybody else does." I accuse myself. I dig for faults. I am frantic, restless.

"What do you feel in your body?" he asks me.

In my body? "I feel like I want to jump right out of this chair," I say. I think to myself: "What is this, some kind of a come-on?"

"I have an ache in my head," I continue. "My feet feel like cement. My stomach is rolled into a ball."

I bluster, I recite.

Dr. Andresen listens to this for weeks. Then one day he says,

"Don't extinguish the meaning out of things by trying to define them too carefully. Don't crush the life out of them."

Then he slams his hand down on the arm of his chair. "What color are its legs?" he asks, opening his hand as if to reveal pieces of the imaginary object he has just smashed.

I am shocked at first, and in my confusion I think I have missed a literary reference. I think the broken figure must be a symbol from a story I have forgotten or don't know. I think about what he says for several days. Dr. Andresen has shown me he is a most kind and patient man. His anger is unusual, so I take notice. I feel I had better pay attention. As I think about his words, allow the events of the last few weeks to run through my head, remaining attentive to the parade of images, attending to my mind's eye as he suggested, I sense, through the mists, that he is offering me a new way of thinking.

"The inquiry," he says, "should be illuminating rather than reductive."

The next night, in a dream, I enter Dr. Andresen's office and find there are many other people there. I see this and go away.

After I tell Dr. Andresen the dream, I start to talk about writing. I mention that I have been looking over my journals, and I am struck by the deadness of their tone.

"There is nothing in them," I say. "No details, no stories."

He looks at me. He is quiet for a few moments. "In your dream," he says, "you came into the room. You wanted to talk, but there were too many other people talking. You could not be heard, so you went away."

I am quiet for a few minutes. His comment changes the dream. It is as if he had taken a few steps away from me and offered a new view.

That night, I have a dream in which I am sitting in a classroom, trying to fold up a map. There are vellum overlays on the map, and I am trying to keep them all together while I work the folds. The teacher, irritated, walks over to me, grabs the maps away from me and crinkles them into a ball.

With dreams like this, who needs an analyst? Here, Dr. Andresen wasn't breaking statuary, but he was snatching away the maps whose personal escape routes I was trying to secrete away.

Dr. Andresen says, "You might try to become more attentive to spontaneous thoughts and retain an openness to unbidden images and emotions."

What he wants is simple, but it seems so desperately hard. I think I know what I am supposed to do. Keep my attention focused on my mind's eye, that movie screen in my head that runs round the clock.

It's much easier to tell everyone else's story. How can I tell my own story, when watching everyone else seems so much more important? I come across a passage in Edith Wharton's autobiography that seems to fit: "I had to fight my way to expression," she wrote, "through a thick fog of indifference."

Instead, it has become my lifelong habit to offer judgment, criticism, condemnation. Dr. Andresen asks me one day, "If you wanted to know what a butterfly looked like, would you capture it, kill it, and pin it to a board, or would you observe it in its natural state?"

It is some time before I allow myself simply to describe, without trying to analyze. I twist and wriggle and "explain myself away."

THE DREAMS COME in a steady patter like rain. At times, they are whipped and seesawed by winds, blown into squalls, pelting their images against my eyes before swirling into rivulets and flowing off to sea.

Unlike Schliemann at Troy, I am not digging for treasures; the masks and statues appear on their own. In the morning when I wake, the storm has left them jutting from the sand, stern talismans whose eyes are fixed on the distance, as if on still-buried companions, once-loved views.

Certain dreams seem now to me to be a map, an outline of everything else to come, an array of clues connected together with a wobbly plot. The images form my own Rosetta stone, a key to the voyage, as if somewhere deep inside me a force were organizing my own revelations, bit by bit, as it saw fit. I am humbled now by the command of this arbiter, this force that controls my knowing, giving up messages when it wants, flooding me at times, then drying to a trickle, leaving me frantic for more.

ALTHOUGH I EARNED an undergraduate degree in psychology, it takes me a while to master free association. Why do I think of writing after telling Dr. Andresen of a dream in which I feel no one is listening? What is the logic of the association of one thought to the other? Could they just be random thoughts, the result of odd neuron firings? I try to examine the logic of the connections, but there is no simple cause-and-effect relation, or easy categorical ties. Dr. Andresen has encouraged me to continue with the process, to let it evolve, rather than trying to define its meaning too narrowly. Although it is against my inclination, I decide to wait and see. I try to learn patience. I am here, after all, because I feel the need for new insight. And I feel protected in this journey into the unknown because of the serious integrity I sense in Dr. Andresen.

In time, I understand the work is like inviting my dreams into this room, following connections of memories and thoughts that are linked by samenesses—of emotion, perhaps, or of ideas. It is like following the path in an old garden back to a familiar spot and stumbling upon a formerly unnoticed shrub, noting a familiar but slightly different fork in the road, and understanding it differently. In time, I see I am traveling back through the organization of my mind. I am looking at nothing less than the architecture of my own personality.

One day, I notice a print that hangs over Dr. Andresen's couch. I swivel in my chair, interrupting my story to face it.

"Is that a Cézanne?" I ask.

Yes, he says, and I burst into tears.

When I stop, he says, "You were so engaged when you asked about that painting."

"I was just so happy to see a Cézanne" I say. This room seems so unlike the rest of Dallas, so different from the morass into which I feel I have fallen.

"AND WHAT IS YOUR BOOK ABOUT?" Dr. Andresen asks me one day. I am suddenly stopped in my tracks by the realization that I have yet to speak of it, though I spent four and a half years reporting and writing it.

I tell him what it is about.

"So it is a love story," says Dr. Andresen, nodding gravely.

I am silent. I look up at him, confused. "Love story?" I ask. "I don't think so. There's no sex in it. Too bad, probably. It won't sell." I laugh. He does not.

"It is a love story," he says, taking a breath, pushing his folded hands toward his knees, looking at me with a combination of gravity, compassion, and concentration.

I look at him. After several minutes, Dr. Andresen says, "It is a story about what people love, what is most important to them."

I am silent again. Suddenly, the idea of love has metamorphosed in front of me. Why did I assume that a love story was a story of romantic love? I sit silently, lost in thought.

"Well," says Dr. Andresen, placing his glasses on the small table beside him, indicating the hour is up.

I AM DREAMING BECAUSE I have a place to dream into. Dr. Andresen is exquisitely attentive. His eyes meet mine and never turn away. Sometimes, when he is sitting with one leg crossed over the other, his top foot gives a little kick, as if to help me push away interferences. On his desk is an etymological dictionary, leather-covered, well worn, with gilt-edged pages. Dr. Andresen reaches for it often and when he finds a meaning or an origin that extends the discussion, his face is lit with an expression of sublimity. He seems to believe we choose words with full knowledge of their extensive meanings and associations in literature, and even their origins. This belief suggests to me the existence of a great unconscious intelligence, and stirs me to occasional thoughts about God.

AS I SETTLE INTO OUR ROUTINE, I realize that I fear that every session will be the last one. I enter with great excitement and expectation and leave with a foreboding that once I leave his room I will not return. I realize this fear is unfounded and doesn't make sense, but it is there nevertheless.

One day I decide I would like to try to lie down on the couch. My idea is that it might allow me to free-associate more easily. Maybe I will be able to look off into space and let my thoughts go. But when I do lie down, I feel tense and uneasy. After a couple of tries, I tell Dr. Andresen I don't like it. I realize I am afraid he will go away when I'm not looking.

"And where do you think I will go?" he asks

"I'm afraid you'll go right out the window," I say. He nods, as if he understands something I do not.

ONE DAY, as I am leaving his office, the door closes behind me, and before I take a step down the hall, I stop and think to myself, "Damn, I did it again, I talked the whole session." I feel shame and a sharp fear. Next time, I swear to myself, I will shut up and let the doctor talk. If I don't let him talk, I'm sure, he'll get bored and go away.

THE DREAMS CONTINUE. But now I dream of drains: drain pipes, sinks, joints. Sometimes I hear the sounds of drains gurgling, whooshing, tinkling. In one, I see an acrobat, a girl with her feet in the air. She is balancing on a trapeze on a straw, which she holds between her teeth. She stays balanced, in the position of a diver in midair, for a long time until suddenly, without a sign, she nudges herself forward, and dives straight down. At the bottom, as she nears the ground, she is in water, and glides forward like a fish. I look closer and see she has in fact glided down the pipe and trap of a sink, the sink in the downstairs bathroom in the house in which I grew up, a common S-curve trap on a bathroom sink. I feel a most powerful but unknown force in the girl-fish, frightening and other worldly.

More drains. Later, the same S-trap, behind which is a hole stuffed up with a black plastic garbage bag. Then I dream about a murder. A woman has been murdered, and the black bag is a clue. Something is being covered up. I think of a dream I had in high school in which I was Raskolnikov. I murdered my neighbor and spent the rest of the dream in terror, waiting for the investigators to find me. I walk past an elevator bank with an armful of black plastic bags. I have a terrifying dream of an elevator that doesn't work. I step in, push a button, the doors close, but the elevator doesn't move.

Then relief, the flying dreams, when I flap my arms as if I were swimming the breaststroke until I get airborne and soar over my elementary school. In some dreams, I am being chased and cannot take off.

"What is flying?" I ask Dr. Andresen.

"Otto Rank believed that flying in dreams represented wishes for an easy birth."

"Easy birth?" I ask.

He waits a while, then says, "Easy separation from the mother."

I DON'T KNOW how my mother chooses this time for her visit. Perhaps she has a sense of impending crisis, and her motherly instinct leads her to me. But I don't think I could be more unnerved about her arrival, as it is the worst time possible for her to come. The reporter with whom I began my first piece under the new arrangement at WFAA developed a disc problem that has sent him to the hospital for back surgery, and I don't think my job at WFAA will be resuscitated again. Not to mention that Craig and I are about to split up for the final time.

Before my mother arrives, I have a dream that she is pregnant with my cat. I can see the cat inside her belly, jumping, diving, doing somersaults. The cat is like the famous Egyptian statue in the Metropolitan Museum.

"You gave her something," Dr. Andresen says.

"What?" I ask.

"She is fecund with something you have given to her."

I am overcome with emotion. I don't know why.

* * *

I WONDER WHAT MY MOTHER will do when I go to my sessions with Dr. Andresen. Should I bring her to a store? No, she hates shopping. Shall I point her toward Turtle Creek and a relaxing walk? What I imagine is her sitting in the car, waiting for me, as if she were the child and I the adult.

"Ah, you had the thought of bringing her along," says Dr. Andresen the next time. I am thrown into silent consideration again by Dr. Andresen's choice of words. He has offered me a completely new thought.

I think then of another moment when he did the same thing. I had told him that when I was a child I had asked my mother to help me finish a story I was writing. I couldn't think of an ending, and I had told her about my problem. She offered me three lines. I still remember how I scribbled them at the bottom of the page, squeezing them in by wrapping the lines up the sides of the paper. When I got the story back, the teacher noted that she had liked it, but thought the ending didn't quite fit with the rest. I didn't tell my mother about the comment. I was even uncomfortable telling Dr. Andresen about it; I felt mean-spirited.

But Dr. Andresen had said, "Ah, you left room in your story for your mother."

It was his gift, it seemed to me, to see the loving intentions that I no longer could.

"You wondered where your mother might go while you came here," he says the next session. "You had a thought of bringing her along with you. Perhaps you can show her the birds."

Birds?

He looks at me with a smile.

"What birds?"

He doesn't say anything.

"They are fantastic," he says with one of his appreciative grins.

"Did you know my mother was a birder?" My mother is a bird-watcher of sorts. I stop, think back, "Did I tell you she was a birder?" I am searching my mind for clues. Does he know something I don't know he knows? Why is he suggesting she look at birds?

Dr. Andresen smiles, jokes, "I want to make sure you don't take me for granted."

After the session, I follow his directions and walk over the hill toward the parking garages. In an elbow of land carved out by a loop in Harry Hines Boulevard, I see a cluster of trees in what looks like a primeval swamp. I look into the trees and I see they are full of gigantic white egrets. They look like Carol Channing in white boas. Every few minutes, a bird will slowly take off, miraculously lifting its impossibly huge body into the air currents.

Once airborne, the birds look like images from a Hiroshige print, oddly two-dimensional, their necks pulled into tight S-curves. It is an astonishing sight, these birds building nests, taking off from and landing in a small city of tremendous industry: building, feeding, nesting, leaving in search of food. For generations, perhaps centuries, these birds have made their nests here, and someone—God love him—had the foresight to save this spot. Imagine Dallas, the town of cigar-chomping, blow-dried, slick-polyester-suited real estate sharks, passing up this prime corner for a thousand big birds who look like Las Vegas showgirls.

My mother arrives two days later. Craig asks if I want him to accompany us to dinner, to act like everything is all right between us and I say yes. I don't like to tell her bad news. I am just hoping to last through this visit without falling apart. I also have a vaguely defined but intense feeling that I want to communicate something about the tears I am shedding for her, I want to soften the walls between us, but I do not know how. Dr. Andresen's idea about showing her the birds intrigues me.

On the morning of my appointment, the sky is gray and overcast, and my mother does not seem eager to go and see the birds. She tells me she'll drink coffee, putter around the apartment, and meet me when I get back. So I go to my session and leave her behind, just what I hadn't wanted to do. When I return, she is dressed and ready to go out. Again, she seems hesitant to go see the birds, though I can't imagine why.

Finally, seemingly resigned to this duty, she gathers together her binoculars and her bird guidebook. We climb into my car and drive over. She asks me about Craig, and I tell her things are not going very well.

"He is not a very nice person," I say.

"All men are mean, Emily. You have to get used to that."

I am quiet. Is she trying to tell me I should stay in this relationship? Does it occur to her that perhaps it is not up to me? Is she implying that the failure of the relationship is due to my inability to endure?

I try to shake it off. We are nearing Parkland Hospital now, and I wonder if she'll recognize it. It looks a little different than it did in 1963, but there is still the low overhang of the emergency-room entrance, the angular hospital behind. She notices it, but without the kind of intense curiosity I had expected. "Is that it?" she asks vaguely, and I say yes. She doesn't really look back at it. I am surprised. This area of Dallas is filled for me with a strange energy. I remember the day of President Kennedy's assassination very well, though I was five years old.

"Are you completely convinced that this is where you want to stay?" she asks me suddenly.

I am stunned by her question. "Of course I'm not completely convinced." I am thinking that I would rather do nothing more than leave, instantly, but I cannot tell her that, nor can I explain why my feet have become suddenly leaden. I can't tell her how frantic I feel about breaking up with Craig. I can't tell her that when I think of his face, I am filled with a searing pain.

"I guess I've decided it's best for me to stay until I have a better plan," I tell her.

"But you don't have a job now."

Why is she saying this? I have always been able to get magazine assignments when I needed them. However, it is true that through the years, without my asking, she has sent me money when she suspected my finances were tight. In this way, she has made it possible for me to continue being a writer.

She pushes once more. "You know your sister wouldn't be able to live as she does with only one income." And I burst into tears.

All I can choke out is "Mom, it's not so easy to find someone."

She leans over and brushes my hair back from my forehead, as if I were a child.

"There's no reason to cry," she says, her voice rising with impatience. "Now just don't worry about it. Everything is going to be fine."

I can hardly see the road, I am so upset by this exchange, but I am determined to follow through with my plan. I turn left just past Parkland Hospital and enter the medical school campus. I feel I am on automatic pilot. I am going to ignore what just happened, because I want to show her the birds, the tremendously graceful white manifestations of muscle and feathers, perched on the edge of a primordial swamp in the middle of this ugly city. History in the middle of antihistory; astonishment in the midst of utter banality. I pull up to the swamp and look over at her, to see the expression on her face. But she isn't looking at the birds. She is gathering together her binoculars and her book, preparing to step out.

We walk over the wet grass toward the nesting area. I look up and see a large bird ten feet away from us picking its way toward a large stick. It promenades carefully, like a woman in spike heels. After a few tentative jabs, the bird picks up the stick and walks away with it, revealing elegant, wispy tail plumes that drape off its ample derrière. I smile and look over to my mother again. Has she seen it?

My mother's face is buried in her guidebook. She is on the page marked "Egrets."

"Do they have black legs?" she asks. "If they have black legs, they are great egrets." She doesn't look up. She is more interested in the categories in the book, it seems, than in looking at the astonishing birds right here.

"How about the beaks, what is the shape?" She is narrowing it down now, helped by my description of the actual birds.

She concludes that the birds are indeed great egrets. I nod. I am disappointed that she hasn't stopped to look, just enjoy this extraordinary sight with me, but I feel I can't prompt her. It is time for me to say what I have planned.

"Mom," I say, turning toward her. "I want to let you know I brought you here for a reason." I hear myself speaking like a machine, an automaton, and I try to adjust my tone a register or two, but am only partially successful. "I know you don't like psychiatrists. I know you think they turn people into monsters and make them hate their mothers. I wanted to bring you here while I went in so that you wouldn't feel I was leaving you behind. I wanted to show you that we could go out together, part, and come back together."

I realize this sounds incredibly odd, but I go on. "I wanted you to know that I am not becoming a monster with Dr. Andresen." My voice rises with the strain of controlling my emotions, but I continue. "That's not the purpose, and that's not what's going on in that room."

She walks over to me and puts her arms around me. I notice how skinny she is, how small and wiry. We are hugging each other, but, still angry about the conversation in the car, I feel no catharsis. However, I have done what I set out to do, and for that I feel glad. I don't cry. I am numb.

"I don't think that's what they do," she says. "Don't you worry. Everything's going to be fine. If it helps you to find out what's important to you and make the important decisions you need to make, that's fine."

I hear her words, and they are good words and fitting. But as I stand there, I wonder to myself why they don't reassure me.

When I tell Dr. Andresen about our visit to the birds, he is very interested in my description of my mother burying her head in her book while I was watching the birds take off and land like space shuttles.

"You and your mother have very different ways of seeing," he says. "You look at the poetry of the birds. Your mother is more interested in classifying them."

And like everything else he says to me, it disturbs my thoughts, shakes them up. It's like digging up a plant, freeing clots of dirt from its roots, and sticking it back into the garden bed in a slightly different spot. It never occurred to me that we simply think differently, only that there was something terribly wrong between us and that it was my fault.

"She said something funny as we were leaving," I say. "She used a birder's term for a bird she's likely to see only once in her life, but will always remember. She said, 'I guess that was a life bird.'"

"Did she really?" Dr. Andresen says, clasping his hands together and shaking his head with an expression of great appreciation.

It is time to go, and I leave feeling hopeful, thinking the trip to the birds may, in the end, have been successful. Perhaps my mother was trying to tell me that we had indeed spoken deeply to each other—

each in her own way—while observing the birds—each in her own way.

THERE IS ONE MORE THING, though, that I must talk over. Next time, I tell Dr. Andresen about the infuriating conversation I had with my mother in the car on the way to the birds, in which she pulled me this direction and that with questions until I finally burst into tears in confusion and frustration.

When I finish, Dr. Andresen is quiet. Eventually, he says: "I'll tell you a story. Once after I gave a talk to a community gathering, a woman called and told me she was having trouble with her daughter. The daughter was lying, and every time she was caught, the mother beat her. The child continued to lie, and the mother continued to beat her. The mother was very distressed, because the girl knew that lying would bring on a beating, and yet she continued to lie. During one episode, the child even cried out, 'Beat me, Mama, beat me!'"

Dr. Andresen told the woman that when something is going wrong with a child, he usually looks at the family. Was anything happening, he asked her, of an unusual nature?

"Oh, no," she had said, "no, nothing unusual." He was quiet for a while to give her time to think, and then she said, "No, nothing is wrong, except my husband lost his job."

After more silence, she said, "He lost his job and he is having trouble finding a new one, and we're in danger of losing the house."

"So there was trouble," says Dr. Andresen, "and the mother was likely quite anxious and unhappy about the situation. What I surmise was happening was that the little girl was offering herself as a victim so that her mother had an outlet for her anger. The child gave the mother an opportunity to relieve her own anxiety and fear and anger by breaking a clearly stated rule."

I think of the girl, beneath her mother's blows, crying, "Beat me, Mama," and I cringe.

Dr. Andresen nods. "I suggest that these conversations that you have with your mother—that you have noted having on several occasions—work the same way. As soon as she has provoked a reaction of tears or anger in you, she has relieved herself of her anxiety. You are helping her release her anxiety."

I listen quietly, and when it is time, I walk out, lost in thought. My mother and I have been having the same conversation, with different words, for years. My mother has been trying to hand off her anxieties to me. We have ritualized this communication, never understanding the meaning behind the words. How different is the conversation now that I understand it. She is asking for help. Now, I no longer have to respond with tears or fury. I can hold off my reaction and listen for what she is really saying.

WHOEVER IN THE great cosmic scheme of things engineered my detour through Dallas was not only fiendishly cruel but fiendishly clever as well. Had I not been marooned in that city in the midst of my personal meltdown, I might never have been given the insight that solved the central mystery of my childhood.

There is not much sightseeing in Dallas except Dealey Plaza and the Book Depository, the grassy knoll and the hairpin turn. These spots draw tourists and newcomers to Dallas every day of the year. In fact, after the Thanksgiving meal at Craig's and my apartment, our guests spontaneously piled into cars and drove down to the site. When we got there, we weren't quite sure why we had come, but we walked around, as if needing to touch that spot, whose horrific crime had colored all of our childhoods.

During my mother's visit, I drive her downtown, past the *Dallas Morning News*, and the WFAA-TV offices next door, showing her the places I had worked. Both buildings are just across the square from Dealey Plaza and the Book Depository, right near the train station and the small area that makes up downtown Dallas. As we pull around Grackle Park, I see an eerie tableau of vintage cars. Chevrolets and Buicks, their fins and bulbous bodies conjuring the sixties instantly, are parked in a line. As we drive on, I notice a gathering of old police motorcycles, with men in wide-hipped breeches and boots astride or standing alongside them. Then, a long, open, black limousine flying U.S. flags on its fenders; parked along the hairpin turn is a replica of JFK's final motorcade.

And then I remember reading in the paper that Oliver Stone's movie *JFK* is being shot downtown. My mother looks on in interest as we park the car. She tells me she would like to see the memorial erected by Jackie Kennedy and designed by I. M. Pei. We walk toward the grassy common, around the motorcade, and see extras in uniforms leaning on old black and white police cars, smoking cigarettes, talking quietly. There are women in knee-length skirts, pillbox hats, cotton shifts, white gloves.

It occurs to me now that if Oliver Stone had not been filming his movie the very week of my mother's visit, I may never have understood how that day changed my own life forever. We find the Pei monument, four walls of white limestone enclosing a shiny black marble slab that looks like the base of a statue. A plaque describes it as a monument to an unfinished work. My mother looks at it appreciatively. I don't sense any particular emotion in her. I ask her if she wants to go up to the sixth floor of the Book Depository, which now is a museum.

My mother shakes her head. She is sure. She has seen enough

and wants to go home. Since it is lunchtime, I head for the Highland Park Village Shopping Center, a Moorish mall of stylish, expensive boutiques, which has a small bakery that serves sandwiches.

The bakery looks like a confection from Disney's *Babes in Toyland*, with a Victorian banister painted pink that sweeps like a heavy swirl of frosting up a curved stairway to a small eating area decorated with ice-cream-parlor chairs and marble tables. We climb the stairs and set down our trays.

"You know, JFK's death had a very big effect on me," my mother says after taking a bite of her sandwich.

"I know," I say. "I remember you weeping. I remember the TV on for all those days, I remember the horse walking down the street with the boots backward in the stirrups. And, of course, I remember you tacking up black cloth over the front door."

"Oh," she says, "it was much more than that."

"What do you mean?" I ask.

"I was home alone after the assassination. You girls were out with Dad. The television was on, and all of a sudden, right in front of God and everyone, Jack Ruby shot Lee Harvey Oswald. I started screaming and I couldn't stop."

I am surprised to hear this. My mother seems eager to talk, and she continues without prompting.

"I felt that nothing made sense anymore. If this could happen, anything could happen. It began a very difficult period for me."

"How is that?"

"I was afraid to go out, I was afraid to go to the grocery store. I didn't feel safe."

"Did you ever go for help?"

"Oh, no," she says, shaking her head disdainfully. "I knew I could take care of it myself."

I nod. Of course, seeking help is a weakness, to her. But how frightened she must have been. Not only from the fear itself, but her conviction that there was no one to help her.

"And how long did it last?" I ask.

"Oh," she says, "about ten years."

TOWARD THE END of the next hour, I tell this story to Dr. Andresen. He gives me a look. I look back.

"Now do you understand?" he asks me. I have told this story with a half smile on my face. It seems like so much else about my childhood: it makes no sense. It makes no sense that my mother would let such a thing go on for so long, yet it makes all the sense in the world.

"Don't you see?" he asks.

He is looking at me as if Orson Welles had just walked in the door pulling Rosebud behind him.

He waits as I silently review what I've just told him. I don't know what to say.

After a time, he says, "A fear like the one your mother described is imperious. It can occupy almost all the attention of the sufferer. It is very likely that the attention she was able to offer her family changed radically."

Dr. Andresen takes off his glasses, places them on his table, takes a deep breath.

I walk out. Over the next few days, I think about his remarks, and I think about my fear of losing his attention when I was on the couch. Where did I think he'd go? I thought he'd jump out the window. I think about my need to sit up and keep my eye on him and his reactions. I recall my regrets one day that I'd talked the whole session and surely lost his attention. It occurs to me I am acting toward him as I used to behave around my mother. Knowing I had to be watchful, perhaps feeling I had to watch out for her. Afraid of losing her attention, fearful of a disaster. Afraid that all might end.

I call my father that night and ask him if he remembers anything about this period of time. He pauses, tells me there is static on the line. He says he'll have to call me back. He does so, but seems anxious. A couple of days later, he tells me that my mother barely spoke for a year.

AFTER MY MOTHER LEAVES DALLAS, toward the end of a session, Dr. Andresen says he doesn't feel my usual "avidity."

"It occurred to me," he says, "that you might be missing your mother."

I choke out the following words: "I noticed I haven't put the towels she used into the washing machine yet."

"I think it may be useful to review some of the things we've seen in the past week," he says. I nod.

"We have learned that your mother suffered from melancholia and fear. This fear may have occupied her attention to such an extent that you sensed she had been separated from you. The fear had no name, it had no face. You could not understand what had taken her away. It is my belief that one of the strongest forces operating on children is the desire to restore life and vitality to a parent. We have already seen your impulse to do this, in the dream of your mother being pregnant with your cat. You gave her something alive. Then we see also that you have expressed a desire to take her along with you. You wondered where she would go when you came here. You left a place for her in an early story. You are concerned about bringing people along with you as you journey into the world. Further, we have seen that you and your mother see the world quite differently. And it may be that at some point you felt that your own thoughts, being true to your own understandings, your own adventurousness, had taken you away from her."

I sit, looking at him, thinking.

He reaches over to pick up his glasses.

"No!" I say. "You can't stop there." He puts his glasses back down and looks at me attentively.

I look at him, wanting to hear something that will quiet the riot in my head. But then I realize that I don't need him to settle things, because I can go home and continue by myself to think about all that has transpired. Perhaps I'll get a new idea or have a transforming thought. I stand up, my eyes still on his, and smile.

"See you," he says, smiling himself, as if he understands my change of heart.

OVER THE NEXT SEVERAL MONTHS, I begin to recognize how every cell of my body has been colored by the experience of my mother's withdrawal following the Kennedy assassination. So many aspects of my life that I could not understand now seem to have an explanation. And I begin to understand why the breakup with my college boyfriend had been so terribly painful, and why I so feared a repeat with Craig. In these breaks, it seems reasonable to imagine, I was reexperiencing the first withdrawal of love, the inexplicable, world-shattering disappearance of my mother twenty-five years earlier.

I know the entire country was thrown into a state of shock by the assassination, but why did my mother react so strongly? I call her up and try to ask her, but she says the same thing: "If that could happen, anything could happen. I didn't feel safe."

* * *

SUDDENLY, I FIND I AM FEELING a great desire to write fiction. But, "How can one write stories when the world one inhabits has no narratives?" I ask Dr. Andresen. "Just scenes with huge gaps between them."

My mind starts to wander, and I tell Dr. Andresen about a fantasy I used to have of watching my mother sitting before a vanity, surrounded by powder puffs and perfumes, dressed in feathery lingerie and telling me stories about her life, to which I listen in rapt attention.

"I never saw that," I say. "When I watched her looking at herself in the mirror, she usually had a quizzical expression on her face, as if she did not recognize the person staring back at her. She never luxuriated in her image. She never talked about her past, or her dreams. When she looked in the mirror, she appeared irritated, mainly with a cowlick that wouldn't stay in place. Occasionally, she'd snip at it with scissors, trying to cut away the pieces that would not behave."

I tell him that I do remember watching her one day in the barn in Jaffrey, putting the top on a plastic box of screws. I noticed that her fingernails were nicely filed and covered in clear polish, and I felt a surge of pride. She was also calm-looking, and I remember this clearly, as if it had been unusual, maybe even unique.

"Ah, so you liked the state of dreaminess, where she was comfortable, even lost in her own thoughts."

"Yes," I say.

After a while, he says, "This kind of reverie is a state of mind that is beneficial to creative work. It is like the mind state of children at play, calm, open to new findings, undirected but alert. Quiet attentiveness is necessary for certain forms of self-discovery, for a finding of one's own mind."

*   *   *

"YOU SAY YOUR STORIES have no plot," Dr. Andresen says.
"That's right." I think for a minute, then ask, "What is plot?"
"Plot," says Dr. Andresen, "is the movement of desire."

I AWAKE WITH GREAT ANXIETY. I feel I am sinking, as if my feet
were stuck in quicksand. I have the vague feeling I am caught in an
early childhood trauma from which I can extract myself only if I tap
into my deepest reserves of strength.

On my worst days, I sit in front of the computer, blocked. Then I
get anxious and feel like a failure. Then I start to call everyone I
know. To hear my own voice?

I am occupied with the idea of being good or bad. Am I good or
bad? Was I good or bad to Craig? Was I good or bad at WFAA?

At the end, I feel disgusted, hollow. After I walk out of Dr.
Andresen's office, I realize I did not even mention what I wanted to
talk about: why can't I sit down and write a story?

I realize the writing has something to do with feeling I have been
good or bad.

You can talk if you're a good girl. Are you a good girl?

Dream: My mother asks me to go down to Cape Cod with her for
a horse show there. I am a bit afraid, as I haven't ridden for a while,
and I'm not well prepared. I look over the bridles hanging in the
barn, and recognize that one belongs to my old horse, Apropos. It has
a terribly harsh bit on it, with long shanks and odd pieces of sharp
metal. I look at the other bridles, and they also have bits that are too
severe. I say I will not ride with such a bit. My mother says, "The relatives will be very disappointed."

* * *

WHERE ARE THE STORIES? What did my mother teach me? For sure, she taught me to love learning and adore books. She encouraged my sister and me to express ourselves in music and art. She sacrificed hours of her time driving us to lessons and to the horses. She taught me, through her own example, about fidelity to obligations and a strict moral code. Yet she seldom spoke of herself or told stories of her own life. I tell Dr. Andresen that the Navajos sing songs that tell stories: how to plant and care for the corn; how corn came to be given to the Navajos by their gods; explain what knowledge is needed in caring for sheep. I tell him how Ella, the Navajo woman I have written about, values the lessons her mother taught her, which are all in the form of stories, and how my book is full of stories passed down from mother to daughter.

"Your book is like a reliquary," he says.

I stop and look at him. "Reliquary" is a religious word. Reliquaries hold pieces of things thought to be holy.

"Like a reliquary of stories to substitute for those I don't have," I say.

AGAIN, DREAMS OF DRAINS, SINK TRAPS. I think again of the strange fishlike girl in the dream who dove down the drain.

"What else happened in a bathroom?" asks Dr. Andresen.

I think about this. I don't know, what?

"Your mother had a miscarriage in the bathroom, didn't she?"

My mind races. I did tell him this. I have always known it but never felt it particularly important. It happened the summer I was four years old, when my parents had rented a wonderful old farmhouse on Cape Cod. In the living room was a painted folk-art figure of Uncle Sam, about six feet tall, mounted in a stand on the floor, and a wicker monkey that hung by an arm from the rafters. There was an old 1940s table radio, on which my father listened to classical music. Outside the front door was a small vineyard, and I remember watching the grapes ripen on their twisted vines, soften, fill with sugary syrup, then rot and fall to the dirt. The bathroom that my sister and I shared was papered with green sea horses and, most remarkably to us, had a Dutch door, like the door of a horse stall, whose top and bottom opened separately.

I am astonished that I remember so many, many details of that fantastic place, since I was just a small child when we stayed there. It had been a grand, memorable summer. We had sailed and swum and watched tadpoles turn into frogs under a raft. We went back years later, after it had been sold to a developer. I was crushed to see it had been savaged by a bulldozer. The property had been divided into quarter-acre lots, all the way down to the pristine Spectacle Pond, divided into a neat checkerboard of driveways and concrete slab foundations. I was probably eight or nine at the time, but even then I felt a tragedy had befallen the place. I picked up some stones from the beach and put them in my pocket.

As I describe all this to Dr. Andresen, I begin to weep, harsh, wracking sobs. Something very sad was registered in this fantastic place full of life and ripeness and color, imagination and adventure and mystery.

On the way to Dr. Andresen's office a few weeks later, I stop off at a women's room. As I push open a stall door, I realize I am peering with some trepidation into the toilet bowl. All of a sudden, I realize that every time I walk up to a public toilet, I fear that I will find in it a bloody, discarded baby.

I realize that I have had this reflex for years, as long as I can remember, but have not been consciously aware of it until just then. My head starts buzzing and I feel slightly disoriented.

I tell Dr. Andresen about the image I had in the bathroom and that I always have when entering a public lavatory.

"Do you really?" he asks with surprise.

"Always."

I return to Spectacle Pond in my mind for weeks. I feel that I have found here a huge cache of memories, memories that have provided main branches for the organization of my personality, my under-standing of the world. I go back and forth over the wicker monkey that hung from one arm, the Dutch door to the bathroom, the feeling of the hot sun on the sandy beach, the woods beyond the house in which old Indian trails led off into the tangle of underbrush.

"What do you think is the significance of the house?" I ask Dr. Andresen.

He looks at me and shrugs. "I have no idea," he says.

I am so curious, I call my mother. We reminisce about the house and that summer. I tell her what I remember. After some time, she mentions that she suffered a "slight misfortune" that summer. I pick up on her opening and I ask about the miscarriage. I try to find out how my sister and I may have reacted.

"Oh, you girls had no idea what was going on," she says.

I am silent. "Were you upset about it?" I ask.

"Oh, no. I was glad. It wasn't planned."

"I remember that something happened in that bathroom," I say.

"Oh, that's impossible," she says. "You kids were asleep." She explains that she began to bleed heavily in the middle of the night, and my father woke up my sister and me and bundled us into the car and headed for the hospital. It was a stormy night, because the Cape had caught the tail of a hurricane. The skies were squalling and the wind was blowing hard. At the hospital, my sister and I waited with my father until the procedure was completed. It seems impossible to me that this event would have passed me unnoticed.

I HAVE A PICTURE in my mind of that summer that keeps recurring. I am standing at the doorway of my parents' bathroom. My perspective seems low to the ground, as I was a four-year-old. I remember a large expanse of green tile in front of me, and at the far side of the room, my mother on a toilet. Behind her is a window. This image must have come from daytime, because the window in my image is light. Across the room from my mother is a small sink with an S-shaped trap and pipe beneath it.

The image is of me, a short person, looking at my mother from the door of the bathroom. I see tiles extending out from me like the green of the field around the house, like the green of Spectacle Pond.

"The S-shaped trap!" I say, looking up at Dr. Andresen in astonishment. I realize, in one dull, calm second, that this is the drain from all my dreams.

I look at Dr. Andresen and see he is looking at me intently. I look away and the image comes back into focus. All these months, I have seen dream images of the S-shaped trap and I have heard sounds of water rushing or tinkling through drains. I dreamed of a girl acrobat throwing herself down the drain. Was that an image of the otherworldly and now dead baby? Or is it an image of myself, fearful at some faraway point of being flushed down the toilet as well?

"Why exactly do you think I would have selected the drain as the reference for all that happened that summer?" I begin. Then, I interrupt myself, remembering Dr. Andresen abhors questions that try to pin down specific meanings. "OK, never mind, I know you hate those kinds of questions."

He laughs. After a few moments, he says, "I will tell you something, though. There were studies done on soldiers badly wounded during World War I. It seems that in the moments just after the mine explosion or artillery attack that wounded them, they made a photographic image of their surroundings, and afterwards, if they had not suffered a brain injury, they could recount with astonishing detail the scene of their terror. It is a well-documented phenomenon that the picture recorded by the eyes at the time of a trauma remains in the memory in heightened detail."

I am quiet for several minutes, and then I tell him that the night before, I had a memory of an old dream, a dream I had when I was nine years old and recorded in a small white diary that I kept that year. I dug up the diary, which I still carry with me. In the dream, something yolklike had dropped out of my mother, and I gathered it up and gave it back to her. I had this dream five years after the miscarriage.

Dr. Andresen looks at me, takes a breath, and says, "You were trying to give her back her baby."

Two days later, I awake in the middle of the night in a sweat. I'd been planning to move out of the apartment I shared with Craig, who is already gone, and to leave Dallas. But having packed my things, I hesitated. Why am I going, I wondered, just now? Am I reenacting my own mother's withdrawal from me by pulling away from Dr. Andresen just as I am growing more dependent on him? Just as I am seeing the benefit of our work?

I didn't get on the airplane, and it seemed less a decision of my mind than of my feet. I couldn't get them to turn me east. Instead, my friend Nancy invited me to share her apartment in University

Park. Now, the night before my move, I awake from restless dreaming, thinking I will be sleeping in a small sunroom off the living room, with no door and little privacy. Further, there is one bathroom in the apartment, accessible through Nancy's bedroom. Will this arrangement be tolerable?

I talk about this the next day with Dr. Andresen. Why am I concerned about such an inconsequential matter?

"Will you have to give up too much to fit in?" he says. I look at him blankly.

"You have been describing a period during which you were seeking increasing independence, and your mother was trying to get you to behave in the ways she thought appropriate. She also expressed some longing for you and your sister to remain babies. That summer she had a miscarriage. You may have sensed a sadness in her, and may have put a few things together. She had a baby and lost it; you were learning about tadpoles and frogs from your father. Perhaps you felt you could restore something to your mother by somehow restricting your rich imagination, the imagination that led you away from her, the imagination you have seen does not allow you a meeting with her."

Thoughts spray around me in all colors. Perhaps I wanted to please my mother by staying young, though I was trying desperately to become more independent. Perhaps I felt that summer that life was changing, from a time of pure mystery and polymorphous excitement to a world with restrictions, rules, beginnings and endings. The baby ended, there was talk of the farm being sold and divided up.

I was trying to fit in, not be exiled, trying to control some of my energy and imagination.

"Could I have throttled my imagination?" I ask Dr. Andresen.

"You could have started to compartmentalize it. You still have it inside you."

* * *

DR. ANDRESEN HAD ASKED if we could reschedule one of our meetings because he had to go out of town. During the time we usually met, I drove to the medical school anyway, but instead of walking to his office, I headed to the library. I looked up his name in a medical periodical guide, noted down the many citations, and walked up and down the library stacks, pulling down armfuls of bound volumes of journals. I carried them over to an easy chair, stacked the volumes on the floor, and read them through.

Today, before mentioning the papers, I ask, "How do you pronounce that word 'analysand'?"

"Ahh," he says, "what do we call you?"

Again, I am stopped short by his comment. I think about this for a few minutes, then I proceed to stammer out the truth of my evil ways: I have looked up his writing and read all the articles I could find. I look up at him. He is looking at me with some energy and intense concentration. I am afraid I have done something very wrong. I think this is probably a breach of the understood relation between doctor and patient. I am waiting for my punishment.

He says, "I was away, and you wanted to continue our conversation."

I am stunned by his generosity, and how he has turned my prying into an effort at intimacy, a gesture toward him.

I weep silently. When I recover, he asks, "And what did you see?"

"Well, I read some very interesting papers, from which I took pages of notes." I hold up a pile of yellow-lined sheets. "But I didn't recognize your voice."

He nods gravely.

"You don't usually speak using the terms you used in your papers, terms like diadic and triadic relations."

He reddens and says, "I don't write like that anymore."

After a pause, during which time we are both quiet, he says, "I had the thought of giving you one of my papers." He gets up from his chair and walks to his desk. I am touched by his admission, and I feel a sudden tender protectiveness for him. He no longer writes using the lingo of the psychoanalysts. He has developed his own ideas, and he is about to share them with me.

Dr. Andresen opens a file drawer, flips between folders, and pulls out a small booklet bound in light blue paper. The paper is called "The Motif of Sacrifice and the Sacrifice Complex."

THERE ARE MOMENTS in which the reshuffling of the cards in the card catalogue is so great, it seems to challenge the entire structure of the system. I don't know if profound mental reorganization is possible normally, but I felt that there were certain moments in my analysis when I was as malleable as a plant being grafted in the spring.

I had never given much thought to the idea of sacrifice, but as soon as I actually see the word on paper, I realize it is a religious concept. Although my first reaction is that it is a Christian idea, I read in the paper that many different cultures practiced real or symbolic sacrifices, and in fact, the story of Abraham and Isaac, one of the most famous in the Bible, symbolizes Judaism's rejection of human sacrifice.

The paper elucidates Dr. Andresen's belief that people often give up something very important of themselves in an unconscious attempt to restore the health and well-being of a loved one. He reviews the psychoanalytic literature on sacrifice and shows that the behavior of his patients is in accord with both Freud's and Jung's analyses of the intentions of practitioners of sacrifice. "The offerers of sacrifice," he writes, "including my patients, interpret certain strivings or life events as harmful to the deity (or loved ones). This mobilizes a need to restore the wholeness of the deity or beloved, and the offerer gives something of his own—an offering, a victim—which benefits his god or loved one. This restores the desired relationship between the deity or beloved and the offerer."

Freud believed that the sacrificial victim is "simultaneously a gift, a transforming agent, and a creator of communion."

I put down the booklet and think that this fits exactly with my understanding of the sun dance, a Plains Indian rite with which I had opened the first chapter of my book. In the ceremony, young Indian men undergo extreme physical rigors for the purpose of offering strength to their people. They also hoped in their individual strivings to experience a vision. So the Indians felt their ordeal was a gift to their people, and they hoped it would contribute to a transformation in them. By hoping to receive a vision, the Indians made clear it was also a rite of communion with the gods.

I read on that Jung believed that religious offerings were always in part self-offerings. And surely the Indians who were dancing and piercing their skin were offering up pieces of their own flesh. And I, in Dr. Andresen's formulation, may have offered up important pieces of myself—the gift—in the hope it would accomplish a transformation—in my mother.

But why would I do that? Do children care enough for the welfare of their parents to do such things? I look back at the paper and read references to scores of analysts who have observed children's and even infants' deep concern for the affective states of their mothers. The analyst Sandor Ferenczi noted that "children have the compulsion to put to right all disorder in the family, to burden, so to speak, their own tender shoulders with the load of all the others."

And why, I wonder, would I keep this conversation with my mother going for so long? Why even now would I keep in place a mechanism for relieving the suffering that presumably had ended?

I ask Dr. Andresen.

"There are several reasons," he says. "If suffering is involved in a big way and if there is unfinished business, the need and urge to console can be very powerful. Not many psychoanalysts hold this view, but I do very strongly, that people have a very strong impulse to make right what was wrong, to relieve suffering. If they have no opportunity to right the suffering, they continue in ways to have a dialogue with the affected party.

"You were never able to console your fearful mother. Her fears had no name and no face. You could do nothing either to understand them or to bring her out of her melancholia. I think you continue to have a dialogue with her about it. Freud has written about this phenomenon in 'Mourning and Melancholia,' and Karl Abraham had thoughts about it. Freud in fact believed that hysterics were overcome by memories."

I think about all this.

"Where might the dialogue go now?" I ask.

"There is no easy answer."

Dr. Andresen continues: "You have revealed your loving intentions toward her. You left room for her in an early story; you dreamed about giving her back her baby. People manage in astonishing ways to keep up a dialogue with certain people in their lives. You had a dream the other day about standing in a stream and shouting at someone."

"Yes, and then you walked up and I put my arm around you and you put yours around me."

"That is a representation of continuing dialogue. And water is often a symbol for a woman. You have shown your sensitivity to your mother's plight by your tendency to befriend people who were in trouble, who were struggling with something unusual. That may reflect your awareness of your mother's special needs and special problems."

Just then I have an image of falling through human tissue, as if I were an egg rolling through a Fallopian tube.

"Like a birth," he says.

"I don't know, maybe. A little thing, calm, sure, radiating a soft energy is fighting to emerge from a dark place."

"Perhaps it is a baby."

"A baby? Whose baby?"

He pauses. When I remain clueless, he says, "A baby of yours."

"You mean a metaphoric baby."

"Not a metaphor, something new."

PERHAPS I WAS READY FOR A BIRTH, but a baby is not what arrived just then.

The first day offered only a hint of what would come: a subtle but unmistakable disturbance in my sight. It happened as I was driving to Dr. Andresen's office. After I arrived, I sat in my chair and said nothing about the almost inarticulable upset in my eyes. Instead, I talked about this or that, distracted, warily awaiting a return of the sensation.

Then, taking myself quite by surprise, I covered my face with my hands and wept. When I stopped, I said, "I think there is something the matter with my eyes."

I looked up and saw Dr. Andresen watching me very seriously. He asked if I could describe what I was feeling.

"It's happened three times," I said. "I'd say my sight seems like a film that has slipped for a fraction of a second from its sprockets."

"Would you like me to make an appointment for you with an ophthalmologist?" he asked.

"No," I said, shaking my head. "I'm sure it's nothing." I returned to what I was saying, trying to pretend that nothing had happened. I babbled on and on, though my thoughts were wandering wildly.

After a time, I stopped and sat quietly.

"I think I will take you up on your offer to call an ophthalmologist," I said.

The next morning, I awoke with double vision.

IT SEEMS SO FITTING TO ME NOW, just after I had been given transforming new sight, or insight, that my eyes should close up shop. Too much, too quickly, perhaps. My perceptual apparatus needed a complete rest.

Or perhaps the explanation was more mundane: my body was finally reacting to the cascade of setbacks that had beset me in the previous six months: my book not yet published, my breakup with Craig, a TV job begun with great promise but ended in confusion, an apartment given up, all of which perhaps conjured up another time of rupture and bewilderment long ago.

What an appropriate curse, though: a malfunction that can come and go, or perhaps never go away, or go away and return days or maybe years later without warning seems such a fitting affliction for me, mirroring my mother's unpredictable comings and goings. I am familiar with this inconsistency, though its familiarity makes it even more oppressive: goodness comes and goes, but never stays.

It also occurs to me that the fate of a child with a depressed mother is to become hypervigilant, ever concerned with the mother's state of mind. And it is with my eyes that I watched her, recorded the anxious face, the frustrated vacuuming, the thousand-yard stare. It was with my eyes that I registered the effects of my own attempts to soothe and rejuvenate her. I wonder if I am punishing my eyes now for my failure, or perhaps for learning her secret.

Here I am, almost thirty years later, in the very city that precipitated her crisis, experiencing my own breakdown. Am I repeating her disaster? If I went so far as a small child to unconsciously sacrifice pieces of myself in hopes of restoring her, as Dr. Andresen suggests, could I be doing the same again, only now offering up my sight?

My eyes worsen the first week. I try to calm myself by thinking of Dr. Andresen. Even when I am not in the office, I see him, I speak with him. I fix an image of him in my mind, and turn to it like a talisman. I think of him sitting in his chair, calm but very alert, taking in everything I say, absorbing every blow.

I reflect on the fact that several times during the analysis he has surprised me by characterizing my intentions as generous or loving. He perceives good in me, and in so doing, he makes me good. At those times, I have turned to him and said, "Seeing that is your gift." I want to be like him. I try to listen to others as he listens to me. In my best moments, I feel I am moving in the right direction. Those are the moments I feel very, very gentle and again think about the divine.

After a week or so, I settle into partial comfort with my impaired vision. I can still do almost everything I did previously. I can run and read and write and see friends. I can drive with one eye closed, but not at night, because the oncoming headlights confound me. My increasing comfort with the blurriness seems to accord with what I have been learning with Dr. Andresen: Don't try to force answers. Sit with my thoughts and allow ideas to come, even unbidden, unanticipated ones. In the same way, I don't try to force my eyes to focus, which I cannot do anyway; rather, I look at the world through the blur.

How much faces mean to me now! Since I cannot see them clearly anymore, the only vivid faces are those in my memory. In my fear and confusion, I think of Craig's face, and I trace its every curve and line. I watch him talking to me and replay his gestures. Where does someone put four years of memories, I ask Dr. Andresen. Do I cut his image out of all the old snapshots in my head? Dr. Andresen nods with an expression of pain.

In time, Craig's image becomes fainter, and Dr. Andresen's replaces it. I love to watch the ovoid, vessel shapes he draws with his hands as he talks. His gestures seem to me inclusive, female, held, and somehow consistent with the work of Wilfred Bion, whom Dr. Andresen cites frequently in his papers, and whose theory of mothering refers to "the container" (the mother's active holding in reverie of experiences induced in her by the child) and the "contained" (the representations of those experiences).

I fantasize about helping him. Perhaps our work will give him an idea for a new paper. I have a dream in which I am Wilhelm Fliess to his Sigmund Freud. I am the muse, the quickener of spirit. I know enough about psychoanalysis to realize that the transference is deepening, and so, also, is the analysis.

How odd that in Dallas, after the catastrophe of feeling unseen, I am seen for the first time. When Dr. Zimmerman calls to say she wants to treat me for Lyme disease, I have a strange reaction. I am afraid of losing something I have gained, a sense of fragility and femininity that I feel I was not allowed before. I feel somewhat fearful of regaining my sight, the tyranny of clear sight, as Dr. Andresen has put it.

Dr. Andresen says, "Perhaps you feel you've done enough."

I PICK UP COPIES of the MRI pictures from Southwestern Medical Center and bring them home. It has been thirteen days since I first experienced the crinkling of space.

I walk into the living room and place them next to each other on a long table. I pick up the heavy four-by-nineteen-inch images one by one, and raise them to the light from the window.

MRI scans take pictures of body parts in slices, as if one were carving a vegetable into slivers. In the first pictures, I see sections of my head from ear to ear, as if sliced like a hard-boiled egg. Another set shows slices from the crown of my head to my chin, as one would slice a tomato held in the palm of his hand. Another shows slivers from my face to the back of my head.

I see the orbs of my eyes attached to thick white funnels of nerve tissue, the optic nerve, leading to my brain. I trace the delicate shell-like shapes of the bones and cartilage in my nose. I see portions of molars and vertebrae transformed into Picasso sketches, Miró doodles. I look at the cartilage of my ears, folding away from my head like a space alien's antennae, and I look at the mysterious butterflies and hollows and valleys throughout my skull. I see my cerebral hemispheres: curly, winding, folded, dense. I see shapes I remember from high school biology: the thalamus, the pons and medulla oblongata. I see the pituitary gland, my midbrain, and the cauliflower-shaped cerebellum.

I look at the pictures until the sun goes down and I have to turn on a light. I see the abnormalities that the doctor pointed out, a half-dozen small bright spots, the "unidentified bright objects" or UBOs, the spots of water drawn to the inflammation. They are oval-shaped, about a half centimeter in diameter, like small pebbles. I stare at these odd foreign objects in my head and become very sleepy. I put the plastic sheaves back in the envelope and climb into bed.

That night, I have an astonishing dream whose clarity and color are unlike any other dream I have had, before or since. It is particularly affecting, since in real life I can't see clearly and have no depth perception. The dream has extraordinary clarity and depth, like an IMAX 3-D movie.

In the dream, I am walking along a dark road surrounded by lush trees whose branches are thick and gnarled and shaped like a head of cauliflower. I step off from the ground and begin to fly. Opening up before me, outside of the forest, I see a fantastic river of brilliant blue water, hundreds of feet below, at the bottom of dramatic, sharp cliffs.

As I rise in the air, I see below me a spit of land on which lie ancient Greek ruins and statues in various stages of brokenness. One statue is sitting up, his back against a building and his legs stretched before him. Another is lying on the ground. The limbs are shattered into pieces, but lying exactly in place. Grass is growing up over and around the figures, which are gradually being absorbed by the earth.

I double back to look at the brilliant water that flows around the ruins, then I fly on toward an ancient Italian city whose stone and stucco buildings are built up against each other and into a hillside. I fly into the old section of town and land on my feet in the street, where I run into a gang of street urchins whom I join as they enter the cellars of various houses. There they root out old pieces of statuary and pottery and throw them down onto the floor, shattering them into pieces. I am appalled that they are breaking these precious things, and I run back and forth trying to catch the pieces before they break. The pieces are oval-shaped, like the little pebbles in my head.

As soon as I tell Dr. Andresen the dream, I realize that the heavy curled trees through which I walk at the beginning are the same shape as my cerebellum. I realize that the dream represents flight through my own, damaged, brain. The frozen statues around a temple I associate with the Oracle of Delphi, the place where the future is foretold, represent my fear of my own possible future: paralysis. And at the end of the dream, I am running around trying to catch the stones the thieves are smashing on the ground. But if the ovoids represent the spots in my head, doesn't it make sense that I should let them be smashed? Isn't it helping me if they root out the spots and shatter them? But on the other hand, if the pot shards represent antiquity, valuable objects, maybe they should be saved.

Reimagining the dream conjures again the great euphoria I felt on waking. I feel no pressing need to solve the puzzles the dream poses, nor to analyze them. I feel I have been offered a glimpse into another world. The brilliance of the colors and their photographic superrealism have left an intense emotional residue in me. I feel I have been given a supernal glimpse of some unworldly manifestation.

As I flew through my brain, I had glimpses of what the future might bring—the statues, broken, fallen in their places—yet I felt no fear. Rather, the island on which the statues lay was surrounded by the brilliant sapphire waterway, sparkling, the waves rippling on it, containing great energy and transformative power. The great dazzling river returns to my thoughts over and over, and revives me as if it carried an electric charge.

I return to the image of the water, so exquisitely blue, because it makes me feel euphoric, and all of a sudden I realize the water is the blue of Dr. Andresen's eyes. The broken future is mediated by the transforming power of the blue water, the new way of seeing that he offers me. Dr. Andresen stands and walks to his desk.

"I have a paper here about patients who have suffered near-death experiences," he says, "that have striking resemblances to your experience of this dream."

I SUPPOSE THE most important word that I learn here is "ineffable." I have to look it up, and I see it means "indescribable." A few years ago, I would have dismissed the entire idea as hogwash. If you can't explain something, I would have scoffed, then you just don't understand it well enough. Or that is something my father would have told me and that I would have parroted to others.

I had heard of near-death experiences, of course, and found them interesting: the phenomenon is experienced by people who die momentarily and are then revived. Many survivors report similar experiences: Some see a bright light and feel an intense welcoming presence. Others see their lives flash before their eyes. Many have the experience of leaving their bodies and watching themselves and the unfolding medical crisis from afar.

The paper Dr. Andresen handed me describes the aftermath of such an experience for a group of people who later sought psychotherapy. Rather than being frightened or bewildered by their brush with death, these people felt that the experience brought about significant changes in their personalities. They came spontaneously to understand a form of thinking that Freud determined to be the "sina qua non of the search for self-understanding," namely, "the receptivity to spontaneous experiences of the mind, with a prerequisite capacity to bear the uncertainty critical to the creation of new knowings." This kind of thinking is similar to that of artists, writers, scientists, and religious contemplatives, but what impressed the authors of the paper was that this skill, usually honed over years of practice, seemed to be understood overnight by the patients. "What is remarkable in these survivors is that they apparently grasp the nature of these methods in but a few moments of time—in fact, in the duration of the brush with death."

The patients indicate a new responsiveness to sensory experience, a new appreciation of the rich power of silence, and the feeling that a whole new world has opened up. They report a greater tolerance and forgiveness of others and a newfound sense of connectedness with the human experience that has something to do with an awareness of sorrow. A few people expressed an increased interest in children or in bringing forth new life.

One patient felt he had had a "'look into a far-off place,' as if he had been 'somewhere,' suffered and returned with special—but completely ineffable—knowledge. It was if he had entered a cave and 'discovered' another civilization."

I find the play of opposites fascinating. A "newfound sense of connectedness" is associated with sorrow. Dying, even momentarily, leads not to panic over what has not yet been accomplished, but rather to a new state of mind in which patients no longer feel pursued by time. A brush with death increases interest in bringing forth life.

And so it is with my eyesight. After the initial horror, I began to feel oddly enlarged by my impairment. When Dr. Zimmerman proposed treating me for Lyme disease, I was momentarily apprehensive about losing my new relation with the world. The blindness led me, also, to lose the sense of being pursued by time. I too began to experience a different connection with the world around me, one that was more reciprocal and responsive. And for the first time in my life, I am able to stand uncertainty, to allow opposing ideas to remain side by side in my thoughts, to be open to the workings of my mind in a new way.

"WOULD YOU CONSIDER listening to this?" I ask Dr. Andresen one day, fishing an audiotape out of my handbag and holding it up. "It's a Garth Brooks tune that I heard last night."

He looks at me with an expression of curiosity, then nods.

The next session, he hands the tape back to me.

"Did you like it?" I ask him.

"That is a question I will not answer," he says with a coy smile.

When I get home, I am mortified to see that the name of the song I gave him was "Shameless."

The next day, I bring in another tape. It is George Strait's "Chill of an Early Fall," and I ask him if he would listen to my favorite cut, called "Milk Cow Blues." The next time we meet, he returns the tape, and I see he has played it to the end of the song. The conversation veers here and there. I ask him if he'd listen to a third song, and he pauses. I realize he wants to talk about what I am up to here. I don't know really, so I remain quiet.

Dr. Andresen looks reflective and begins to talk about the human voice, and how it was the first musical instrument. Then he tells me about a letter he received from a friend who had been listening to chamber music and feeling that the instruments were calling out to each other as if they were voices, each in turn reaching out for the others in an aching, searching way.

As Dr. Andresen describes the interplay of instruments, he draws a round shape with his hands in the air before him. Suddenly, I have a vivid image of a circular opening in the wall of the synagogue I had attended a few times as a young girl, from behind which the voices of a choir could be heard. I remember the ribbed support of the arch, the grayish cloth covering the porous space.

Then, I have a very strong image of standing beside my father in synagogue and hearing his voice praying. I hear it momentarily at first, then it disappears. The image reconjures itself, and the voice comes back. I hear my father's voice chanting beside me. I am flooded with a feeling of familiarity so intense that it wipes away any words I can find as explanation.

"What are you thinking?" Dr. Andresen asks me.

I look at him and see he is watching me intently. "I am having the most vivid image of standing next to my father in synagogue," I say. "And I can actually hear his voice." I look at Dr. Andresen with an expression of puzzlement.

"That's where the music was leading us!" Dr. Andresen says, inhaling quickly.

I look at him.

"The music led us to the synagogue," he says, shaking his head in an expression of surprise and awe. "You asked me if I'd listen to the tapes. You wanted to bring someone along with you."

I am quiet for a few moments.

"And you came with me," I say.

"Why do people cry?" I ask, grabbing a tissue. "I am not sad. Not sad at all."

"A wonderful teacher of mine named Elvin Semrad taught that people cry in the face of what is important," he says.

YEARS LATER, I mention the experience of hearing my father's voice to Yitzhak Buxbaum, a compiler of Chassidic tales and a maggid, a teacher and storyteller, and he tells me it reminds him of a story of his own, which took place at the beginning of his journey back to Judaism. "When I first went to pray with the Lubavitcher Chassidim," he tells me, "there were a thousand people in the synagogue. This was in Brooklyn, in the main building on Eastern Parkway. They pushed me to the front, to the rebbe. And as I was getting close to him, being jostled by these guys, singing, their faces all joy, I heard my father calling me by my English name, "Bobby, Bobby." I turned around but of course he wasn't there. Now this was not some whisper. I heard his voice loud and clear."

Buxbaum then tells me that a similar thing happened to his brother, when he too became interested in the Lubavitcher Chassidim. "After this happened to me, my younger brother went to Lubavitch as well, following in my footsteps, you might say. He attended a Lubavitcher weekend for a few hundred male college kids run by a panel of five rabbis. In the middle of a session, around twenty-five young Chassidim came into the room and quietly arranged themselves along the walls, and began to sing a Chassidic melody. As my brother sat there, he heard my voice. Not for just a second. He heard my voice singing this melody along with the others for five minutes."

"What do you make of this?" I ask him.

"You see, it didn't just happen to you. It happened to both me and my brother. It's remarkable. From what I have learned, it shows that everybody gets his or her transmission of Judaism from someone, usually a relative. It's your father, your mother, a grandparent, aunt, or uncle. The transmission is received and it stays in your soul someplace. And one day it comes out.

"That's one reason they say that when God spoke to Moses at the burning bush, the words came out in Moses' father's voice."

Chapter Five

❦

FIRST STEPS

WHAT I FIRST NOTICE one morning at Beth Emunah, where we are gathered to meet Rabbi Yerachmiel Fried, is his hat. It is jet black and firmly constructed. It is not on his head; rather, he has set it beside him on a table, crown down, open like a wine goblet.

This is a hat unlike any I've ever seen before. It is not a homburg, nor a derby. Is it a fedora, or a Borsalino? No, it is more than that. It is not a hat worn by a man of this world. The brim is a tad too wide, the curve a bit too raffish. There is brio in that brim, though I can't fathom it, can't decode it.

Sitting beside the hat on the table at the front of the room is a trim, energetic man with a short red beard, carefully barbered hair, and a merry smile. He speaks quickly, his breath a beat behind his words, so he seems breathless. On his head is a black yarmulke, and he wears a dark suit and white shirt with no tie. His accent tells me he is American, but he says he recently moved to Dallas from Jerusalem. At the request of the Dallas Orthodox community, he has set up a kollel, a group of adult men whose full-time occupation is studying holy texts. For eight hours a day, they study Talmud and Torah, and in the evenings they and their wives teach in the community.

Although Rabbi Fried is friendly and humorous, I sense he is a very intense, directed man. I glance at the hat again, and realize the idea of devotion to a journey *in extremis* interests me. Rabbi Fried is here to introduce himself to us, let us know about the programs the kollel runs, and do a little studying with us. Except he doesn't say "studying"; he calls it "learning." Studying is what one does in secular school; "learning," from the German *lernen*, he explains, is a more intimate endeavor.

He begins his presentation by telling us the story of a man who loves to walk right up against the edge of a waterfall to watch the torrents crash down on the rocks hundreds of feet below. One day he comes up to his familiar spot at the falls and he sees that a fence has been erected around the edge. He is disappointed and angry that he can't approach as closely as he would like, and he asks the guard who has erected the fence why it is there. The guard says, "Perhaps you will see a little less, but you won't run the risk of being swept over the edge."

Rabbi Fried then hands out a photocopied page of Pirkei Avot (Sayings of the Fathers) and reads the first lines: "Moses received the Torah from Sinai and transmitted it to Joshua; Joshua to the Elders; the Elders to the Prophets; and the Prophets transmitted it to the Men of the Great Assembly. They [the Men of the Great Assembly] said three things: Be deliberate in judgment; develop many disciples; and make a fence for the Torah."

"What the sages of the generation were trying to say," says Rabbi Fried, putting down the paper and looking at us, "is that the mitzvahs, the six hundred and thirteen commandments that Jews are obligated to observe, carry great power. We don't realize how much energy is in every mitzvah," he continues, "how much potential good. And the greater the good, the greater the potential for danger.

"Surrounding a high-tension wire," he continues, "you don't just have a sign, you have a fence to keep people out. The electricity has so much benefit for mankind, it can bring so much good. But if you get too close, if you trip over it, you run the risk of being electrocuted.

"The sages of the Talmud and the Mishnah, those who have a window into the secrets of the Torah, who can see back to Mount Sinai, they know. And that is why they wrote about building fences. You can see through fences, but you can't pass. That is very revealing about the essence of a mitzvah.

"For example, there is a rabbinic prohibition against blowing the shofar on Rosh Hashanah if that day should fall on Shabbos. It is not because blowing the shofar breaks the rules of the Sabbath. It is that the rabbinic authorities thought that people would be so enthusiastic to blow the shofar, they might forget it was Shabbos and carry it to a public place for the joy of blowing it, and in so doing, desecrate the Sabbath."

I am fascinated that Rabbi Fried has introduced himself to us, by, in effect, telling us to back off. It seems to me it is just the danger of the power he has hinted at that is interesting, and I wonder if it isn't the danger that attracts him as well. I also note that he used the old-fashioned Ashkenazi pronunciation of the words "mitzvahs" and "Shabbos," the pronunciation that was taught to people of my father's age. Most Jews nowadays use modern Hebrew, in which the words are pronounced "mitzvot" and "Shabbat."

After his brief words, the congregants bring out some cake and drinks. I notice that Rabbi Fried doesn't partake. I realize later that although we have a rule that any food brought into the synagogue should be kosher and dairy, he doesn't trust it. We are not kosher enough. I ask Frank Joseph why we met in the "dining salon" rather than the sanctuary, and he tells me that Rabbi Fried is more comfortable in this room. Like a child who asks only as much as she wants to know, I do not pursue this, though I wonder about it for years. Later, I will learn that Rabbi Fried and other Orthodox Jews consider any sanctuary that is not Orthodox to be a desecration. Some Orthodox will not even step inside a building in which non-Orthodox services are held.

Before we leave, Rabbi Fried hands us some papers with schedules of upcoming events sponsored by the kollel. In a few weeks there will be an event called a Shabbaton. A member of the congregation tells me a Shabbaton is a weekend gathering during which you celebrate the Sabbath with a community and attend lectures and meals. I hear Rabbi Fried say there will be a guest named Rabbi Ezriel Tauber, who is an esteemed rabbi from Muncie.

"Muncie, Indiana?" I ask, puzzled.

"No," Rabbi Fried says. "It is M-O-N-S-E-Y and it's in New York." Later, I learn that about 6,000 very Orthodox families, including several Chassidic sects, live in an area including the town of Monsey in Rockland County, about an hour's drive north of Manhattan.

As I leave, I ponder the image of the high-tension wires behind the fence. The Navajo reservation was strung with such wires carrying electricity from several coal-fired plants to Tucson, Las Vegas, and Los Angeles. The coal that fired those plants was dug from Navajo and Hopi land, and the plants that burned the coal stood on Indian land and befouled their air, but most of the Indian people themselves had no electricity, even those who lived under the crackling lines. The people do not have access to the fruits of the electricity that emanates from their own natural resources.

Similarly, I am a Jew, but I have not experienced the fruit of the treasure behind the fence. What could be so powerful that it must be guarded and parceled out? The image of people getting so carried away by the joy of hearing the shofar delights me. I want to see the treasure, touch it, see it glitter. I want to understand the brim of that hat.

IT IS A FRIDAY AFTERNOON, a good hour before sundown, and I am driving past a row of ranch houses in a comfortable North Dallas neighborhood. I have signed up for Rabbi Tauber's Shabbaton, and I have been matched up with a family at whose home I will stay for twenty-four hours, until sundown on Saturday. With images in my head of a reverential weekend, I am embarrassed to drive my low-slung black Mustang, which looks like a drug dealer's car, right up to the front of the house, so I park a few doors away.

I step out and walk along the wide, peaceful street. When I find the house, I head up the flagstone path and knock on the front door, feeling a tingle of anxiety at the prospect of sleeping in a strange place.

The door is opened by a short plump woman in a shapeless cotton shift, carrying a newborn infant at her breast, her head wrapped up in a long rag. I am quite surprised to see a woman dressed this way in Dallas, and I feel a surge of dismay rise to my throat. She is overweight, sloppy, scuffling along in slippers, yet beatifically attached to her baby. I step inside the door and realize there is no flooring: the Mexican tile has been ripped up and we are walking on the cement underfloor, which is crisscrossed with marks of what once was glue. She mentions something about a new floor being laid down but seems not the least concerned that her house looks like a bomb crater.

In the kitchen, she offers me something to drink and introduces me to her five children, who are respectful and handsome. The little boys wear velvet yarmulkes and strings hanging from their pants, which mean they're wearing tzitzit, a rectangular undergarment of light cotton with a hole cut out for the head, that hangs like a soft sandwich board over the chest, beneath the shirt. From the four corners of the garment hang knotted strings, which the religious wear hanging out of their pants. Tzitzit are worn by men and boys according to biblical dictum. The girls wear dresses that cover their knees, and with sleeves long enough to cover their elbows but no additional mark of religiosity. I think it's interesting that the boys get all the toys and accouterments. At the sight of the children, I warm up, however, which serves to dispel the despair I feel looking at their mother.

Conversation is awkward at first. A piece of me wants to make up an excuse and rush back out to my car and drive straight home. But then something else kicks in, my reporter's habits perhaps, and I separate from my own anxieties, my own needs, and settle in to absorb the world into which I have just stepped. I will register my feelings, but I will also suspend judgment. I want to get beneath the surface and find out more about this family and this world. I am sure to learn something, and it may be something I didn't expect.

I am soon rewarded. When one of the little ones starts to fuss, my hostess soothes him with a most charming question. "Would you like a little piece of delicious Shabbos chicken?" she asks him. "A little Shabbos chicken?" I have never heard this phrase, "Shabbos chicken," which seems an entirely new category of food, food with special forms of sustenance, extraordinary restorative powers. After this moment, I can relax. I have entered the zone. I have left my world and entered another.

After a few minutes, a tall, handsome man walks in. He doesn't touch his wife, but they seem to have an unspoken intimacy. He wears a white shirt, black yarmulke and dark pants with strings hanging out at his hips, like his sons. I stand and put out my hand. He hesitates, then takes it. I flush, wondering if I have done something wrong.

We exchange a few pleasantries, then I ask him if I did something improper in extending my hand.

Out of respect for women, religious men do not touch women other than their wives, he tells me, an expression of resigned discomfort crossing his face, but since his work as a school administrator requires daily contact with a largely secular world, he has learned to reconcile himself to these social graces. I say nothing, but I am put off by his manner. If he didn't want to shake my hand, why did he do so?

He didn't touch me out of respect for me? Then why did he look so uncomfortable after grasping my hand? Later, I learn that Orthodox Jews believe in a strict interpretation of Leviticus 18: "You shall not come close to uncovering her nakedness." The Oral Law elaborates on the steps that might lead to this, and they include kissing, mixed dancing, and touching.

He suggests we take my bag out of the car before dusk, and I tell him I'm happy to get it myself. I don't particularly want him to see my Mustang, a truly goyishe car. However, there seems no way to dissuade him from accompanying me. I fumble with the key and lift my bag from the front seat; he takes it from me without a word. He shows me to a room with twin beds where I see an additional bag, and so learn that I will be sharing the room with another young woman.

Before we leave for synagogue, my hostess asks me if I would like to light a candle. I say yes, not sure exactly what she means. She leads me to a gorgeous, ornate silver candelabrum that holds many candles. There are also a few white candles in metal cups on a tray beneath, two of which she points out to me. I watch her as she strikes the match, lights her candles, then puts her hands over her eyes. After a moment, she waves her hands over the candles and recites the familiar blessing, "Baruch atah adonai, eloheinu melech haolam asher kid'shanu b'mitsvotav v'tsivanu l'hadlik ner shel Shabbat." When she is done, she nods to me, and I take the matches in hand and, hoping to get the prayer right from memory, I begin to recite it before striking the match.

She stops me with her hand and tells me first to light the candle and then to say the blessing. She explains that once the Sabbath has been ushered in with the blessing, one can no longer strike a match, because it violates the prohibition of lighting a fire. But you can't make a blessing over nothing, so the idea is to light the candles first, then close your eyes as if the light had not yet been struck, recite the blessing over the lit candles, then open your eyes to the glorious flame. With this sleight of hand, you circumvent the problem of order.

"Why do I light two candles?" I ask.

"Zachor ve shamor," she says. "It means 'to remember the holy day' — which stands for the positive commandments — and 'to guard the holy day,' which refers to the negative commandments. There are a lot of things on Shabbos that come in twos — you hold up two challahs, for the same reason."

I look into the flames, and let my eyes unfocus for a moment. The lights blur into one, and then back to their own shapes. She has lit a candle for every member of her family. They seem like little hands waving, little souls struggling to stand up.

Afterward, I climb into a minivan with my host and three of the children, and we head to the synagogue. We have seven minutes until dusk and the official beginning of the day of rest. "When you light the Shabbos candles," my hostess told me, "keep in your mind that you're going to get in a car, so you won't really accept the Shabbos until you get out." Although it sounds absurd, I think about this, and try to do as she says.

At Shaare Tefillah — Gates of Prayer — my host greets other men in dark suits as we enter the synagogue and walk past offices, a library, and a large gathering room, which I see has been set up for dinner. There is a sea of people, a far wealthier and more established crowd than that at Beth Emunah. The sanctuary is modern but remarkably warm for its austere, angular design. The men enter by the center doors; those on either side are marked WOMEN'S SEC-TION. I grab a prayer book from a bookcase and open the left-hand door. The carpeted floor leads up a few stairs to a narrow section that runs the length of the sanctuary. Between this and the other women's section running along the opposite wall, and beneath us by a few feet, is the men's section, whose pews face the Ark. Our benches face each other and the men. To look at the Ark, in which the Torah is stored, we women must either sit at an angle on our seats, or twist our necks forty-five degrees to the side.

A wooden screen separates the women's benches from the men's, and I see its design is composed of interlocking Stars of David. I'm not sure what I think of the symbol of David, author of the hallowed psalms, being used as a barrier between the women and the men and as a barrier between the women and their clear sight of the Torah. And why on earth, I wonder, do the women's seats face the men's, if we are not supposed to look at them. Why don't our seats face the Ark?

I walk up toward the front and sit down, aware of the well-behaved girls and women watching me. I look toward the men's section, where boys tumble over their fathers' laps, men stand and talk with each other, some rock with prayer books held close to their faces. I feel a flush of jealousy at the community of activity and the camaraderie in the area before me. I turn and look to my left, and then glance to my right. The women and girls sit quietly, or speak quietly with each other. Some look toward the center with dark eyes and silence. I feel angry for them and myself. I feel left out.

In a few minutes, the praying begins. Although there is a man sitting up front in a chair whom I later learn is the rabbi, another man leads the prayers from a pulpit closer to the center of the men's section. The praying sounds like an ancient wail, a wail interspersed with mumbling. The men rock back and forth from their waists as they pray and sometimes turn left and right. One man tips forward and back so dramatically it is as if he were making violent love—to God, I suppose. A counter that marks the page of the prayer book is turned by a young boy in a hat. After fifteen minutes, the synagogue is full of men in black hats or yarmulkes and women in suits or dresses and hats. I see Rabbi Fried praying with his hat pushed high on his head, the brim pushed back from his brow. In spite of my irritation over the women's segregation, I am quickly lulled by the sound of the prayers and the appearance of the beautiful Hebrew words on the page.

This is the first time I have used a real prayer book on Shabbat. At Beth Emunah, our service is guided by the booklets designed by Rabbi Groesberg, which I now realize include a highly selective choice of prayers. And I see from the translation in the book I now hold that there is a prayer here that we have never said in its entirety, but only in very short pieces. It is called the Shimoneh Esrai, and I can see from the notes that this is the central prayer of Sabbath worship. Why haven't we recited it in full, I wonder? As we begin, I see people bowing all around me. I watch a woman standing in front of me who seems to be praying with great feeling. She bends her knees, and bows forward at the waist, then twists left and right before straightening up. I notice that while the men sing and chant, the women move their mouths and whisper the prayer just under their breaths, as if offering a quiet supporting rhythmic line to the men's prayer. I am almost completely lost, but I try to act as if I were following along, and I scan the Hebrew letters for something I recognize.

Children wander through both sections, leave, visit another parent or a friend's parent and return. I remember being surprised during Navajo meetings or religious ceremonies that the many small children in attendance seldom cried or threw tantrums. I am equally surprised here. I see little of the agonizing struggles for attention that seem so much a part of the relations between children and their parents in the secular world.

I wonder for a moment if the children behave well because of the self-discipline they develop while learning the strict religious rules regarding food and other behavior. Or is it that they are simply more respectful because of the constant devotion in their families to a power and movement greater than them all?

The service is concluded with a few announcements, after which the people stand up. A murmuring begins as the men greet each other and start conversations. The women offer each other polite greetings, and wait in line quietly to file out. As I walk toward the dining area, Rabbi Fried appears next to me, a happy, conspiratorial look on his face, as if we shared a good secret.

"Good Shabbos," he says with a smile, and introduces me to his wife, Miri, a thin woman with a dark wig whose shy manner doesn't obscure her evident intelligence and competence. She is pushing a baby carriage bearing twins. Rabbi Fried points out a book-lined room where the kollel meets and learns, and he introduces me to a couple of open-faced, friendly-looking young men who are rabbis in the kollel. I do not reach for their hands; rather I say hello and nod, feeling a small thrill at being able to enact what I have so recently learned.

We all move slowly into the dining room and sit down. A man recites the Kiddush over the wine, and I swallow the contents of the small plastic cup beside my plate, enjoying the taste of the sweet wine on my lips and tongue.

Then I notice people are getting up from their places to walk toward the back of the hall. I catch the eyes of the woman who was praying with great intensity during the service. She asks me if I know about washing, and I shake my head. I follow her into the women's room nearby, and I watch her fill a plastic, double-handled pitcher with water. She tells me we will wash our hands, recite a blessing as we dry them off, and refrain from talking until we return to the dining room and say a blessing over the bread. I watch her pour water over her right hand, then switch hands and pour water over her left. As she dries them with paper towels, she murmurs under her breath a prayer whose words are printed on a sign on the sink. The blessing has the usual start, "Baruch atah adonai, eloheinu melech haolam," then concludes with the words, "al netilat yadaim." I know that the pointer one uses to keep place while reading the Torah is called a yad, and it is in the shape of a little hand, so I figure "yadaim" means hands.

I take the pitcher myself, fill it up, pour the water over my hands. I think how primitively satisfying it is to feel the water flowing over my hands, and how different it is from the busyness of washing them under the faucet, rubbing them together with soap and then rinsing them off. Like lighting candles to prepare for the evening, pouring water from a double-handled pitcher is a special ritual, an action infused with meaning and expectation and full of association with the past. I recite the prayer under my breath, hoping that I get the words right.

I return to my seat and sit quietly. The enforced silence gives me a chance to look around at the crowd. I see children who are eager to eat, parents who seem relaxed and happy. The mood is boisterous, informal. I can look at people's faces without feeling I am intruding, and I see people with whom I can imagine being friendly. I also see several couples I have already met through work and other friends: lawyers, businesspeople, doctors, both male and female. It is a sophisticated, worldly crowd, sprinkled with the more traditional people like the kollel rabbis and their wives. Many, but not all, of the women wear wigs, and some wear skirts slightly above the knee.

When the room is quiet, a man lifts up two loaves of challah, recites the blessing, then quickly cuts a piece for himself, dips it in a pile of kosher salt he has poured on the breadboard, and brings it to his mouth. Then he cuts into the bread with deep, forceful thrusts of the knife, picks up a handful of slices and dips them in the salt, and passes the bread out to the people at his table. The same is then done at all the other tables. I bite into my heavy, even-textured piece of challah, and taste a delicious sweetness. The second bite brings the burn of salt on my tongue and the feel of the smooth, brown crust.

The platters of food on the buffet table look fresh and nicely prepared. At the end of the table, on a warming plate, is a pot in which meat and beans and barley are slowly bubbling.

"What is that?" I ask a woman standing nearby.

"That's cholent," she says.

"Cholent?" I ask, repeating the soft "ch" sound of the word "chicken."

"The mortar of the Jews," she says, laughing. I take a closer look.

"It's a traditional Shabbat meal," she says, "as it is made Friday and kept warm all through the Sabbath."

"People say it is cholent that has bound the Jews through the centuries," says a man beside her, smiling. Back at the table, I taste the cholent, which is redolent with flavors from the Ukraine to Morocco.

I am sitting with a group of professionals: a psychologist, a real estate developer, a woman who owns a clothing store. All are a little older than I am; their Judaism, they tell me, has been revived and deepened since the arrival of the kollel here a year and a half ago. I notice that the women manage to dress quite stylishly while still keeping their legs and arms covered. They are an interesting group of people, connected through business and friendship with other Jews in the community whom I have met.

When I arrive home with my host after a pleasant walk that we shared with several of my dinner companions, I notice that the house has been picked up. The wife waits for us in the living room, nursing her baby. She has put on a brown wig with a straight Dutch-boy cut and bangs. Her full lips are rouged red, and her face exudes a sensuous expectation that startles me. She looks like a lollipop for her husband, and I remember reading that Friday night is the time for conjugal lovemaking. My first impulse is to retreat to my room, but she asks me to sit with her. She asks me about myself, where I grew up and what brought me to Dallas. I tell her, enjoying the possibility that I will shock her with my sad tale. She tells me she is from Los Angeles and that she met her husband in an ice-cream parlor. They dated for three weeks before becoming engaged. I can't believe this. Three weeks? She tells me that religious people tend to have brief courtships. The husband sits with us for a while, then goes to bed. It occurs to me that I should let her go to him, but I stay.

"But how did you know you were suited for each other?" I ask her.

"We had the same goals," she says. "And we both liked ice cream."

I am shocked, but then I wonder if maybe that's the key—perhaps I have always been looking for far too much in a man.

We talk on. Soon she becomes sleepy. Her baby dozes in her arms. I excuse myself, wishing her a good Shabbos, and return to my room, in which the other girl is already asleep. I undress quietly, thinking about my hostess's appearance as we came home, how this plump, homely woman had transformed herself into a red-lipped treat for her husband. She appeared to me for all the world as a sacrificial offering, straggly hair of the afternoon pushed up under her wig, lips painted, the house clean, the weekend's food prepared, the children tucked cozily to bed.

I step into the bathroom and see the light switch has been taped in the ON position, so that no one will inadvertently switch it off. I see the toilet paper has been taken away and replaced with a box of tissues. Tearing paper qualifies as one of the thirty-nine categories of work forbidden on the Sabbath. I splash some water on my face and realize there will be no shower tomorrow because the hot-water heater is probably turned off as well.

I quietly change into nightclothes and settle under the covers. I lie on my belly and hook my toes over the bottom of the bed, and my fingers up over the top. I stretch, feel out the boundaries of my new, small space, then roll into a fetal position and fall asleep.

The next morning, I am awakened by a knock on the door. One of the children announces that morning services begin at nine. I reach over and look at my watch. It is eight o'clock, not much time to get ready, since the walk is about twenty minutes. I look over toward the other bed. The girl is there, the covers over her head. I get up and walk to the bathroom with my toiletry case. I look in it and see toothbrush and toothpaste and I wonder if I am allowed to brush my teeth. I wonder if I can brush my hair. I walk back into the bedroom and see that my roommate is up and dressing.

"Do you know, " I ask, "what the rule is about brushing hair on Shabbat?"

"You're not supposed to brush it unless you use a very soft brush," she says, "so as to avoid pulling out any hairs."

"Oh," I say, looking in my bag and finding only a wide-toothed comb.

"And what about makeup?"

"Well, you're not supposed to draw anything, because you are forbidden from creating anything new on the Sabbath."

"How about brushing teeth?" I ask.

"Well, smoothing or smearing is considered work."

I guess that rules out toothpaste. I go back into the bathroom and look at myself in the mirror. That girl had nice straight hair that fell in place as soon as she got out of bed. My long wavy hair is a mess. I run my fingers through it, hoping to straighten it out, and am horrified to see three hairs wound around my fingers when I'm done. Oh my. Have I already violated the Sabbath?

I look in the mirror again. I need to do something about my hair. I will feel uncomfortable heading out into public looking like this. I wonder if I use the comb just to make a part in my hair, perhaps I won't pull out any strands. I think for a few seconds, and then I pull the comb slowly in a line from the crown of my head to my brow. Nice straight part, hair put in place, and no hairs, I see, left on the comb.

I look at the bottle of face cream in my bag. My face feels very dry, and I'd love to put a little moisturizer on it. I wonder if that's legal. It's a screw top. What about some concealer to hide the dark circles under my eyes? I look in the mirror, then back at the special box of tissues and the tape over the light, and I decide if I'm not supposed to do it on Shabbat, I won't do it. Everyone else is subject to the same prohibitions, after all, and I won't look worse than anyone else.

I dress and walk out to the kitchen. I am dying for a cup of coffee, but, as I think about it, there's no way one can brew coffee without boiling water. On the table are a few pieces of apple cake. I look for my hostess and find her in the back of the kitchen. I wish her good morning, and she asks me if I slept well. She tells me there is a container of hot water if I would like to make tea.

I pour some water into a cup, put in a tea bag that she offers. I ask if I can have a little milk. She nods. I take a container of milk from the refrigerator and move across the kitchen to set it down on the counter.

"This side's dairy," she says to me, and I turn, carton still in hand.

"This counter is for dairy products, and that one is for meat," she says.

"Oh," I say. I knew about the separation of plates, milk from meat, and I knew some people had two sinks and two dishwashers, but I didn't realize the counters mattered too.

I swallow the warm tea and try to pretend that it is coffee, running through me to wake me up. I am trying to feel the peace I imagined coming over me during the observance of Shabbat. It seems hard to feel this peace when I am so afraid of making the wrong move and when I am dying for a shower and in general feeling so disoriented physically.

"Would you mind accompanying the kids to shul?" my hostess asks.

"Not at all," I say. "I was wondering how I'd find my way there."

My hostess will not go to services, she tells me. Women are not obligated to observe time-dependent mitzvot like the communal prayers required three times a day for men, so they can take care of their home and children.

RABBI EZRIEL TAUBER wears a three-quarter-length black silk coat tied with a rope, the dress of a Chassidic man. He has a mesmerizing voice with a strong Yiddish accent that leads him to say "Toirah" for "Torah." As he speaks, he rhythmically adjusts his yarmulke in a hypnotic, lulling gesture. Rabbi Fried has told me in his breathless way that Rav Tauber is not only an inspirational lecturer but also a successful businessman who made millions in real estate in New York. Rabbi Fried feels it is particularly important for secular Jews to see that one can be both religious and successful in the world.

We have attended the morning service and eaten lunch and are gathered for Rav Tauber's talk in the sanctuary. I look around at the other women and observe that far from refraining from hair-brushing and putting on makeup, most of them are meticulously groomed. I feel unattractive and unkempt. I try to determine who is wearing a wig. I find something erotic about the notion of concealing the hair, and as I look at these women, I feel as if I am sneaking peeks where I shouldn't. I can pick out the rabbis' wives rather quickly, from their dowdier clothing and cheaper wigs. I wonder if in the privacy of their own bedrooms, with their hair down, these women become Delilahs, or whether as a result of their circumscribed modesty, they remain in character: plain, unseen.

I am told that women cover their hair because it is considered an overwhelmingly attractive attribute. Once they are married, they reserve the sight of their hair for their husbands. There is much energy and activity associated with the wigs, or sheitels, as they are called. There are women who style and cut them for a living. There are others who make snoods, or head coverings. Sheitels are very expensive. Custom-made wigs start at $3,000. When a woman with a head of blond curls enters the room, someone whispers to me that she has a sheitel made of "European hair," whereas the more standard wigs with heavy straight locks, most styled in a page boy or a pony tail, are made of "Korean hair" that has been dyed brown.

To my surprise, the men and women are allowed to sit together for Rabbi Tauber's speech. Who determined this, I wonder. What are the rules that keep us apart when we are praying but allow us to sit together in the same place, in the synagogue sanctuary, for a lecture?

I sit toward the front, greedy to get close to the action. Rabbi Tauber's speech combines real-life stories, parables, and sayings of the sages, and his Yiddish accent disarms me completely. As he begins his speech on "Life, Marriage, and Happiness in Judaism," I feel the ice that has crusted over me for the past fifteen hours begin to melt. I feel comfortable attending a lecture. It is familiar ground, and once my brain is engaged, I enter his world, and my body relaxes.

"The Hebrew word for man," says Rabbi Tauber, "is 'ish,' spelled aleph, yud, shin, and the word for woman is 'ishah,' spelled aleph, shin, hey. These words share two letters, aleph and shin. And they have one letter that is unique, the yud of 'ish,' and the hey of 'ishah.' Together, the yud and the hey spell the name of God—Hashem. The job of the man and woman is to reunite their unique letters of holiness. If they do not bring the yud and hey into their relationship, if they do not make the focus of their relationship the goal of spiritual reunion, then all that is left is the aleph and shin of 'ishah' and the aleph and shin of 'ish.' Aleph and shin spell 'aish,' which is 'fire.'"

He continues: "If the husband and wife lack the goal of spiritual union, then, like two consuming fires, they will destroy each other." And: "There is a story told of the tzaddik Reb Aryeh Levine. His wife injured her foot and the two of them visited the doctor together and Reb Aryeh said, 'Doctor, my wife's foot is hurting us.' This was no slip of the tongue or dramatized response. He had truly become one with his wife, and her pain was his. This is the unity meant by the Torah's injunction, that husband and wife will become 'one flesh.'"

And: "In the Shefa Tal, a book written several centuries ago, there is described a storehouse of souls, which acts as a kind of way station for souls destined to be divided in half and sent down, one half at a time, into a body. The entire concept is based on the understanding that originally Hashem created one soul possessing both male and female characteristics, which is destined to be divided and put into two separate bodies. Since the husband and wife can be years apart in age, the bodies will not be created at the same time, so the half soul which is born later than the other needs a place to wait.

"The Talmud tells us that forty days before the formation of the fetus, a voice proclaims, 'This soul is destined to marry so-and-so.' Once born into this world, the half souls are separated for many years until one day they instinctively start seeking each other out. The attraction they feel is rooted in the yearning in each of these half souls to reunite with the other half. That is why the potential oneness between husband and wife is unparalleled in this life, because it is a coming together of two parts that were once one, and were then separated."

I am moved by this idea. The welcoming back of the lost knowledge, or the joining of the souls separated for years, creates a wistfulness in me. I feel that Rabbi Tauber's stories are familiar, as if I have always understood their mystical logic and poetic structure.

"The couple becomes one," he continues, "just as the cherubim were one." The cherubim were the two angelic figures—one male and one female—on top of the Ark of the Tablets of the Ten Commandments. "They and the cover of the Ark were actually hammered out from a single piece of gold; it was forbidden to solder any part of them. So too a couple is originally one soul; they are not two entities melted and molded together. They can become one just as the cherubim were one.

"The cherubim made up the connecting point between heaven and earth. And so, when a couple achieves true oneness, the Shechinah, the Divine Presence of mystical Judaism, comes down into this world and dwells between them just as it did between the cherubim. When the love between a man and a woman is strong and produces spiritual oneness and reunion, they and their household are worthy of having the Divine Presence manifested in their lives.

"Furthermore, when the Kohen Gadol, the high priest, once a year on Yom Kippur entered the inner chamber of the Temple where the cherubim were situated, a miracle happened. If the love between Hashem and His people Israel were strong, the figures would be embracing each other; if not, they would be turned away. So too when the love between a man and a woman is strong, and is the kind of love that produces spiritual reunion and oneness, then they and their household are worthy of having the Divine Presence manifest Itself in their lives like It manifested Itself in the Temple.

"The spiritual closeness between a husband and a wife in the privacy of their own home sanctifies all Israel, and from there it spreads and sanctifies the entire creation and universe."

I find myself smiling when Rabbi Tauber pauses here. This idea seems so beautiful. Love between two people is not just a solitary event, but is part of the fortunes of a community and a people. I think then of a most moving ritual in which I took part at the wedding of a good friend from college. Candles had been placed on the seats of every guest before the ceremony. As the bride and groom walked down the aisle toward the chuppah, each carried a long lit candle, which they touched to the candles held by the people at the end of every row, who in turn turned to the people next to them, and so on, until, when the couple reached the chuppah, they turned to see their family and friends as a cluster of flickering flames. Their loved ones were accompanying them to the chuppah, seeing them off on their journey to union with a roomful of light and hope. The couple were not alone.

As I return from my reverie, Rav Tauber asks if there are any questions. One person asks if Jewish law requires a woman to marry. Rav Tauber replies that it is only the man who, strictly speaking, is commanded to marry. A woman is considered complete without a man, but a man needs a woman. Before Eve was created, Adam was "not good," according to Torah. "It is not good being man alone." He becomes good only when he marries the "good," and learns to give.

The Hebrew word for "bone," says Rabbi Tauber, "etzem," customarily translated as "rib," actually means "essence." When God took the rib from Adam, he took the best part, the essence. Later, when Eve is shown to Adam, he says she is the "essence of my essence." The woman is the essence of the man's divine soul. She is literally the "good" of man.

I raise my hand.

"If as a woman I am good," I ask, "why am I not allowed to read publicly from the Torah, nor be called for an aliyah to bless the Torah?"

He shakes his head with what looks like dismissiveness. He says that men and women have different purposes in the transformation of the world, and each needs to perfect his own role. A man needs to perform all the mitzvahs to put himself in line with God's desires for him. The woman, being naturally closer to God's view of her, is freed from certain positive commandments that the man needs to perform daily.

I feel myself wondering: Is this a fancy way of neutralizing the woman, putting her on a pedestal to get her out of the fray? Then Rav Tauber offers something particularly stirring: "The remnant of the Holy of Holies, the Ark of the Covenant," he says, tipping his yarmulke back onto his head, "today resides in the bedroom of the husband and wife."

SOME OF RABBI TAUBER'S tapes and books are available for purchase after the lecture. Since it is still Shabbat, I cannot pay for them, but I arrange to take a book and some tapes and send a check later. Rabbi Fried, a big smile on his face, walks over and asks, "Did you like his speech?"

I nod. I feel like I am in something of a trance. "I thought it was very interesting," I say, though I don't quite know how to explain what I am feeling. Although I cannot abide the suggestion that woman's place is in the home, that is not exactly what I heard from Rabbi Tauber. He made it clear in his comments that women can be doctors and lawyers and journalists and whatever they want. However, I wondered how plausible it was to succeed in the outside world while remaining strictly observant of halachah, or Jewish law. And I do not like the fact that women are excused from most of the ritual observances the men are obligated to perform, and are not part of the public worship in the synagogue.

But there is something stunningly, primitively appealing about the protection offered women within a closed society. At this moment, such treatment appeals to me. I feel fragile and damaged and wouldn't mind being a little bit protected. The idea that Judaism asserts an ethical dimension to human relationships pleases me. I agree that joining with another human being should be considered a sublime gift. I think how different the picture of life with Craig became, how void of ethical obligations, how truly materialistic.

After Rabbi Tauber's lecture, I talk more with the attendees, and then we walk home together, as many of them live on the same block. At my host's we eat a light dairy meal, the required third meal of Shabbat, after which I excuse myself to take a nap. As the end of Shabbat nears, my host marks the event by gathering the family around the table, then lighting a special braided candle, singing prayers, and then extinguishing the flame in wine.

Soon after, I say good-bye to my hosts, load my things in my car, and drive off. I am in a bit of an emotional tangle, my feelings divided. On the one hand, I have caught a glimpse of a precious, rarefied world of poetry and grand, ancient imperatives. On the other, I am disappointed that I did not sense the peace of Shabbat I had heard about. I also had trouble putting aside my initial dismay about the relegation of women to traditional roles, though I sensed there was more to it than I saw in the brief time I was there.

I drive a mile or so through the neighborhoods of North Dallas before I turn onto the Tollway, but as I accelerate onto the on-ramp, I hear the sound of something shattering outside the vehicle. I slam on the brakes, step out of the car into the warm spring air, and walk back a few yards, where I see something shiny in the road. It is the Rabbi Tauber tapes, one, two, three, scattered like pick-up-sticks on the asphalt. I had left the Shabbaton in haste, with the tapes still perched on the roof of my car. Just then a pickup truck whizzes by me, and I realize with some fear that I am standing in the middle of a highway entrance, a very dangerous position indeed. I think of the parable of standing too close to the pounding waterfall that Rabbi Fried told us and I pull myself out of my trance and get back in the car. My calves, my thighs, my hands are shaking. The dark sky is bright with the light of a full moon.

FOUR MONTHS LATER, in October, Rabbi Fried calls and asks if I would like to come and stay with him and Miri and their family for Shabbat.

I don't know what to say. I was uncomfortable the last time I spent Shabbat among the community, though I was moved by Rabbi Tauber's talk.

"Oh, well, that's a kind offer, but I . . . um . . ." I stammer out my hesitation. At the other end of the line, there is silence.

Rabbi Fried is a very nice man and so filled with excitement about Yiddishkeit, that I don't think I can tell him how I felt during my previous visit.

"I got the feeling you didn't have the best time when you were here last spring," he says, surprising me, "and I would like the chance to have you stay with us. Maybe you could write a story about it?"

Oh, that's not a bad idea, I think to myself, wondering how he knows that I will respond better if I can protect myself behind the reporter's shield. My role as an outsider will then be clear, and I can retreat into skeptical distance whenever I want.

"But, if I'm there on Shabbat, I can't take any notes."

"You can come back, though, and we'll talk about everything again, if you'd like. Or perhaps you won't need to. Who knows what might happen?"

I hesitantly agree. Within a week, I obtain an assignment from *Texas Monthly* magazine, something I had been trying unsuccessfully to obtain over the last few months. They agree to my new suggestion to write a story about the kollel. I wonder if this is an omen of some kind.

So I RETURN to the Orthodox community one balmy Friday. Rabbi Fried is running around the house, his tzitzit flying, trying to give the very active eighteen-month-old twin boys, Elisha and Elazar, a snack as they struggle to climb out of their high chairs. With the charming sincerity of a man who has no natural management skills with children, he has succeeded in vacuuming the living room, washing the dishes, and feeding his sons, all the while talking to his two older children, Bennie and Tzipporah, and giving me short sketches of the Talmud chochem, or Torah scholars, photographs of whom hang on the walls.

"That is Rav Shlomo Zalman Auerbach," says Rabbi Fried breathlessly, nodding to the image of a white-bearded man with a face like an angel. "He is one of the brightest lights of the Torah world."

He straightens out the cushions on the couch and continues: "I once went to him to get his blessing on Yom Kippur. In this yeshivah, they learned musser, proper personal conduct, before the davening, and I walked up to him, and he looked up from his book, and his whole face was white like a ghost. He was murmuring about Yom Kippur and the next year, and his eyes were beet red from crying. I never saw such a thing. I just said, 'Have a good year,' and he instantly answered that back to me. He's so good, he didn't say 'What are you bothering me now for?' Immediately, he gave me a blessing right back."

I am quiet for a while thinking about the almost supernal light emanating from this man's face.

"Was this your personal rebbe?"

"No, my rebbe is Rav Moshe Shapiro, another giant of that generation."

"It must have been very hard for you to leave Jerusalem and these people to come here to Dallas."

"It was. At first, I came here only to give a talk. Just a few people knew the visit was a secret pilot program, and if it went well, I would return to set up a kollel. I was scheduled to board a plane from Jerusalem on a Sunday morning. The Saturday evening before, there was a new moon, and there's a special prayer you say for that. You walk out of the shul on Saturday night and you bless the new moon with a special, moving prayer. I was surrounded by sages with long white beards. We were saying this prayer together, and I was thinking, Look what I have here, am I crazy? I am about to fly to Dallas, Texas. Am I out of my mind?

"But then I thought to myself that being there gave me a false sense of security. It's very easy to be secure Jewish-wise when surrounded by Talmudic sages, while the Jewish people are being burnt up, are going through a spiritual holocaust in the United States. And therefore, it's false to stand there and feel secure while all that is happening out here. And I told myself, that is why I'm going.

"I went through a very hard emotional time struggling with myself. Could I really get myself to leave the top of the world? To come down here, which was a desert compared to where I was. Even though there was an Orthodox community here that was devoted to Torah, still, when I compared it to the diamond of the world, it wasn't even close."

"What was it that finally convinced you to come?" I ask him.

"It was the desire and positive feeling of the people here, the fire they had to build Torah in their city. Meeting those people made me want to come. I reported back to the sages of the generation. They believed extremely, extremely strongly that it must be done. They felt that there was a special mission in bringing Torah to a place like this."

"How do you account for the fact that so many people have been coming to your programs," I ask, "and taking tapes from the library, and becoming more observant. Here in Dallas, Texas?"

"If I had to put it in a nutshell," Rabbi Fried says, "I'd have to say it's the Jewish soul. That throughout the generations you see revealed this desire to come close to God and to Torah. No matter how far away a Jew is from exposure to Judaism, the moment he gets exposed is when he wakes up and sees that that's what he really wants."

"When I was a child," I tell him, "I dreamed of becoming a yeshivah student after reading two books by Chaim Potok, *The Promise* and *The Chosen.*" What I don't say is that I was crushed to learn that girls don't go to those yeshivahs.

He looks at me. "It was after reading those two books that I decided to go to yeshivah as well," he says.

"So you are a ba'al-teshuvah?" This term means, literally, "one who returns," and refers to the growing number of nonobservant or semiobservant Jews who are choosing to become Orthodox.

"Yes. I grew up in Indianapolis in a secular family."

"What do your parents think of your becoming religious?"

"They've always looked at me as some weird sort of fanatic who's always doing this extreme stuff. But they just spent a week here, and they're happier about the whole thing now that they've spent time here in the community, and they've seen what kind of people are involved, normal people. We've always been on good terms. But now, they no longer say, 'Well, he could have been on drugs, or in a cult.' There's a tremendous mitzvah of honoring one's parents, and if I can bring them honor, then that in itself is a fulfillment of God's will. They're proud of me because I've been publishing books, but I'm still human, I guess—I want their approval."

He then tells me he's written a book on Jewish philosophy, a commentary to the Talmud, and a handbook on Jewish law regarding the two-day observance of holidays in the diaspora. He has also written other books for the yeshivah community.

I am quiet, absorbing my growing knowledge of this man. We continue to talk, in spite of the vacuum cleaner, in spite of the ringing telephone. The twins are now playing with blocks on the floor.

"I have some ideas about the connection of music and religion," I say. "In a very odd way, I was drawn to the synagogue through a series of associations that concern music."

"Is that so?" he asks me, moving the coffee table out of the way, so he can vacuum beneath it. "I wrote a paper about the connections between Judaism and music. I think I may even have it here somewhere, though most of my books and papers are still in Israel."

"I would love to see it," I say.

"It's in Hebrew."

"Oh," I say, thinking I could have read it had it been written in French or even Spanish. But not Hebrew, the language of my own people.

"I'll try to describe the ideas to you later, after dinner."

ON THE WALK BACK FROM SYNAGOGUE, Rabbi Fried tells me that the midrash says that two angels accompany a man home from synagogue on Friday night—a good angel and a bad angel. If the Shabbos table at home is all ready, and peace prevails over the home, the good angel talks to the man, making blessings for him, and the bad angel says, "Amen." If, however, God forbid, Shabbos is not ready, the house is not peaceful, the bad angel will make his curses over the house.

When Rabbi Fried and I enter the house, we are greeted by Miri, who wears a silky white blouse tied with a bow at the neck and adorned with gold chains. She is smiling broadly, and seems relaxed and happy. I feel I am looking at the Shabbos bride herself. She is radiant even though she has probably been working all afternoon to prepare food for the next twenty-four hours, not to mention taking care of her four children. Miri is a pharmacist, and when the family was in Jerusalem, she worked in her mother's drugstore. She is now studying to get certification here in the States.

Before the meal, we wash in the kitchen, using an ornate double-handled silver pitcher. I realize I don't remember the blessing. I wonder if I should fake it and just mumble something to myself, or ask Rabbi Fried to remind me of the words. I am saved by one of his children, who recites the blessing aloud, and I am reminded of the words, al n'tilat yadaim.

The apartment complex in which the kollel rabbis live is humble and the furniture here secondhand, but Miri's Shabbos table is beautiful. We eat on pretty china and drink wine out of crystal glasses, and the table is covered with a beautiful hand-embroidered cloth. Everyone is dressed in their best clothes, making it clear to family and guests alike that this is a special day with special pleasures. In fact, the table and the entire room seem to be illuminated with a special warmth. As we eat, Rabbi Fried asks the children questions about this week's Torah portion. He encourages them to offer their insights and congratulates them on their responses. When they say something funny, he giggles. He is not the slightest bit doctrinaire; in fact, he loves to pun, and does so ceaselessly.

Rabbi Fried tells a story about a relative of someone he knew in yeshivah. This relative was the servant of an old rabbi who was known to commune from time to time with Elijah the Prophet. In the evenings, on occasion, the rabbi asked his servant to prepare tea for him. But oddly enough, he always asked his servant to bring the tea in two separate glasses and then go away and leave him alone to learn. In the mornings, the servant would gather up the empty glasses. One night, he became so curious about the second glass that he positioned himself in front of the study door and watched the goings-on through the keyhole. He saw his master drinking tea and holding forth—with the second glass tipped in the air across the table before him.

The man fainted dead away and made such a noise that the rabbi came out to see what was the matter. He woke up his servant and scolded him: "I told you not to look in here when I am learning." The servant hurried away, promising that he never would look again. Rabbi Fried has a wide smile of pleasure on his face when he finishes, and his children light up with questions and comments.

This Shabbat table, it occurs to me, which not only celebrates the

people seated around it but also their shared beliefs, is the center-
piece of Jewish culture, encompassing everything—family, abundance, learning, happiness. Although my family never discussed
Torah at the table, something of the archetypal Shabbat table was
preserved in our nightly family dinners, when we sat down and ate
together, talked about our day, discussed the news of the world,
debated and laughed.

What we missed out on was the idea that one day a week we
would be offered a glimpse of the world to come, a whiff of the Garden of Eden. Never did we imagine we were participating in the
world's redemption, nor did it occur to us that we might have a role
in it. My sister and I did develop a strong sense of responsibility to use
our own gifts, whatever they might be, to contribute to the good of
the world. Our father was doing medical research, and our mother
was involved in the area of land conservation and environmental
protection. What we all lacked was the belief that anyone—or any
One—was helping us along or that we had a purpose beyond our
own private reckoning.

At the end of the meal, Rabbi Fried reaches to the top shelf of a
bookcase and grabs a bottle of chocolate liqueur. He pours it into two
glasses, then adds some selzer water.

"It's like a chocolate soda," he says, laughing, handing me one.
And so it is. I am amazed by Rabbi Fried's disarming enthusiasm. My
eyes wander to the photograph of Rav Shlomo Zalman Auerbach,
and in it I see the same transcendent expectation that I see in Rabbi
Fried's face, yet it is more concentrated, as if the additional forty years
of study had filled his every cell with knowledge, until his complexion resembled nothing less than a page of holy scripture itself. I wonder if Rabbi Fried's face will in time become similarly charged with
light.

After dinner, Miri puts the children to bed and Rabbi Fried and I go into the study. We sit down in captain's chairs around a circular wooden table.

"So, you want to know about the connection of music and Judaism?" he asks, folding his hands. "There was a great Torah scholar named Shraga Feivel Mendilovich. He lived in the 1940s in Flatbush. He was such a humble man that he referred to himself as 'Mister Mendilovich,' not even as 'Rabbi.' This was his greatness. When they eulogized him, they called him 'Nister Mendilovich,' because 'nister' means 'hidden, or secret, one.' He was a very mystical person, and he liked to walk in the forest. One day, as he was walking in the woods, one of his students absentmindedly plucked a leaf from a tree.

"When Mr. Mendilovich saw this, he started trembling, and he asked the student, 'How could you do such a thing? How could you pluck off a leaf? Don't you know that the whole universe is a song? It is like an orchestra playing, and each part of the world is like an instrument in the orchestra, and by plucking off that leaf, you've diminished the song.'"

Rabbi Fried becomes very animated as he talks, as if he himself had been right there in the woods with Mr. Mendilovich himself. He looks at me, his eyebrows raised, his hands up, as if inviting me there as well.

"So, there you hear the idea that the world is a song," he says. He pauses. "Then, there was the Vilna Gaon," Rabbi Fried continues, "the genius of Vilna, who lived about two hundred years ago. The Vilna Gaon went into self-imposed exile a couple of times in his life. During one of them he finished a commentary on Shir Hashirim, the Song of Songs. The whole song is about the connection between husband and wife, a man and a woman, which is an allegory for the relationship between God and the Jewish people. After he emerged from his exile, he said only someone who really understands the science of music can truly fathom the depths of Kabbalah, Jewish mysticism, and understand the Book of Creation."

I ask him if he thinks that songs hold mystical power.

Rabbi Fried smiles. "I once heard the story of a yeshivah student," he says. "He was studying with Moshe Shapiro in Israel. Now, even though the guy was just a regular student, Moshe was quite friendly with him, very close to him, and one day Moshe decided to sing him a song that he had received from someone in the last generation, a great Kabbalist.

"After hearing the song, the guy was never the same. Before, he had been just an average student, no better or worse than anyone else. But afterward, he became incredibly diligent and studied far into the night. In time, he became an awesome Torah scholar. And all because of hearing the song."

Rabbi Fried tells me that he has also heard some miraculous tunes, one of which he heard in Israel from a rabbi who broke out in song after offering a novel interpretation to a difficult Torah problem during the weekly Kiddush at his yeshivah. Rabbi Fried says the tune was so beautiful that it caused him to weep. When I asked him if he ever sang it himself, he said he did so only occasionally, and only when he was in the mood.

The songs and their mystical secrets are, by custom, closely guarded, he lets me know. The young man whose scholarly career was changed by Moshe Shapiro's song innocently taught the tune to someone else. But when Rav Shapiro found out about it, he became very angry. "I did not give you permission to teach that song," Rav Shapiro told him. "You don't teach it to just anybody."

"Jews are constantly singing," Rabbi Fried continues. "When Jews study Torah, they're singing. If you ever walk into a yeshivah, they're not just reading like in a library, they're singing Torah, they're swaying. And when we learn musser, the study of desirable character traits, suddenly the whole sound changes. The students are thinking about 'Where am I and how I should be and I'm not.' So they're singing a mournful song, and it sounds like three hundred guys sort of crying in unison. It could just rip your heart in half to hear it. If you get too close to the big sages when they do it, you'll almost faint. You can't imagine it. You just can't imagine it."

Jews sing during Shabbos, they sing at meals, they sing when they learn Torah, and when they chant from it. They sing when they're davening. Jews sing when they take out the Torah and when they put it back. "The heavens are singing, the world is singing, everything is singing," says King David in Psalms. "And the Jews are singing."

I ask Rabbi Fried what a song is.

"Good question," he says. "First of all, look at the Hebrew word 'yoffi,' which means 'beautiful,' and is understood in terms of harmony, in terms of how things blend together. I heard a series of talks from Rav Volbe, the world leader of the musser movement, about beauty. The epitome of beauty, he said, is when you have a landscape with a mountain and a valley and then a desert over here and blue sky and green leaves. The more opposite the parts are, the more stark the differences, the more beautiful the picture.

"The idea is that beauty is a harmony of opposites. We find the same thing in the spiritual world. God created animals, which are totally physical. They don't have souls with free choice. And He created angels, which are totally spiritual, and they don't have free choice either. So, God's creation includes opposites—physicality on one hand, spirituality on the other. Each is beautiful in its own right, but there's nothing blending the two together."

"Then you have a human being," he continues. "That's where you find true beauty. Man was created on the last day of Creation because that's what God really wanted out of the world. The world was created for the sake of man. The reason is that God wanted all this physical world to be elevated into something spiritual. In Christianity, a monk is somebody who goes out on a mountain, doesn't talk to anybody, doesn't get married. That's holiness. But with Judaism, that's considered a sin. Truly holy people, they get married and they participate fully in the world. They're not supposed to abstain from things. They're supposed to enjoy the chicken and enjoy the candy and enjoy everything else. But they should enjoy it the right way. They make a brachah, a blessing, before partaking. They stop and think about God, and they taste it, and so they're tasting how good God is.

"In Judaism, we're supposed to take the physical world and elevate it to the spiritual. By doing so, we connect the things that are finite with those that are infinite. The secret of the world is this connection. And the one that keeps it connected is the human being."

"So the purpose of humans is to elevate the mundane and the physical to the spiritual by being aware of God's presence in it?" I ask. Rabbi Fried nods, and I feel at once excited and calm. This seems to me to be the perfect answer. It is said that when a child is in utero, an angel teaches it all of Torah. But when it is time to be born, another angel touches it on the center of the top lip, on the "Cupid's bow," and all the baby's Torah knowledge is forgotten. However, when the child grows up and begins to learn Torah again, the knowledge is felt as revelation, rather than something learned for the first time.

"Each time you go and sit down to eat a piece of chicken, you can eat it just to fill yourself up, or you can eat it to elevate yourself to keep up your strength so you can study the Torah, keep mitzvahs, and be a healthy person. If you do that, then eating a piece of chicken becomes as holy an act as putting on tefillin—it's a big mitzvah, because it's an act of holiness in the world. You've elevated the physical world to something spiritual.

"If you watch the way the true sages eat, that's the way it is. Imagine, I've seen this so many times, after Shabbos, Rabbi Zalman Auerbach, with all his holiness and grandeur, sitting there eating a chocolate bar." Rabbi Fried laughs. "He's breaking off a little square and drinking a cup of tea with a sugar cube between his teeth. But he's doing a holy thing. He's making it holy."

"But how does this connect with music?"

"A truly great piece of music is not something that's all bass or all treble, all high or all low, all loud or all soft. The great symphonies are made up of as many possible kinds of tones and notes as you can imagine. True music, true song, integrates tensions and opposites. That's beauty and that's music.

"So the secret of the world is that the physical and the spiritual form a masterpiece of music, and what blends it all together is Torah. The whole world was standing in limbo from the time of Creation until the time of the acceptance of the Torah. If humans accepted Torah, the world would evolve into some type of completion. If they didn't, the world would revert to the state of chaos it was before creation, tohu v'vohu."

I remember learning from a Lubavitcher rabbi at the Jewish Community Center, where I continued to take classes, that God offered the Torah to all the people of the world, and none would accept it because it asked too much. The Jews were the last people to be offered the Torah, but when it was their turn, God gave them less a choice than an ultimatum. Either they accepted Torah, or the world would cease to exist. The midrash says that God lifted up the mountain that Moses had climbed to get the tablets—and literally held it over the Jews' heads as they considered. At the time of God's proffer, the rabbi said, the world was so quiet there was not even an echo, because every bit of the world, including the rocks and the canyons, were listening so carefully.

"It even says in Kabbalistic works that if there should ever be even one instant that there was no Torah being studied," Rabbi Fried continues, "the whole world would disappear from existence."

I look at him, my eyebrows raised.

"There's a story that illustrates this perfectly. There was a great rabbi in Europe who had no children. One Purim, as everyone else was making merry and drinking, this rabbi was sitting and studying the Torah. All of a sudden, he saw a great lightning strike—boom—and he was blown out of his chair. When he woke up, he didn't know what had happened, and he climbed back onto his chair and resumed learning. That night, he had a dream that for that instant he was the only one studying Torah in the world. The whole world was existing on his merit and his merit alone. And for that he was to be rewarded with a son. Well, it turned out the dream foretold the truth, because he had a son, and that was the beginning of a big Chassidic dynasty, the Kotzker dynasty, which we still have today.

"The Torah keeps that connection. It's like the wires through which God stays connected with the world. If for one moment the physical should have nothing spiritual going into it, it couldn't exist anymore. We have to ensure that we keep the connection. This connection between the physical and the spiritual," Rabbi Fried continues, "is the great song, the song of the world, the song of the universe. The more you delve into Kabbalah, the more you see it holds the secrets of the makeup of the world, of exactly how God connects with this world. The more you get to the Torah's secrets, the more you get to the song that's coming out of the world. Those hidden parts of the Torah reveal hidden songs. That's why some of these rabbis, if they get deep enough, can come up with songs that change the life of the person who hears them."

I think about how much music has been enfolded in my own story. My mother's distant relatives were cantors, and my father told me that his father loved to sing, knew all the songs in the liturgy, and often sang Jewish songs at home; my father's mother came to this country to study music, and playing the piano soothed her troubled soul. My father loves opera, but he also owns recordings of old cantorial music. It was a song I heard in the synagogue that first conjured my father's presence there for me, and Dr. Andresen's comment about the sound of instruments seeking out each other in a string quartet that stimulated a recollection of the sound of the choir emerging from behind a panel in my childhood synagogue and the vivid memory of standing there beside my father. Moreover, Jews are always singing, Rabbi Fried has explained, and, although most of Judaism has disappeared from the lives of my family, a hidden but vital connection has remained tied to musical memories.

I ask Rabbi Fried what the sound of angels is like. He says it is the sound of joy mixed with fear. "There are choruses of angels singing all the time for God," he says, "but it is taught that they can only sing when the Jews sing down here first." During the recitation of the Shimoneh Esrai (during which time we believe we actually stand before God), it is customary to stand with our feet together, like angels, as it is said that angels have only one leg. We bring a bit of the angelic to our very bodies in those moments.

I look away from Rabbi Fried for a moment and feel overcome as I did one day on the Navajo reservation, when I realized it was so utterly quiet that my ears were pounding. I felt a reverence then that made me think of Freud's description of the religious as "something limitless, unbounded, as it were . . . 'oceanic.'" Now, I am having that experience not over the wonder of something strange and new, over the differences of another culture, but over my own, over ideas that are not strange but seem to have something very much to do with me. I see from the clock on the wall that Rabbi Fried and I have sat up for many hours, and the sun will soon lighten the sky. I look at him and smile. I feel warmed, as if by a roaring fire or a bountiful meal. And then I realize I have been warmed by Rabbi Fried's stories, and I am reminded of something a Navajo once said to me: "A good story is like a foundation."

Finally, I am hearing the stories of my own people, and they are like a foundation on which I am building the beginnings of a home.

Chapter Six

The True Lives of Stories

ONE MORNING, as I stand to leave Dr. Andresen's office, I suddenly remember a dream fragment from the night before. I look up and say, "I had a dream last night in which you told me that you and your wife were taking a lot of photographs." I stop for a moment, wondering why I have brought this up just now. It is a joke in psychiatry that a patient will mention a crucially important fact, in an offhand manner, just as he or she is leaving the doctor's office.

I am caught up by the returning dream, however, and I continue.

"You were taking pictures of a cliff in Cottonwood, Arizona, on top of which sits an old prospector's cabin. Below it, in the curve of a stream, is a house owned by Senator John McCain and his wife, Cindy. I knew John McCain from the Navajo-Hopi issue, and also because I wrote a long magazine story about him when it seemed he might be chosen to be George Bush's running mate in 1992. I visited the McCains one summer weekend at their cabin, and John wanted to cross the stream to explore a small island. I was carrying his toddler, Jack, while he carried his daughter Meghan. I couldn't believe McCain trusted me to carry his baby into the swiftly running stream, as it was rocky and slippery underfoot, but everything went fine, and we made it across safely."

I stop here, then turn to leave Dr. Andresen's office. "You called your wife Kitty in the dream, or Kitty-a." I try to pronounce this word as I picture it, but it doesn't quite make sense. "Kitty. You called her Kitty at first, and then you called her Kitty-a, and after I woke up, I thought to myself that word must be Katya."

I take a step toward the door and look over at him, preparing to say good-bye. He has a very strange look on his face.

"What is it?" I ask.

He doesn't say anything.

"Do you call your wife Kitty?"

He looks like he is about to say something, then he stops.

"Is that your nickname for her? Kitty?" I hear a surprising insistence in my voice.

He waits a few beats, looking as if he were arguing with himself, then he says: "My daughter's name is Katherine. When she was small, a Russian professor told us we could call her Katya, and so it was, Katya."

"That's strange," I say.

He shakes his head and smiles. I say good-bye and pull the door closed behind me. As I walk to my car, I am caught up in the bizarre fact of my having dreamed Dr. Andresen's daughter's name. For a few minutes, I indulge myself in the fantasy that I am getting so close to Dr. Andresen that I am reading his mind, or receiving telepathic messages from him. But though I would dearly love to believe such a thing, I eventually let the idea go, as I can't begin to defend it logically. I think of the fact that McCain had been a Navy pilot, and Dr. Andresen had also served in the Navy. I wonder briefly if their paths had ever crossed. And I wonder if a key to the dream lies in the Navy connection.

But my thoughts keep returning to the name Kitty and away from the details of the image of McCain's house, the cliffs, and the stream. After I get home, I take out my copy of Tolstoy's *Anna Karenina*, one of whose main characters is named Kitty Shcherbatsky.

I haven't looked at the book for years, but as I flip through the pages, I quickly remember the characters. My favorite, Levin, lived on an estate far away from the social activities of Moscow and St. Petersburg, and spent much time thinking about issues of faith and science. I read on with increasing excitement, as if with every page I turn I am closing in on something of great portent, until I am flabbergasted to find what I believe I am after: a passage in which the name Kitty and Katya appear on the same page.

How could I have remembered something as obscure as that? My unconscious memory of this passage surprises me profoundly. I read on. The passage comes about two-thirds of the way through the book, just after Levin's marriage to Kitty, when Levin hears that his brother Nikolai is dying of tuberculosis at a roadside tavern. Kitty insists on accompanying Levin to his brother's bedside, but Levin is horrified by the idea of his pure young bride at the squalid death scene he imagines. Kitty will not be dissuaded, however, and Levin finally assents. But after they arrive at the tavern, Levin's worst fears return. His brother rests in a small, filthy room, his wasted body twisted under a dirty blanket, his hair soaked with sweat. Levin, who is tormented by what he calls the "enigma of death," is terrified by the sight.

For her part, Kitty sweetly but insistently sends Levin off on an errand and cleans Nikolai's room, brings in fresh linen, calls for a doctor, arranges the bedside table with drink, a candle, and powders. She changes Nikolai's bed shirt, props him up on fluffy pillows, and fills the room with fresh scent. When Levin returns, he sees his brother has been transformed. He is clean, smiling, peaceful. His coughing has subsided. Further, through Kitty's goodhearted persistence, Nikolai has agreed to allow a priest to administer communion and extreme unction.

The next day, as I'm telling Dr. Andresen about my searches through *Anna Karenina*, I look up and say, "It is just at this point that Levin begins to call Kitty Katya."

He is watching me intently.

"I kept reading," I continue, "and I saw this moment triggered a change in Levin's thoughts about death and the limitations of rational thought. Levin was aware that though he was more learned than his wife, and better prepared to discuss death philosophically, he had no idea how to confront it in real life, nor how to comfort the suffering. But seeing the transformation that Kitty had wrought on his brother, Levin remembered a line from the Gospels." I read from a sheet of paper on which I have written the words "Thou hast hid these things from the wise and prudent, and hast revealed them unto babes."

I continue: "From then on, when he was close to Kitty, he felt shielded from despair. It also marked Kitty's passage in his eyes from a girl to a woman.

"And, you know what else?" I say, looking past him, out over the pots of blooming African violets to the blue sky. "The next thing we learn is that Kitty is expecting a child. After the loss of the brother and the confrontation with fear and death, we learn that a new life has begun."

I look up at Dr. Andresen, but as soon as I see his expression, I freeze. His face is red. He looks straight at me, kindly, a little defiantly. I look away in surprise. When I look back, I see tears running down his cheeks.

We sit there for quite a few minutes together in silence until it is time for me to leave.

I think about Dr. Andresen's reaction for days. I know that the idea of the limits of rational thought has resonance for him. And he also appreciates moments of grace, for example, the discovery of Kitty's pregnancy after Levin's confrontation with death and fear. But I wonder what could have provoked the strength of his response? Had there been special moments in his life in which a woman offered life-transforming care? Did the story remind him of an episode of his own daughter's maturing? I spend many hours letting my mind wander over this territory. Something of the magic of psychoanalysis takes place in these hours of intense thought and regurgitation, I come to believe. It is as if I were making unconscious corrections in my memories and brain structures. I am rewriting my past with new understandings, filling out my present with new implications.

What remains with me after the *Anna Karenina* episode is the astonishing, mind-bending, epoch-turning experience of seeing his tears. This time, I moved him to tears.

Toward the end of the next session, I hesitantly remind him of the Tolstoy novel and ask him if he could tell me what made him react so strongly to my story.

"I had a theophany," he says.

I am confused. I search my brain for a definition. I don't know what this word means.

He says, "A religious experience."

DR. ANDRESEN HAS TAUGHT ME to be patient with my thoughts, and I have learned that if I allow ideas to stay unmolested and untied in my mind I can be assured they will offer up new meanings over time. This is very different from the way I had become used to thinking, which was to seize answers quickly. The quicker the better. The rules had seemed quite clear to me in school: the quickest, funniest one gets heard. These habits of mind, though perhaps good for exam-taking and attention-getting, can lead one to remain bound by shallow thoughts.

I wonder if Dr. Andresen was moved that a work of literature played a crucial role in deciphering the dream? I know that he is a deeply informed student of Freud's, whose own analyses made great use of the symbols and tropes of literature. I will never know, of course, what affected him so strongly unless he chooses to tell me. But the fact that my storytelling moved him to tears marked the first time I knew I could tell a story.

I CONTEMPLATE. One day Dr. Andresen reads me the origin of the word "contemplate" from his etymological dictionary. It is "to gather in a temple to receive the auguries."

Dr. Andresen not infrequently sprinkles his observations with biblical references. He also quotes from ancient myths and poetry, but it seems to me that he holds a particular reverence for the Bible. One of his papers uses the story of Job as a trope around which to discuss the productive and unproductive ways of psychoanalysts. The paper draws me to study the ancient poem, just as it leads me to appreciate more fully the intellectual underpinnings of the psychoanalytic work. Elsewhere, Dr. Andresen writes about awe and the transforming of awareness in psychoanalysis. His comparison of religious experiences and analysis—and his acknowledgment of and delight in religious references when they come up in my sessions—grants authority to the religious. Gradually I have come to believe that a search for the self is inseparable from an examination of belief. Furthermore, the sudden insights and epiphanies of analysis create feeling states similar to those of religious experiences. I don't think I would have taken the religious feelings seriously if I hadn't been able to read scholarly papers that tied them to psychoanalysis, the secular religion that seemed far more acceptable in my world. If Dr. Andresen had not encouraged the inchoate religious hints in me, and if I had not seen the importance he placed on religious strivings in his own work, it is unlikely I would have continued pursuit of Judaism at this time. Perhaps ever.

One of many ironies of psychoanalysis is that the patient is not supposed to know anything about the analyst, yet is filled with thoughts about him or her. The relationship formed with the analyst is referred to as the transference, and the particulars of the patient's thoughts and emotional reactions to the analyst tell a great deal about her, and her previous relationships with significant caregivers. It is assumed by many analysts that every idea the patient has about the analyst is a product of the transference, rather than a perhaps insightful intuition about the human being that is her doctor.

Dr. Andresen believes otherwise. He thinks a patient's thoughts manifest ceaseless fashionings of meaning and perceptions both of and within the encounter he or she and the analyst are creating together. "The patient perceives a lot and does so from points of view of which the doctor is blind," he once said. One day, in a quiet moment after we had gone through some particularly difficult terrain, he told me that during his own analysis, he had sensed qualities in his analyst that the doctor denied were so. Though the analysis was in many ways productive for him, this lack of candor, he came to believe, may have kept him from discovering, with that doctor, certain areas of his life experience. Later, the experience informed his own thoughts about analytic practice.

I'm not sure the added responsibility this understanding engenders makes his job any easier. However, I felt privileged by his treatment of me not simply as a patient but also as a potentially reasonable—and empathic—adult. And I think this sped up the analysis and encouraged me toward increased independence from him and the singularly quirky hothouse of the analytic chamber.

Dr. Andresen has written that the mutual search for and finding of the other in psychoanalysis is felt as love. If all goes well, that love offers a new model that eventually finds its way to expression in the patient's real life. Dr. Andresen's art of psychoanalysis made me the beloved, which was his therapeutic responsibility. But it also made me the lover, which was, for me, his special gift.

ONE DAY IN EARLY SPRING, I see a new film by Akira Kurosawa titled *Rhapsody in August.* It is the story of an old Japanese grandmother whose husband was killed by the atomic bomb that dropped on Nagasaki on August 9, 1945. The woman lives a life of quiet ritual in a country home of breathtaking beauty. She serves tea to her neighbor as they sit on the porch of her house, overlooking her magnificently orderly garden.

A couple of days before the anniversary of the bombing, the old woman's children and grandchildren arrive from the city for a visit. They are restless, unaccustomed to the rhythms of the country. One day, her grandchildren go into town to visit the school where their grandfather was killed. In the playground is an iron jungle gym melted and twisted by the force of the nuclear wind. It is a fantastic and fantastically horrifying image. Underneath is a simple plaque marked 1945 8 9 11:02 AM.

The bomb hit in the middle of the school day, and the silent children understand everything just by looking at the jungle gym.

They walk through the school yard over to a memorial, a granite block on which is written in Japanese PLEASE, JUST A SIP OF WATER. The children read the words aloud, and then together, they splash water from the pool in which the granite block is set. They splash water until the words uttered by the dying are completely wet. When I tell Dr. Andresen about the film, I point out the children's attempt to give what has been asked for, a big theme in our work together.

Back home, the grandmother seems haunted by the upcoming anniversary, and she wanders out to her garden in the serenity of a full moon. She looks to the sky often, as if she were anticipating a ghastly revisiting of the vision she saw that day, the sky roiled with clouds and what seemed like a human visage bearing down on her. The next day, a memorial service is held in a Buddhist temple, and one of the children, who has been singing a Japanese song about the rose that grows after the storm, sneaks out to watch. The camera follows him over to a position beside the temple, where he fixes his eyes on a column of ants climbing the stem of a brilliant red rose.

That night, the grandmother wakes up and hangs her dead husband's clothes all over the house. The wind is picking up outside, and the clothes blow in the breezes. She sees her son and calls out to him with her husband's name. She returns to bed, but one can see she is unnaturally unsettled. Early the next morning, the neighbor, whose husband was also killed by the bomb, runs over and wakes everyone up. She tells them that their grandmother is running down the road toward town. She says the sky looks just the same way as it did on that day, and we see cruel, eerie clouds, bestial eyes in the sky, and then we hear a tremendous clap and a burst of rain. First the youngest child, then the rest of the family runs out of the house and down the road after the grandmother. The camera stays on each of them for long minutes of slow motion as they run, soaked, in the pelting rain, each one slipping in the muddy road, falling, and struggling up again. The camera moves from one to another until it reaches the grandmother, who walks serenely, purposefully, her umbrella held high, not wavering, not falling. Her face seems rapturous, radiant. She has already passed over to the other side and is no longer burdened by her humanity, the dross of her emotions. She is on her last journey. Failure is not possible.

I look up at Dr. Andresen and see he has walked to his bookshelves and pulled down a thin volume. He returns to his seat and opens the book. I can see his face is red. He seems to change his mind, gets up and hands me the book. It is T. S. Eliot's *Four Quartets*.

"Do you want me to read it to myself?" I ask. "Bring it home?"

"Why don't you read a little now," he says.

He has opened the book to the last section of the Fourth Quartet, called "Little Gidding."

I begin to read:

What we call the beginning is often the end
And to make an end is to make a beginning.
The end is where we start from.

I start to feel sad, because I know that in some way, this is the beginning of the end of my time with Dr. Andresen. He has set me off on a journey, on which I will soon travel by myself. As I read on, I recognize the poem and realize it is Eliot's farewell to poetry.

And every phrase
And sentence that is right (where every word is at home,
Taking its place to support the others,
The word neither diffident nor ostentatious,
An easy commerce of the old and the new . . .)
Every phrase and every sentence is an end and a beginning. . . .

As I read, I think about how sensitive Dr. Andresen is to words, how he loves words, and how he was able to reignite that love in me.

We shall not cease from exploration
And the end of all our exploring
Will be to arrive where we started
And know the place for the first time.
Through the unknown, remembered gate
When the last of the earth left to discover
Is that which was the beginning . . .

We sit quietly for a few moments after I finish. Dr. Andresen mentions a dream I told him in which I planted a rose beside a desiccated house. He goes on to remind me of other associations and actions that indicated my choice of planting a garden in spite of what had been stripped bare, in spite of death, impairment, blood. In the poem, as in the Kurosawa movie, as in my experience, life grows out of death. The dead give life and color to the living.

He says he was struck by the images in *Four Quartets* that seemed so similar to the writing of the contemplatives. "There is an intense focus on the present without the pressure of the not yet," he says. This observation exactly describes this room: here is an intense focus on the present without the pressure of the not yet.

"I also appreciate the intimations of the Divine that intensify that presentness," he continues. "And the poem in its own way brings into being the idea of union with others in that state of intense solitary presentness." Again, I feel the similarities between these qualities and the experience of the work with him, specifically his understanding that in silence, by following our own thoughts, sometimes we can gain insight into the thoughts of another.

Dr. Andresen changes tack here and points out that earlier sections of the poem are in rhyme. He says when he read them, he felt that the anticipation of the approaching rhymed sounds had moved him into a different sense of time from that produced by the unrhymed portions. The poem's form had thus induced varying senses of attention and time, a central concern of the poem. And, I think, a central concern of psychoanalysis.

Again, his reaction to my words—the offering into the room of a poem and his thoughts about it—startle me, transform me. Later, I understand Dr. Andresen believes that "cure" in psychoanalysis is possible to the extent that a patient learns that he or she has changed the mind of the analyst. That is, that the patient has been able to produce new thoughts in another. I realize, many years later, that this is the ultimate corrective. He shows us that our words have the power to create new thoughts, whereas our life experience is usually the opposite: a never-ending struggle in our unconscious but continuing—and often unresolved—dialogues with our parents or caregivers. They never hear us and they never change. We are never able to bring them relief or show them a new way. Dr. Andresen helps us write a new ending to the story. He allows us to change him.

ONE DAY, I am thinking about being bound to others. I am bound to my mother by her suffering and by my desire to relieve her. I have a strong image in my mind of a statue I saw at the Louvre as a small child. It is *La Victoire de Samothrace*, a massive marble figure of a bowsprit—a figure lashed to the bow of a boat to protect her and her passengers and cargo from danger. Interesting, I say to Dr. Andresen, that a woman's figure is bound to the front of a boat to endure the wind and waves and weather for the purpose of ensuring safety for the men inside. And I think of the common female fantasy of being bound.

"Her sacrifice leads the man on his own journey of discovery," says Dr. Andresen.

After a few moments, he says, "How different that is from the story of Odysseus binding himself to the masts of his ship and telling his crew not to listen to any orders he may make while he listens to the singing of the Sirens."

Indeed.

"I HAVE TO TELL YOU SOMETHING," I say one day at the beginning of summer.

"Beth Emunah is buying a Sefer Torah because the congregation has been asked to give back the one we have been borrowing. So one of our members went to New York to buy a Torah.

"The way the congregation is financing the purchase is one apparently used by other congregations. The congregants give money, and in return, they are told they have 'bought' a book or a chapter or a passuk or a word." At this point, I burst into hot, forceful tears. "I want to let you know," I say, "that I have donated the book of Exodus to the synagogue in your honor. I thought that was very appropriate and the least I could do to show my gratitude to you."

Dr. Andresen stares at me and remains silent.

I get uncomfortable with the unspoken emotion, so I joke, "Of all the gin joints in all the world, I happened to walk into yours." We both laugh.

He says, "Well, it is a wilderness story," and we laugh more. Then he takes off his glasses and wipes his eyes.

WILL I BE ABLE to hold on to him when I am gone? Will I be able to conjure up the energetic peace of that room? Strangely enough, the closest I get is when I am in synagogue, reading the commentary to the Torah portion.

MY NEXT-TO-LAST SESSION with Dr. Andresen. I must try to remember the feelings I have when I leave his office. I am often exhausted, almost in another state of consciousness—but also full, content, balanced, warm. When I look at people, I feel like I can see into their hearts. I feel very sympathetic. I feel close to God.

"How do you stay open and soft with the press and pull and idiocy of everyday life?" I ask him.

He pauses his usual pause, just a bit shorter than usual. He says, "See that telephone? It doesn't ring. See that door? It doesn't open until you go."

"You mean, you make sure you have enough quiet time to think?"

He looks a bit flustered. He says, "This journey is a two-way journey."

"So it's in this room, there is an honest communication that takes place in this room?"

"I try to listen rather than be critical," he said. "I try to have no ambitions."

"That's trying to defy gravity," I say.

"I watched a resident with a patient the other day," he answers.

"The woman said she had trouble asking for help. 'My son asks for help,'" she said.

"'Ahh,' said the resident. 'You let him ask.'"

"You see how the resident turned it? Instead of the person saying something about not having confidence or self-esteem and the child had it, the resident held the moment. . . . 'Ahh, you let him ask. . . .' A comment like that invites a lot of thinking."

Dr. Andresen continues.

"Remember when you were at the *Observer*? And a woman came up to you and said, 'I'm a nobody'? And you turned to her and gave her your full attention and she began to talk. And she asked you, 'What is it that you have?' And you looked at her and showed you wanted to know what she had."

Yes, I remember. Several months after the television job ended, I was hired as the managing editor of a newspaper. At a staff party, one of the employees was tipsy and upset and wanted to talk to me. I was thinking as hard as I could of being like Dr. Andresen and she responded as if I had opened up a door for her. She walked through it, but it was I in the end who had felt transformed.

DURING MY FINAL SESSION with Dr. Andresen, I spend a long time looking around his room, trying to remember everything on the walls, memorizing not only the lines and shapes but also trying to absorb the peacefulness of this chamber. The African violets that fill his windowsills are in full bloom. They have all reached a flowering cycle together and his windows are lined with a profusion of colors: white, purple, magenta, blue, the colored petals flared over the woolly green leaves.

I talk about this and that, touching, I realize later, on words or moments of the past two-and-a-half years that signified important things, moments when it seemed we had come to a meeting, moments when I looked up and saw tears on his face, or moments when I learned something extraordinary, or when he told me he had come to understand something in a new way. It is not just Dr. Andresen I want to hold on to; the experiences of his chamber have mysteriously led me to a belief in God. I hope I can hold on to that belief after I leave.

After a while, I am quiet, and I think he realizes I now need to hear something from him.

"Do you remember the little violet you gave me?" he asks. I remember a tiny specimen in a one-inch pot that I saw in a garden shop a year or so earlier and brought in for him. I couldn't resist it because it was so cute, though I wasn't at all sure it would survive.

"Yes," I say.

Dr. Andresen reaches around behind him and pulls out a strapping plant with lush greenery that is ablaze with flowers.

"This is it," he says.

I weep for several minutes, my chest pressing in with sharp, hard pains over the thought that I will no longer look into this kindly, generous face.

"It's been a wonderful journey with you," says Dr. Andresen.

I am stopped short for a moment and say, "You didn't say it was a wonderful journey for you. You said it was a wonderful journey with you."

"Yes," he says. "I'm a better doctor now."

"How is that?"

"I have learned many things."

Almost six months ago, Dr. Andresen told me that he had taught me all he could. That may or may not have been the case, but I think he knew I had to get back to New York to continue my life, and he was giving me his blessing. The analysis lasted two-and-a-half years.

He looks off and is quiet. Then he looks at me straight on for a long time, then away.

"What," I say.

"I was thinking of my uncle, whom I loved. He was full of fun. And I'd wake up early to see him and he'd be gone," he says.

"Gone?" I asked.

"He didn't like good-byes. He avoided them."

And there it was, the subject was out. I was about to leave. "I will miss you terribly," I say.

"Last time," he said, "you asked me if I have time for myself. And I said that I do in here, when you come in. Perhaps you haven't realized this, but it has been a very enriching time for me. I find myself in here with you."

The last time he said this I thought he meant with all his patients, but I realize today that he means me. He was speaking to me about his experience here with me. I look straight at him. These words seem to flow into their own designated place, as if a spot had been held for them. Something was settled then, finally settled, and I could go on.

"I realize," I say. "I've known." I hold his eyes in mine without strain or discomfort. "I know because it can't work only one way."

"No, it doesn't work one way," he says.

And then there it is, the end of the final session. I ask if I can shake his hand. It is warm and firm. I gather my things and turn. He is watching me, kindly, seriously. I pull the door closed quietly behind me.

WHY IS PSYCHOANALYSIS so bitterly attacked by its opponents, I asked him once.

"Well, I'll give you a hot-dog answer," Dr. Andresen said. "As in myths, the treasure is always guarded by a dragon."

After a few moments, he says, "There's a parable from Matthew that goes something like this: A man bought a field in which he had found a buried treasure. He paid everything he had for it.

"The key to understanding the parable," he explained, "is that the law at the time stipulated that treasure found buried in a field or under a house, or at least part of it, belonged to the previous owner. What this says is that treasure must be pursued with intense desire — the parable states that the man paid all he had for the field. Yet the wonderful paradox is that that which is most valuable — the treasure in the parable is actually the kingdom of heaven — cannot be possessed. That which is most valuable will first be sought as possession, but then prove incapable of being possessed. The greatest treasure seems to be that which is destined to be given away to others."

Chapter Seven

❦

HOME

IN NOVEMBER 1993, I load my belongings into a U-Haul truck, drive across country, and come back home. I move into the third floor of a brownstone on the Upper West Side of Manhattan with a terrace large enough for the roses and hydrangeas I have dug up and replanted in pots. I renew old relationships with friends and editors and make new ones, and very quickly I find freelance work. From ten to six, I inhabit the fast-moving world of magazine reporting and writing, and in the evenings and on weekends I segue centuries back to Judaism, in classes and in worship. It is a division that doesn't seem at all unnatural. In every way, I feel I have returned to the center of the world.

In late winter, I receive a telephone call from Monsey, New York, an outpost of Orthodoxy in Rockland County, the same Monsey that Rabbi Fried mentioned in Dallas during his visit to Beth Emunah. In fact, Rabbi Fried is responsible for the call; Sarah Shira Berman invites me to come up and spend Purim with her and her husband, Rabbi Daniel Berman, and their family. She says I can get a ride up from a young woman who also lives on the Upper West Side.

Rachel picks me up in the late afternoon of a misty March day. When I walk out of my building, I see her moving bags to the trunk of her late-model economy car. She wears a bulky sweater and baby blue skirt that reaches almost to her ankles. Like other religious Jewish women I've seen, she wears brand-new white Keds and short white tennis socks, like a girl's, decorated with gold beads. Her outfit is shapeless, at once like that of a young girl and a matron. She is a pretty woman with full lips and lustrous long hair. I guess she is in her late twenties. We say hello and I get into the car beside her. Between us on the seat are boxes of molded chocolates covered in cellophane and tied with ribbons.

"They're mishloach manos," Rachel says. "On Purim, it is customary to bring baskets of treats to people." We settle into the car and head for the George Washington Bridge. I ask if she made the chocolate herself and she says yes, in fact she was up until 4 A.M. making and wrapping the candies with a great deal of effort and care.

The motion and confines of the car lull us into the temporary intimacy of a shared ride. She tells me that both of her parents are lawyers, and she is an only child. When she learns I am a writer, she tells me with pride that her mother is also a writer, that she has written a coffee-table book about Tiffany windows. I see she wears a heavy gold necklace, expensive gold watch and bracelets, and I imagine she is a much-adored and privileged child. I wonder what her parents think about her turn to Orthodoxy, and I ask her.

"Oh, they're OK with it," she says with a breezy laugh that seems to conceal as much as it reveals. She says she was raised Reform, but became more religious in college. She gradually gave up nonkosher foods and began to keep the Sabbath. She tells me she hopes to find a shidduch, or a match, with a brilliant young student, and to live a life of penury devoted to God with him. To that end, she is training to be a special education teacher, an acceptable line of work for a woman who is frum, as she puts it, or proper. A bright light comes over her face as she describes her dream of being the breadwinner of the family so that her husband can dedicate himself to learning.

I wonder if her romantic dream of poverty has ever been informed by actually having to worry about not having enough money to pay the bills. I wonder if she has any idea of the corrosive reality of adding up one's expenses and seeing they fall far short of one's income. She lives in an apartment on Columbus Avenue paid for by her parents. The car, also, is provided by them. I ask her where she went to college, and when she answers Yale, I nearly fall out the door.

I have never met a Yale graduate studying special education. I stop and try to redigest everything she has told me. I think of my old friend Judith, who went to Yale. I knew her in seventh and eighth grades, during which time she completely reeducated me. I believe my IQ jumped several dozen points as a direct result of her influence. The daughter of MIT and Wellesley professors, she was so sophisticated and knowledgeable that I spent hours on the telephone with her, silent, trying to absorb everything she said. It was at her house that I ate takeout Chinese food for the first time. I will never forget when she pronounced, "I love Szechuan food, don't you? It is such a wonderful purge." She was all of thirteen years old.

Judith took my breath away. I knew I wanted to learn everything I could from her. When she applied to Yale, she wasn't just accepted to the college, as I was. She got a personal letter from the dean saying her application essay was so superlative it demanded a personal reply.

Rachel went to Yale? I think then of the girls on the Yale soccer team, Harvard's traditional rivals, a tough bunch of competitors against whom we played a game my freshman year that left me injured from a kick that broke right through my shin pad.

How strange. I think, that a Yale graduate would train to teach learning-disabled children so she could have babies and support her husband while he studied ancient Jewish texts. Did she ever think of his supporting her while she did the same?

Rachel tells me that she goes up to Monsey almost every Shabbos, because she likes the atmosphere. She speaks in a baby voice, high and soft, though it is clear she has very strong opinions. I wonder if she feels she must mask her willfulness behind a façade of childishness or timidity. As she talks, I feel she is speaking inside a bubble, a world in which she finds comfort, a world she at once creates and reaffirms. Sometimes she snaps her tongue against her teeth when searching for the right word, a mannerism I later see is common to both religious men and women. It suggests a certain sincerity of effort in trying to explain. Rachel seems prodigiously uninterested in anything outside her bubble, and she is definitely not interested in anything I have to say.

The traffic is heavy. Rachel turns on the radio, and we hear that a tractor-trailer has rolled over on the bridge. She says it looks as if we won't make it to Monsey in time for the megillah reading or dinner; we'd best stop in Washington Heights to hear the reading, so we don't miss it. She attended a seminary for women up here after graduating from college and knows something about the community. After turning off the highway and pulling away from the traffic, we enter a dark, quiet residential area. Rachel parks and puts her chocolates in the trunk. I grab my handbag from the seat beside me.

"Do you want to lock the doors?" I ask. She has overlooked my briefcase and some cut flowers that remain in the car, unprotected.

"OK, I suppose that is safer," she says, with her airy laugh. As she locks the doors on her side, it occurs to me that this woman is extraordinarily self-absorbed. "We have to call the Bermans," she says suddenly, stopping. I stand beside her as she thinks about where to go, when suddenly a man in a dark suit and bowler hat materializes in front of us. Rachel speaks to him in Hebrew, and I follow as he ushers us through a parking garage and up to his apartment. Inside, we are met by the intense fragrances of Jewish cooking. He introduces us to his wife, who stands in the kitchen in a bathrobe, with her head wrapped in a cloth. Her cheeks are flushed pink, and a gaggle of small children peer at us shyly as Rachel makes her call. I try to play with the five dark-eyed, serious-looking children, each separated by about two years from the next in line, but they are reticent. After Rachel hangs up, the man says in English that we are welcome to return for dinner after the megillah reading if we'd like. My eyes light up. The kitchen is warm and friendly and the smells are like those of my Hungarian grandmother's kitchen in full steam. My journalist's appetite for adventure has already kicked in, but Rachel apologizes that we won't be able to make it for dinner because we are expected in Monsey.

We thank the man and his wife for their kindness and walk back outside. I feel as if we had entered and departed from a Yiddish story, where messengers materialize out of the dark, shepherd strangers to safety, offer food to travelers. I think the man's ready generosity was astonishing, and I am amazed that such a community still exists, in which one can perceive from dress or manner that a stranger is in fact a member of the tribe and thus the ready recipient of the greatest courtesies.

We turn a corner and walk toward a modern building, which I see is the synagogue. In front, many people are gathered—men in beards and black coats talking, young men in oversized black hats pitched jauntily on their heads, women in wigs and hats, and children, of course, everywhere.

The women have a separate entrance, which leads upstairs to the balcony. At the top of the stairs is a table with a silver plate on it, in which have been tossed some coins and dollar bills. Rachel mutters a word to me, which I don't understand, then she says, "It's charity for the poor. We give money to the poor on Purim." So I fish out a couple of dollars and place them on the plate. I realize then that she said tzedakah, which means "charity." But it also means "justice," I recently learned, which is very interesting, as it implies that it is not just money for which people are in want.

As we walk on, I remember learning that Jews are instructed to use extreme care to preserve human dignity when offering tzedakah. I read a story about a rabbi who was opening his purse to leave some money for a man down on his luck, when he saw the man approaching. Rather than embarrass him, the rabbi threw himself into a flaming oven.

Wooden pews fill the large U-shaped balcony. Only those few seats near the front offer an unimpeded view of the goings-on downstairs, but most women don't seem to care, as they sit in the middle, where Rachel steers us. As she greets her friends, my thoughts wander off once again. I remember learning that pain and suffering can bring redemption. But so also can charity. And, a rabbi told me, God prefers charity.

I smile at the sweetness of this story and look around me. I catch the eyes of a few women, who look at me searchingly, as if trying to place me. I am self-conscious about the frumpy clothes I have put together in an effort to look modest. I walk away from Rachel and look over the railing to the main part of the shul, where several men pray energetically, rocking back and forward from their waists. I see the men have desktops on which to rest their books. There is a great sense of excitement and anticipation downstairs. Up here, the mood is subdued, attentive. The women wait, settle their children. It strikes me that I feel a stranger in women's company.

I pick up a gray-covered book from a seat and flip through the beautiful etchings that illustrate the story of Queen Esther and King Achashuerosh, the historical Xerxes I. Purim commemorates the failure of a plot by one of Xerxes' viziers to murder all of the Jews in Persia, where the Jews had found refuge after the destruction of the Temple. Esther, revealing to the king at great personal risk that she is a Jew, seeks to nullify Haman's plans. With the help of her cousin Mordechai, who uncovers a plot to murder the king, she succeeds in saving her people.

In a few moments, the chanting begins. I cannot see who is reading, but a strong, expressive tenor fills the sanctuary. When the name Haman is mentioned, the children twirl their noisemakers, and the adults pound the backs of the pews or their tables.

I settle inside the melodies of medieval Eastern Europe, and I follow the voice of the ancient tale bearer. I remember descending into a Hopi Indian kiva to attend a winter bean dance, a rare privilege for whites. As I sat on a dirt bench carved from the mesa, I watched the kachinas, men dressed as Hopi bird-gods, climb down a ladder into the subterranean chamber and chant and dance in a circle before us to the beat of a skin drum, turtle shells rattling on their ankles, just as they had done for more than a thousand years at the same location, their voices meeting at a frequency that I could imagine matching the earth's own vibrations. I remember having the thought that I wouldn't be surprised if the Indians successfully communicated with the earth's very center during those dances.

Here, I don't have the feeling of communication with the earth;

instead, the voices seem to swirl up to the decorated ceiling and beyond, as if singing to the choruses of angels who pass their songs along to the heavens. I look around at the beautiful wood carvings and gold decoration of the sanctuary, and it strikes me how well hidden worlds can be, especially worlds that wish to remain hidden, and how it isn't until one has stepped inside that one has any view at all.

WE ARRIVE IN MONSEY after nine o'clock. The Bermans live in a sprawling house on a large lot in a suburban town of widely spaced houses. We enter a large, light entry that leads, to the right, into the kitchen, and straight ahead through French doors into a dining room. We are greeted by Sarah Shira, a very pretty, youthful-looking woman with a big smile and freckles over her delicate nose. I imagine she is in her late thirties, and think we cannot be separated in age by too many years, though she is the mother of nine children—seven boys and two girls. The children are attractive and charming, with small features and freckles. All the boys wear dark pants and white shirts with the strings of their tzitzit showing. I am introduced to the children one by one, and the names, biblical appellations, sometimes two strung together, are hard for me to catch, for example, Yehuda-Aryeh, Chana-Bayla, and Binyamin-Alter. I am embarrassed once again that Hebrew is so unfamiliar to me, and I have to learn Hebrew names as if they were foreign words.

I hand over the bouquet of fancy tulips with variegated edges that I have brought up from Manhattan. A vase is produced, and I trim the stems, and arrange the blooms in it. The children gather around, asking the name of the flowers, looking at them with great interest.

As Rachel and I stand with Sarah Shira in the kitchen, Rabbi Berman appears. He is a good-looking man of medium height and build, with dark hair and short dark beard. Although he is not tall, he commands attention and seems "with it" in a way one wouldn't ordinarily expect in a rabbi. We have spoken together several times on the telephone since my initial talk with Sarah Shira, and he seems to be well read and to have many thoughts about the outside world.

"Emily. How are you?" he says, looking me straight in the face and smiling, as if saying, "Yes, you look as I imagined." I smile and nod, saying hello, knowing I cannot put out my hand for a shake. I am aware of a space, a pause, in that time. We remain silent and unmoving for those few beats, and continue to look toward each other, nodding, and it occurs to me that because I am not reaching toward him with my hand, I am doing so on other levels. I realize there is an intimacy to a greeting that does not require a handshake, that a welcome without a touch may in fact may be heightened by the absence of touch. I think I remember that handshakes grew out of gestures among prehistoric peoples to indicate that they were not armed. It is a gesture of propitiation.

Dinner is long past, and I am hungry. The kids go back to whatever they were doing, and Rachel moves around the kitchen as if it were her own, making herself some macaroni noodles; though it seems she has forgotten that I am here, and perhaps it has not occurred to her that I am less comfortable opening up my host's refrigerator than she is.

When Sarah Shira returns from putting the children to bed, she tells me to take anything I would like, and she suggests eggs or salad. After a while, I make some scrambled eggs, being careful to observe the rules of the two sinks, two sets of plates and silverware, two stoves, and two sets of counters, one for milk and one for meat. There are quite a few dishes and pots and pans stacked in the milk sink, and when I am finished eating, I clean up everything I see and wipe down the stove.

The Bermans' house is similar to those of other religious Jews I've met: the rooms are very simple, with few decorations except for the family Judaica. In the living areas, a few couches and chairs line the walls, and the center is open for children to play and run. Rabbi Berman has a study, whose walls are lined with books, all of which are either sforim—religious tracts—or concerned with Jewish matters. I don't see any secular literature at all. What seems unique are the family photographs of hiking vacations in the Adirondacks, Montana, and Wyoming.

It is clear that the dining room is the emotional center of this home. The house's energy seems to be located around the long table, beneath the modern glass chandelier. The principal decorative element in the room, and the house, is the dining-room cabinet, which contains Kiddush cups, Sabbath candlesticks, siddurim. On the wall above the fireplace at the head of the table is a large, ornamented family tree, tracing the Berman ancestry back for centuries to such illustrious rabbis as Rabbi Yehudah Ha Levi. I stand in front of it, amazed, trying to imagine what it might be like to locate oneself in a lineage going back twenty generations.

The house is filled with a sense of anticipation, comfort, and love. It occurs to me that there is a tremendous difference in emotional tenor between a family grounded in belief and knowing its place in history and a family struggling to discover and create both from whole cloth.

"My husband takes the older kids on a trip every summer," says Sarah Shira, pointing to the 8 x 10 photographs that adorn the walls. One of the younger children materializes with a packet of snapshots and shows me pictures of their hike and canoe ride in New York State. Although the boy didn't go himself—he was too young—he shows me the pictures with great excitement and pride. The children look healthy and outdoorsy. Though wearing yarmulkes and tzitzit in the photos, they are dressed in climbing clothes.

Sarah Shira shows me to my room, which is a small addition off the first floor that Rabbi Berman built himself.

"Your husband actually built this addition?" I ask. "He was up on the roof with the kids, hammering and sawing?"

She laughs. "Yes. My husband is a very creative man."

I carry my bag into my room, hang up some clothes in the closet, and pull out a copy of *The Wind Won't Know Me*. I have signed it for the Bermans. I carry it back to the kitchen and hand it to my host.

"This is a copy of my first book," I say. "It's about a family that's quite different, but in many ways the same."

"Very good!" Rabbi Berman says with enthusiasm. "Very good." The children surround their father. They touch the book, open the cover, and flip the pages.

"You wrote a book?" asks one of the little ones, Simcha.

"Yes."

"You spent some time living with Indians?" asks Yehuda-Aryeh, the next-eldest.

"So you've written for magazines and other places too?" asks Shlomo. I tell them a little about what I do and how I lived in Arizona writing about the Navajos and Hopis. I watch them carefully for any sign that what I am saying is not proper. On the contrary, the kids seem to eat up everything I tell them, and they seem very interested in my stories.

It is soon time to go to bed. I double-check in my mind about whether I am allowed to turn off the lights, and I realize it is not Shabbat yet. I ask Sarah Shira, however, what rules apply for the Purim holiday. "Everything is OK," she says. "You can cook, light a flame, everything." But as soon as Purim is over, it will be the Sabbath, and we won't be able to perform any of the thirty-nine categories of work that are forbidden.

I retire to my room, shut the door, undress, and climb into one of the two single beds. I pull the shade away from the window with my hand and look outside. The day has been mild, and the window is slightly open. In the light of the streetlamp, I see several black-suited, hatted men walk by, speaking in low voices, urgently, in the singsong tune of Torah study.

I AWAKEN THE NEXT MORNING to the muffled sounds of little feet. I pull on my sweat pants and sweatshirt and open the bedroom door, wondering if it is OK to walk around in sweat pants here. I find Sarah Shira in the family room with her three youngest children, who are eating cereal. Sarah Shira wears a loose skirt and sweater and a snood. I wave, looking to see if she disapproves of my clothes. I don't see anything in her expression that suggests she does, and I continue into the kitchen and find Rachel there as well, nursing a cup of tea.

Sarah Shira tells me there are tea bags in the cabinet.

"If you want coffee," she says, "there's some instant decaf in the cabinets somewhere." I rummage around, and I succeed in digging out a very old container of regular instant coffee. It occurs to me that I haven't yet met an Orthodox person who drinks coffee in the morning.

Later, Rabbi Berman says, "I hear people talking about their morning coffee as 'their morning ritual.'" He laughs. "We don't need coffee because we have a real morning ritual. We get up, wash, recite our prayers, then dress and walk to shul."

I stand in the kitchen, listening to Rachel and Sarah Shira. I sense from the tone and the words I overhear that they are talking about something connected to Rachel and possible husbands. I decide to dress quickly and get over to the shul for morning prayers.

When I come out of my room, I see Rachel standing in the living room, holding her prayer book, facing east, and rocking back and forth, davening. I ask Sarah Shira for directions to the shul, which is connected with the Ohr Someach (Light of Happiness) Yeshivah at which Rabbi Berman teaches. The air is refreshingly brisk, and there's still lots of snow on the ground. I head off into the neighborhood, and then duck through a few backyards onto a shortcut. I approach a small bungalow, the rear of which has a door marked WOMEN'S SECTION. I step up a couple of wooden stairs, pull open the door, and find myself in a space about ten feet square where a half-dozen women are sitting in wooden chairs behind a heavy screen through which one can see shadows of the service in the men's section. A few women look up and, not recognizing me, return to their prayer books. I sit down, look for a siddur with English translation, and judging by the other books on the shelves, I see that we are sitting in a children's library.

The space on the men's side is about twenty times larger than the space here, and they also have chairs with little desks on which to rest their books. Most of the men are draped in large prayer shawls, some of which are ornamented with silver at the collar. There is a great deal of energy and activity on the men's side, men rocking and praying. Sometimes, I see the men glancing back toward the women's section. The women, for the most part, read their own prayer books intently. They don't mumble and sing like the men, rather they whisper, moving their lips so only they can hear their words.

I open the book and try to figure out where we are from the sounds of the prayers coming from the men's side. I am embarrassed because I can't quite tell. The tunes seem dissimilar from the ones I know, and the service is different. I don't want to rustle the pages of my prayer book too much trying to find my place, letting everyone know I am lost. I look over to my neighbor's book to see what page she is on, but her prayer book is different from mine. So after a minute or two, I make my best guess as to where we are, and I simply listen to the men, and rock back and forth in my chair, which soothes me, as I sound out the Hebrew words from the pages before me. The service is very different from that at Beth Emunah, which was truly a communal gathering. We prayed together and discussed the text. We broke bread and talked. This service seems much more businesslike and solitary, each person having his or her own relationship with the words and with God.

As I sit and listen, I remember that Jews pray as they do, uttering words just loud enough to hear the prayers themselves, in honor of Hannah, who prayed so fervently for a child in the Tabernacle at Shiloh, moving her lips, that the priest Eli, thinking she was drunk, expelled her. After he learned he had misinterpreted her passion, he interceded for her with God, who granted her prayer. Her son Samuel was born, whom she later consecrated to the service of God. And the Jews adopted Hannah's method of prayer.

Most of the women here are wearing wigs or hats. Some young girls sit quietly with their mothers; others look around. The Bermans' youngest daughter walks in, sits beside me, and quickly knocks over a desk. I feel immediately at ease; her shufflings and fidgetings create the opportunity for me to tell her to sit still, and therefore to establish that I am connected with someone here.

When the service is over, the women kiss their prayer books and put them away. We file out into the sun and meet the men, who are nattily dressed in suits and ties. I see Rabbi Berman walking toward me with a couple of his boys.

"Emily, how are you?" he asks in an enthusiastic way.

"When the yeshivah is done," he adds, "there will be a very nice women's section." Through the woods, I can see a brand-new building going up.

"It'll be much nicer. You'll come back and see it."

When we return home, I find Yehuda-Aryeh in the living room, reading a condensation of a popular novel.

"Why are you reading the *Reader's Digest* version?" I ask.

"Because it's shorter. I don't have time to read these books in their long version, because I should be learning Torah," he says.

"There will be a laining for women at ten o'clock," Sarah Shira says, walking into the room. "Just down the street."

"OK," I say, standing up, not sure what this means or what is being asked of me.

"It's a mitzvah to hear a second reading of Esther today," Rachel tells me walking by. I don't ask why there will be a separate reading for women.

I follow Sarah Shira's directions to a small frame house in the neighborhood. An elderly man with gray hair opens the door for me. Several women in bathrobes, looking particularly florid and over-whelmed, are working in the kitchen with children hiding behind their legs. They look out at me and the other young women gathered here as if we were animals in a zoo. I am doing my best not to observe them in like manner.

A slightly roly-poly red-haired man in his early thirties rushes in with a small scroll in his hands. The women of the house place paper cups and bottles of seltzer and soft drinks on the table beside a few paper plates of cake, and we all silently take our places.

The reader stands at the head of the table, in front of a window that looks out into the backyard. I wonder how long this will take and what we are supposed to do afterward. I heard this story just about twelve hours ago, and I wonder how much more I'm supposed to absorb during this second reading, but then I shake myself out of my own patterns of thinking and realize that is not the point. The reason we listen to a second reading is that it is a mitzvah, a commandment, to do so. We do it because we are told, and there is no argument or doubt about its purpose or necessity. I look around and see various children wending their way to the table with their noisemakers. Within seconds, most of the women from the kitchen are seated.

The man takes a breath and lets out his first note, and I snap to attention. He has a beautiful voice. As he goes on, I realize this man isn't just chanting, he is singing a veritable opera, transforming himself into the different characters of the story. I am transfixed by him and his passionate exertions, and exertions they are: He reddens, steps forward and back, swiveling his shoulders, as if battling the forces of evil himself. He wipes his brow periodically with a handkerchief from his pocket. It is such a beautiful and musical rendition, I wonder if he is an opera singer. On the other hand, it occurs to me that perhaps this marvelous singing emerges naturally from the man's feeling for and understanding of the text.

At one point, the reader stops momentarily and backtracks to correct his pronunciation of a word. I look up toward the woman sitting to his right, from whom I thought I had heard a tiny sound before he stopped. I see no expression on her face, though she seems to be following along intently in her book.

Within a few moments, the singer stops again, and I hear the same woman correct him in a low, soft voice. He leans toward her to hear, then repeats the word exactly as she had pronounced it. Later, I find out she is his sister, and very learned. She was one of the women I saw standing in the kitchen, and I kick myself for judging her so quickly by her appearance in bathrobe and slippers. It occurs to me that the rules here may be very different from what I understand. The deferential posture with which the reader leaned toward his sister to hear her words showed me that he holds her in the highest esteem.

When the reading is over, the man gathers up his papers and

leaves the house quickly. I think again about the hidden things in this world, the woman who is a master of the text yet who is shrouded by a head rag, the singer with operatic expression disguised beneath a rumpled suit, and last night, the gilded shul concealed inside the stark, modern building on an icy street in Washington Heights.

I walk back up the hill to the Bermans' house and see that preparations are under way for the big midday feast. The table has been extended, embroidered table cloths laid down, and plastic covers placed on top. The best china is brought out and places are set for twenty-four.

The eldest boy, Shaul, eighteen, is soaking a head of lettuce in salted water and peeling off the leaves.

"What are you doing?" I ask him.

"Checking for bugs," he says. "Bugs aren't kosher, so you have to examine fruits and vegetables to make sure there aren't any bugs or worms in them. The salt water brings them out."

"What's the matter with bugs?" I ask.

Shaul shakes his head. "I don't know, you just can't eat them."

I help clean the lettuce, then chop vegetables for an Israeli salad of cucumbers, tomatoes, and carrots. Sarah Shira is putting huge pans of roasts and chicken into the oven. Malka, the eldest girl, who is about sixteen, is making chicken soup. Happy chatter fills the air. News of babies born, matches made, small miracles observed. There is so much going on in a large family that one never finds oneself without a conversation or a drama to observe or in which to be engaged.

In the middle of it, Rachel arrives, dressed in a housecoat, velvetlike-plush, with a zipper down the front and gold decoration, like that worn by the woman in the apartment in Washington Heights, like the pink-cheeked women in the kitchen where I heard the laining this morning. I can't stop myself, and I blurt out, "Rachel, what are you doing in that thing?"

As soon as the words are out of my mouth, I regret them. It occurs to me that I never would have dreamed of saying such a thing to a Navajo. I would have automatically been respectful of what I didn't understand. Somehow, however, I assumed that both Rachel and I were fighting a metaphoric battle away from the housecoat. I finish preparing the salad and walk away, still peeved, unbelieving. What is she doing? I wonder. What happened to her in college? I imagine she had to have had a terrible disappointment in order to retreat to this world.

I go to my room and sit on the bed. Now why do I assume Rachel has come to this world to escape a disappointment? Is this why I have come?

WITHIN AN HOUR, the house starts filling with people. First the yeshivah bochers, ranging in age from eighteen to their mid-thirties, Rabbi Berman's students, enter in their nice suits and hats, full of energy and pep. They are young men who grew up in nonreligious homes who have decided, for one reason or another, to take time off from their careers and lives in order to study Torah. I walk past the dining room and see the boys sitting, their hats pushed back on their heads, at the table with Rabbi Berman. I linger at the door, watching, until Rabbi Berman gestures to me to come in. I am happy to be included, but, out of respect for the traditions here, I sit at the end of the table, far away from the boys.

Rabbi Berman is looking over a book, and says, "The question was just asked, 'When King Achashuerosh told Esther he would give her anything she asked for, up to half his kingdom, why didn't she ask him right away to free the Jews from Haman's evil decree? Why did she ask, instead, for a party the next day?'"

One of the students recites a line in Hebrew and, pointing to the appearance of certain words, argues that Esther wanted to delay her request so that the Jews would have a few extra days to pray and repent—to do teshuvah.

Rabbi Berman nods his head. "Good," he says. Another boy pipes up. He also recites from the megillah, and argues that since this was a miracle, a ness, it should have an appropriately dramatic setting, a party thrown for the king.

A third student says he thought that Esther was stalling for time, waiting for a divine sign that the time had arrived for her real request.

"Very good," says Rabbi Berman. "That is the point argued by Ibn Ezra."

"The sefer, Megilath Esther," he says, "is often referred to as hester ponim, the hidden face. Not once in the text is the name of Hashem mentioned. But at every moment, his hand is apparent. The Ba'al Shem Tov taught that the importance of the Book of Esther was foreshadowed in the Bible when Hashem told Moshe that the Jews would turn away from Him: "Veanochi haster astir ponai," which means "And I will hide my face." Rabbi Berman explains that we are still in this phase, when God no longer works visible miracles, as in the parting of the Red Sea, or the sending of the plagues, but rather works invisibly, behind the scenes.

"Purim," says Rabbi Berman, "is one holiday that is said will be retained in the world to come, Olam Ha'bah. It is a holiday of today and tomorrow. It is a perfect example of God communicating, not in overt miracles, but through nature, and as such it reflects the overcoming of hester ponim and the way it is expected that God and man will interact in the world to come. Most of the other holidays will disappear. For example, there will be no need for Yom Kippur, because our relationship with Hashem will be open to the greatest degree all the time."

He explains that at the time of the story, God was concealed because the Jews had created a great distance between themselves and God. "The Jews were splintered and confused: 'mefuzar umeforad,'" he says. "And this is exactly what Haman told Achashuerosh. The Jews were disunified and defenseless, scattered and taken apart, wandering like mules. And mules, as you know, are sterile. The word 'meforad' means 'separated, sterile.' And 'preda' is mule in Hebrew."

As soon as Rabbi Berman begins to analyze words, I feel I am drifting away to a most comfortable place. I realize that study provides me with a unique and unmatchable pleasure. It is a resounding excitement bounded by a deep calm.

"It was true at that time, and it is true again now," Rabbi Berman says. "Hashem has been hidden for many years, and many Jews have drifted away. We have become scattered and sterile at the end of golus." Rabbi Berman uses the Ashkenazic pronunciation of the modern Hebrew word "galut," or exile. "We are fragmented from ourselves. People accomplish things when they are focused on a goal. Haman said the Jews aren't focused anymore. He was correct. And we are still unfocused.

"There are so many temptations and our numbers are small. It is difficult to keep all the mitzvahs, but the time will come when we will come together, and like a marriage, the total will be greater than the parts."

Rabbi Berman is a real romantic, I think. He has a very romantic view of the Jews. "It is simply heroic to be a Jew in this world these days," he says later. And when I listen to him, I get caught up in the emotion of his hopefulness and belief. I can't quite step into the self-contained world in which he lives and breathes, though it fascinates me, and though I know that pieces of it make up my own flesh and blood. Understanding the world through a fundamentalist belief in the word of the Bible is too strong a turn for me to take. It would require obliterating my character and everything I know.

I recall the questions I asked myself earlier: Did I come here out of fear? Do I feel inclinations within me to withdraw into a more protected world? Do I think that, if I lead a virtuous life in which I follow the commandments, God will reward me?

It feels to me that my journey is not being fueled by fear, but rather by my desire to gain access once again to the feelings of awe I experienced in my work with Dr. Andresen.

I feel it here, in the midst of this study. I feel it in synagogue during the discussion of the Torah portion. No, it is not fear that has led me here, though after my experiences in Dallas, I certainly feel chastened. Rather, it is a desire to feel caught up once again in that most powerful feeling of connection. With what? The past? Learning? Myself? God?

Within an hour or so, the Bermans' dining room is full, the table is laden with food and alcohol, and we are drinking and telling stories. Purim is the only day of the year when drinking to the point of intoxication is encouraged, although the women, I'm sure, are expected to remain appropriately demure. The idea is that on all other holidays, one experiences joy in the head and spirit, but on Purim, one experiences joy in the body. We are supposed to feel the other side of ourselves. Everything on Purim is turned upside down.

Although the party is getting wild, the seating is highly choreographed. To Rabbi Berman's right, the students extend around the table. Directly to his left sits Sarah Shira, and beside her sit the unmarried women. I notice that men and women do not sit next to each other unless they are married. At the few sections of the table where male meets female, a child is placed between them as a buffer.

The yeshivah bochers are in high spirits, and they joke with great gaiety. One of them, a blond, has a high-pitched giggle, which, as the evening wears on, I begin to imitate, causing Rabbi Berman to laugh until he gets red in the face. The student also uses a particular hand motion that resembles one used by Rabbi Groesberg in that first class I took at the JCC in Dallas. It seems such a very Jewish gesture—a flick of the wrist, with the thumb out—as if one were flipping a cherry out of a pie with his thumb. I repeat this gesture at unexpected moments.

As my confidence increases, I offer little stories into the conversation: caricatures of some of the people I met during my travels through Arizona and Texas, rednecks and yahoos, cowboys and fools, who believe singularly in their right to do whatever they want. I create a character, Joe Bob Trailerpark, who takes target practice on saguaro cactuses. When I get to the part of the story where Joe Bob is convinced, in his beer-soaked stupor, that the cactuses are pointing their arms at him, I am afraid Rabbi Berman is going to have a seizure.

The energy mounts as I get closer to expressing the pure, unadulterated hell at the heart of my spoofs: a character lost in a seemingly meaningless world. I act out, with gestures and accents, a gallery of lost souls who drift to the Southwest to rid themselves of ties to community, family, and culture. These characters are utterly foreign to everyone at this table, though they were my constant companions, the shadows I saw in the corners of every room while I was away from the East—and myself—the beings whose very existence seemed to mock me and my desire to see and understand.

It occurs to me now that although I created characters that the Bermans have never met and never will meet, they knew them even better than I did, though not from personal experience. These characters were the strangers of any Bible story. They were the Amalekites, the Hittites, and the Jebusites. It was among them that I came head-to-head with the forces of meaninglessness and dissolution. In that regard, I am the closest this family has come to being face-to-face with a character in a Chassidic story. I walked to the edge of existence and returned to tell the tale. I proved the truth of their beliefs, that God drops little crumbs in the forest that Jews can follow home.

The schnapps and Scotch are flowing, and the Berman boys open bottle after bottle of wine. Every few minutes, more people arrive at the door with musical instruments and poems, songs and gags. Rabbi Berman intersperses the hilarity with more serious comments about Purim or Torah. This is how I have always envisioned family gatherings—a lot of people telling stories, singing songs. A teacher from one of the local yeshivahs reads aloud a long, rhyming Purim poem he has composed, which he punctuates with flashes from a wallet which, when opened, spouts a flame from a cigarette lighter.

Since I am the only woman who is telling stories or drinking any alcohol, I keep one eye peeled for signs that my behavior is inappropriate. I look at a gorgeous dark-eyed woman with a baby in her arms and elegant clothes, silent, graceful. I see another woman, a blonde, with pale skin and fine features. She doesn't speak, but her body seems musical, her modesty like a song.

I realize that though I admire these women, I can never be like them. And in fact, I think I drink and tell stories to push the limits, see how far I can go before I am reprimanded. It is as though I am waiting for a rebuke from Rabbi Berman.

That is not what comes from him. "It's a brachah," he tells me later, "a blessing, that you have the ability to make people laugh."

I FEEL EMBRACED HERE. I am happy to be a part, if only temporarily, of a huge family, a family in which the present and future seem stable and clear, a family in which the future holds hope, a world where kindness and charity are a part of daily life, a family that believes it is part of a larger whole. It is certainly a new view of life for me, one that I see I am encountering like an "amateur" in the strict sense of the word, a lover, though there are aspects I find silly or absurd. However, I imagine at moments just letting myself be carried away. Wouldn't it be nice for somebody else to make me a match? Wouldn't it be something of a fantasy to give myself over to a system whose rules were absolute? No gray areas to sort through? I laugh to myself at the simultaneous folly and appeal of this wish.

Over the Purim weekend, I learn that my book has made its way into the Bermans' upstairs bathroom. This is the ultimate mark of approbation, I come to understand. Jews are supposed to spend all their time studying Torah. "Walk in them," Jews are commanded about holy texts. Reading for fun is done when and where one cannot learn Torah, for example, while in the bathroom. It is said that the great Vilna Gaon wrote a geometry book in the lavatory. Once I get over my shock at the Balkanization of secular and religious studies, I feel appropriately proud of the place of honor my book has earned.

FRED WASSER, a producer at National Public Radio, is on the phone. He wants to know if I will write him an essay that will run on the first day of Passover. I ask him what kind of piece he is thinking about and he says, "Anything you want."

I tell him I'll call him with my answer in five minutes. I walk out onto my terrace, pluck a few old leaves and dead flowers from the roses, loosen the dirt around their roots, and give them some water. I go back inside and walk over to the computer. The first paragraph comes out very quickly. I am thinking of the four questions that are asked by the youngest child: "Why is this night different from all other nights?"

I write: "Last night was different from all other nights for me, who, like thousands of other young Jewish adults, have chosen to become more religious. The Israelites didn't become the Jewish people until after they escaped from Egypt, crossed the Red Sea, ate some matzoh, and accepted the covenant with God (after a little Sturm und Drang at the foot of Mount Sinai). Like them, it is only after exile and wandering that we, the newly religious, are learning what it means to love and obey our God. Last night, the stories of exile and return meant very different things to me and the 100,000 other Jews who, over the last five years, have begun to return to their faith. Because these events now burn real in our own lives."

I walk back out to the roses, pluck a few more dead leaves, and return to my computer. It occurs to me that my trips to tend to the flowers may be a symbolic offering to my mother, who, in an old formation that is hard to shake, I am betraying by writing, and moreover, betraying by writing about Judaism.

The second paragraph also comes quickly. "Ba'alei-teshuvah are what they are called—those who have returned—and although I don't count myself among them yet and don't know if I ever will, ba'alei-teshuvah don't just go to synagogue on the High Holy Days like the majority of Jews in this country. They embrace Orthodoxy, a twenty-four-hour-a-day devotion to religious life and observance. It is still new and strange to me, but profoundly moving. As a little girl, I read Chaim Potok's book, *The Chosen*, and I desperately wanted to study Torah like the boys in it did. It took me twenty years to begin, but now I know why I wanted to learn, because in studying the texts, in learning from rabbis, in arguing, in thinking, I am learning who I am, who I most deeply am, and who my people are and have been for three thousand years. It's not all unknown to me; although I grew up in a secular home, I now realize that home had embedded in it, in its values and in its style, what was essentially, truly Jewish. Like someone who has played piano all her life and decides suddenly to learn to read music, I am now learning the structure, the complexity, the depth, of what, in a primitive, inchoate form, I always knew."

I call Fred Wasser back and tell him I'll do it—in fact, I'll fax him a copy of the piece in ten minutes. Then I sit back down, and, as if guided by another hand, I finish the piece almost without effort.

"Although I have chosen to study with the Orthodox," I type, "many of my friends in New York who go to less strictly religious Conservative or Reform synagogues, or to none at all, are very interested when I tell them of my studies. When I tell them I have spent the Sabbath with an Orthodox family in Monsey, New York, where I must observe all the confusing dietary and behavioral rules, they give me the requisite funny looks. But they also seem to understand why I go, because they feel a stirring too. In his or her own way, each is trying to study more, learn more, and when my new rabbi comes into the city to teach, they all want to come.

"Ten years ago, if asked, I would have said I was an agnostic. Today I can say with no doubt that I believe in God, and that studying Jewish texts and learning about the traditions and rituals makes everything else in my life richer and more interesting. So, why is this night different from all other nights? Because this night, I have crossed the sea, I have danced at the bottom of Mount Sinai, I have wandered in the desert, and now I am home."

THE FIRST NIGHT OF PASSOVER is on Saturday this year. Not only will I stay Sunday night, as the Bermans will go through the entire seder a second time, but I will arrive on Friday to celebrate the Sabbath with them too. One holiday flows directly into the next, leaving no time to travel.

At Forty-seventh Street and Fifth Avenue, where I've come to catch the bus up to Rockland County, I look toward the windows of the diamond stores that line the street. Although I'd like to walk over and look at the jewelry, I am embarrassed to do so when I'm waiting for the bus to Monsey. I don't want anyone who might ride up on the same bus seeing me, obviously a single woman because of my natural hair, staring at engagement rings.

In a couple of minutes, a huge bus marked MONSEY TRAILS pulls up to the curb. I line up with men in dark suits and peyot and women in wigs. I reach into my bag to pull out my money, and when I look up, there is a short man with gray hair addressing me in a language I do not understand. I lean toward him. It's not English or French or Italian or German or Hebrew. After I have stepped back, it occurs to me that I heard the word "tzedakah." Then I look again at him, and see he is dressed in shabby clothes. I realize he's a schnorrer, a Jewish beggar, something I've read about but never seen. Imagine, a Jew begging! So I hand him a dollar. Suddenly, there materializes next to him a heavyset Russian woman who stammers out a few words of English as she muscles her way in front of me. I look at her and realize I have no spare change. I say I am sorry, and she turns away, saying, "OK, no problem," and I climb into the bus. The driver is wearing peyot himself. I hand him my money, and he is careful not to touch my fingers. I step up into the bus and see there is a curtain running down the center of the aisle and women sit on one side, men on another.

The curtain separating the sides gets hiked up at times when the men move or the bus shifts. A hand usually appears to straighten it out. As the bus goes through a big turn, I find an ample bottom, wrapped in a Chassidic satin suit, almost in my lap when a man loses his footing and twirls in a pirouette, keeping his balance by holding fast to a pole. I try to pull back in my seat as much as possible so as not to touch him, and the women around me giggle. After the man rights himself, he does not apologize, or make any gesture of acknowledgment toward us. I wonder if he is just thoughtless or observing prohibitions against speaking to the women. In either case, it causes me to bristle.

I walk toward the front of the bus as I recognize the Bermans' neighborhood, and the driver drops me off at the bottom of their street. As I walk along, I see other families preparing for the Sabbath, rushing around to get their last-minute shopping done. I feel happy walking up the hill in this neighborhood, it seems somewhat familiar to me now, and I am tempted to say hello to everyone I pass. A man comes out of a house and I nod and say "Good Shabbos."

"Not yet," he says sharply, and gets into his car. My face reddens, and I stop to think: Is there a time when one is allowed to say "Good Shabbos"? Does it have to be after sundown? Did he see my greeting as a rebuke that he wasn't ready? I walk on, recognizing how far I still am from understanding this world.

Sarah Shira greets me with a big kiss at the door. I hand her a bouquet of flowers and greet the children.

"We thought you'd bring flowers," says Yehuda-Aryeh, "because the ones you brought last time were such a big hit."

The family is full of the talk of the massive cleanup they've accomplished over the last week. Every crumb of leavened bread, or chometz, has been removed from the kitchen, every crack scraped, the space behind every piece of furniture vacuumed and washed. Crumbs have been excavated from upholstery and shaken from clothes, and mattresses have been tossed. In a special ceremony with a feather and a candle conducted last night, Rabbi Berman and the children performed a ritual final search for chometz throughout the house, and this morning burned all the crumbs they found.

I see the kitchen has been radically overhauled. There are new plates and silverware, and the kitchen counters are covered with aluminum foil. Even the buttons on the stove are covered with it. Rabbi Berman has just returned from the grocery store, and I help unload the bags. There is a staggering amount of food here—crates of oranges, grapefruits, pineapple, onions, and apples, peppers, tomatoes, carrots, two huge roasts, and several chickens.

I help Chaim cut pieces of tin foil and paper towels, for use later, since tearing is forbidden on Shabbat. We also crack open the tops of seltzer bottles and begin to open cans whose contents we might need. We discuss the fact that if we don't open enough containers of macaroons, we could, if necessary later, open up another cardboard container by slicing through its side.

Chaim makes a salad of olives and hot sauce and mayonnaise for the fish, and he also makes a tomato-and-cucumber salad. I comment about his creative cooking, and Malka says, "He's a good cook. He might go into catering."

I am impressed to see the boys in the kitchen, though I see the responsibility for preparation falls on the women. Malka has made soup, two other young women staying in the house are putting together various dishes, and Sarah Shira is in charge of the meat.

Shlomo, who is twelve, smart, and somewhat diffident, steers clear of kitchen activity, except to pop his head in and make an observation or two about the proceedings.

"Nice story," he says to me as he passes through. I look up at him and see he is holding a copy of my radio essay, which I gave to his parents.

I thank him, and continue to help Shaul trim lettuce for the seder. He has already ground up a great deal of horseradish for the moror, the bitter herbs that as part of the seder ritual remind us of the bitterness of slavery under the Egyptian pharaoh. Most of the preparations must be completed before Shabbat, because as soon as the Sabbath is over tomorrow, Passover begins, and unless we want to eat at three in the morning, everything must be ready. So this afternoon, we are preparing for two evening meals.

Just before sundown, we make a mad dash to finish up in the kitchen and dress before the official start of Sabbath. I go to my room and don one of the outfits I found at home that was long-skirted, long-sleeved, and high-necked. Although I don't feel I am dressed stylishly, or in a way that particularly looks like me, at least I don't appear to have been put together from the Goodwill racks, as I did last time. I arrange my hair with my fingers and imagine what kind of a tangle I'll have in the morning.

Sarah Shira is dressed in a fashionable, peplum-waisted blue suit and high heels. She has on a nicely styled wig in a shoulder-length pageboy cut. I know her real hair is brown and wavy and long. I wonder if it is uncomfortable pushed up under the wig. On the other hand, the wig means she doesn't have to worry about her uncombed hair on Shabbos.

Rachel, who is also here, has put quite a bit of blue eyeliner around her eyes. And it is then that I understand another way that women maintain their appearance on Saturdays: they put extra makeup on on Friday night because they are enjoined from putting it on the next day—drawing a line, as of eyeliner, is creative work. Sleeping in one's makeup seems an unpleasant aspect of the Sabbath, as is not showering. Both seem to militate against comfort and the peaceful repose I seek from the day of rest. I think of what Rabbi Groesberg of Beth Emunah suggested: If you work with your hands all week, on Shabbat, use your mind. If you use your head all week, do something physical on the Sabbath. I thought this philosophy had a sweet creativity to it, but of course, here in Monsey it would likely be considered a lily-livered excuse for not following the mitzvot.

This line of thinking brings me into a conflict I have not been able to resolve, the same division that separates the Orthodox from the two arms of modern Judaism: how much can or should the religion bend to adjust to changes in knowledge and society over the past three thousand years? I respect those who cannot imagine altering a system that they believe was handed down by God to Moses. But, until the Jewish Enlightenment in the nineteenth century, I have read in a Conservative tract, rabbis regularly made creative interpretations of halachah to adapt it to changing mores. After that time, however, Orthodox rabbis no longer felt they had the authority to do so. So, although Reform and, to a lesser extent, Conservative rabbis have continued to reinterpret Jewish law to adapt to the demands of the time, the Orthodox have become increasingly, rigidly aligned with standards of an earlier age.

I have come to a newfound respect for tradition, yet I am wary of strictures that impede individual creative strivings, particularly of women. On the other hand, constant reinterpretation cannot help but weaken respect for the underlying postbiblical law. However, a great deal of practice—such as women covering their hair—is considered in more liberal circles to be dictated by custom, not law. What makes this conflict even more difficult for me is that I enjoy being in the company of believers.

"WHAT IS YOUR HEBREW NAME?" Simcha asks me as we sit together in the study.

"Ilana."

Of course, this is kind of a fake answer, as it's just the name our one-time Hebrew teacher gave me. I wonder vaguely if there is some other name rattling around in the universe that was given to me and about which I am unaware.

"What is your sister's Hebrew name?"

"I don't think she has one," I say.

"What is your father's?"

"Saul."

"What is your mother's?"

"I don't know."

Of course, he is bewildered by these answers. Every Jew has a Hebrew name.

"Does your father have a beard?"

"No."

"Why not?"

I shrug my shoulders.

"Goyim can grow beards," he says.

"He's not a goy, he's a Jew," I retort, and Simcha giggles.

SHABBOS IS SUPPOSED TO HOLD within it seeds of the world to come, a scent of heaven. I want to feel it, smell it, remember it, and I prime myself, as if I were a hunting dog, to be aware of new senses in the air. I tell Sarah Shira I'd like to go to shul to hear evening prayers. She confers with her husband and they decide to direct me up the street to a small praying space, or shteibl, in someone's home. Sarah Shira explains that an esteemed rabbi lived there until his recent death, and the neighborhood men continue to pray there, in honor of the man's widow.

I follow their directions and walk up the street to the front door of a large white house. I stop for a moment, wondering if I should knock. I am not sure if knocking constitutes work, and would therefore be in violation of the Sabbath. I look at the sky and think it isn't yet dusk. Then I wonder what if the people inside had already lit candles—and would that make a difference if I knocked? Then it occurs to me that I shouldn't ring the doorbell—because that would use electricity—but if I knock, it'll probably be OK.

I think of the man who replied to my greeting of "Good Shabbos" with "Not yet." I now understand that this man was probably machmir, or strict. Had he acknowledged my greeting, it was explained to me by a yeshivah bocher, then it would have brought the obligations of the Sabbath on him. Since he was heading to his car, he couldn't possibly do that. Most men accept the Shabbos in the synagogue right after the prayer called "L'cha Dodi," when they say, "mizmor shir l'yom ha Shabbat." Then they mentally bring the Sabbath onto themselves, and they give up all thought of prohibited activities.

I stand in front of the widow's house, trying to figure out how to get in.

I knock.

A young blond girl answers the door and shows me the way past another girl, surely her sister, downstairs to the basement, to the women's side, a book-lined cavern. There is only one other person here, an attractive, middle-aged woman with a blond wig, sitting in a posture of great absorption yet ease. From her posture and bearing, I assume she is the mistress of the house. She nods to me and smiles, a demure but knowing smile. I pull up a chair at the wooden table and notice that we are separated from the men by a wall in which is a very small opening, about one foot by two feet, covered by a screen. I imagine the rabbi here must have been a very strict man. For a moment, a frisson passes through me, a reaction to feeling excluded, locked out. What could we women possibly emit that requires men to come up with such extensive protection schemes? But then I think of the reactions various Orthodox women have offered me regarding how they enjoy the enforced division, as it allows them to lose themselves in prayer without distraction. I am not sure it is convincing. I pick up a prayer book, open it, and decide I will try thinking this way. I listen carefully to the men's side, and I find my place. Now I won't have to spend the entire service trying to catch up or pretending to know where I am.

Sarah Shira told me this woman had married a rabbi whose first wife had died. Sarah Shira also told me that she was a convert. I don't look at her as I read along in the prayer book, but I am filled with her image and her posture of calm repose. After a few minutes, I glance up at her. She holds the prayer book in her hands, its spine resting on the edge of the table. Her feet are stretched out before her, and her body is in a state of easy concentration, as if she were most richly at home here. The room is still and deep, with the particular tranquility of chambers belowground

Rabbi Fried told me that in great yeshivahs the very walls have absorbed decades of learning, so it is thought that students within them learn faster and more deeply. I feel that here. It is dark and deep and quiet and the walls seem to hold their prayers gently, as if offering them back to the people who pray here. The woman of the house exudes a deep serenity and steadfastness. It occurs to me that her tie with Judaism must be very strong. I imagine the temptation when she was faced with the loss of her husband, to turn back to her family. But if she is a convert, that family would no longer be a part of her world. She now lives here on an island of her own creation, the center of which is gone. The community is her family now. I hope it treats her as such.

Her quiet self-possession burns itself into my memory. For years afterward, when I think about piety, the image of this woman comes to mind, sitting alone at the long empty table with her thoughts and her loss and her commitment.

* * *

RABBI BERMAN AND HIS STUDENTS begin the Shabbos meal with songs. They tip their hats back and tap the table in rhythm. It seems to me that they share great camaraderie and high spirits, and they show me the image of a life that I found extremely desirable when I first read about it in *The Chosen*—a community of people who are bound together by intense, shared activities of mind and spirit. I remember hearing that in Israel, tank crews are created from pairs of young men who study Talmud together, because they know each other so well they can anticipate each other's moves.

I notice that the women and girls do not sing, but rush about with last-minute preparations. Women's voices are considered, like their hair, too sensual a temptation, capable of arousing men to uncontrollable passions, and thus women are not supposed to sing in mixed company. I think it is touching that there is such exquisite sensitivity to the utterances of women, but on the other hand, I can see how easily this kind of reasoning is used to still the very voices it supposedly exalts. I sing along softly. Singing produces feelings of happiness and well-being, and why should women be excluded from that? It is this observance of archaic prohibitions—which in fact seems to me un-Jewish, as it doesn't give the individual much credit for resisting temptation—that keeps me from full participation in this world.

After a time, Rabbi Berman performs the Kiddush, pouring himself a silver cup full of wine, singing the blessing, and downing it before filling and passing plastic cups of wine around the table.

After a few minutes, Sarah Shira lets us know it is time to wash our hands, and we get up, a few at a time, to walk into the kitchen and perform the ritual. We then silently walk into the family room, where a picnic table has been set up. Rabbi Berman holds up two loaves of challah and sings the motzi over the bread. We eat it in here to keep the bread crumbs on the linoleum floor, from which they can be swept up easily, as the house has already been cleaned of all chometz. We return to the table and take our places again. I look around me, particularly at the Bermans' nine beautiful, bright children, and I have a sense of how deeply gratifying it must be for Rabbi Berman and Sarah Shira to have such a large family. The children, a veritable soccer team, inspire a sense of solidity as if they comprised a physical structure themselves. It is almost beyond me, imagining so much of one's own flesh and blood out in the world, devoted to you and your common mission. It is almost as if this man and woman had produced a small synagogue, a beacon to the world. I try to imagine the pride they must feel looking out at such a good-looking, respectful family.

I am reminded of a drash Rabbi Berman once offered in class about the mishkan, the Tabernacle, in which the Israelites worshiped God during their forty years in the desert. He said that Chazal, the sages, taught that although the details of the building of the Ark were meticulously set forth in the Torah—for example, it was to be made of acacia wood, covered with gold, fitted with poles for carrying, and decorated with two winged cherubim—nevertheless, it was without physical presence.

"It was a physical structure," Rabbi Berman explained, "with dimensions, but it didn't take up any space at all. So that's telling us something about the nature of spirituality. It transcends space and it transcends time."

He explained that the ancient rabbis predicted that in Jerusalem there would always be enough room for the Jews. "People would come into the mikdash, the Temple, and bow down and they would have enough room. Nobody ever said—as crowded as it was—'move to the side, I need room.' There was always enough room in the Temple."

"I always wondered," he said, "why did Hashem give us Jews Eretz

Yisroel? Why didn't He give us America? China? Great big lands? Kentucky, for example, the lands of Daniel Boone, Davy Crockett, where we could all go out and be rugged individualists?" He chuckled at the thought.

"How many Jews can you pack into Eretz Yisroel? But Hashem wanted us to have the ultimate richness, which is human richness. The richness of being with the people—our people—in a small land that was the opposite of the kind of extreme individualism that America is built on. It's a very different kind of idea. He said, 'I want you to be rich, but I want you to be rich emotionally, spiritually, intellectually. I want you all to cross-pollinate each other and build on each other and live with each other.' And it's a very, very different orientation than, let's say, the myths that America is built on. OK for individualism and OK for every person having their own space and their own territory and their own—their own!

"These are fundamental orientations that come from profoundly different sources."

Back at the Shabbos table, I understand that Rabbi Berman is dedicated to Yiddishkeit and the survival of the Jewish people with all his body and soul. Moreover, he believes he and other religious Jews are doing no less than helping to bring about the world's redemption. Toward the end of the meal, in a tender mood, he says with great sincerity that he believes the Messiah will appear soon.

"During your lifetime?" I ask.

"Yeah," he says. "I think so. I deeply believe so." His eyes are warm and dark brown. He pushes his hat back on his head, nods again.

THE NEXT DAY, Rachel and I have been invited for the noon meal to the home of a family that lives in another section of Monsey. Rabbi Berman jokingly refers to it as Vishnitz because of the density of Chassidic families who live there. Although to me the Bermans are extraordinarily observant, the Chassidim, I am told, are even more so. They are the rarest birds in a collection of exotica. Whereas Sarah Shira keeps her hair long and pushed under her wig or snood, many Chassidic women are required to shave their heads.

Sarah Shira doesn't like the practice and wonders how it affects the marriages. Rabbi Berman explains to me that he thinks the custom to shave the hair comes from Kabbalistic ideas about "good" hair and "bad" hair. Beard hair is good, but some hair on the top of the head is bad—even Chassidic men cut this hair extremely short. He believes that the custom derives from a story in the Torah of the Levite priests shaving their heads. Like many Jewish customs, the origin of this one is not clear, though devotion to minhag, or custom, remains unwavering among many. Of course, minhag differs greatly between groups.

It is raining, and I am wearing a raincoat and one of Rabbi Berman's old hats, under which I have pushed my hair, except for some side curls, which poke out from the side of my head. As we walk through the quiet streets, a man wearing a fur hat with a plastic cover on it waves energetically in our direction and begins to walk quickly toward us. I hear Rachel take in a sharp breath as I'm looking over to see if I recognize him. Is he a former Harvard classmate, one of whom I've already encountered here, ensconced with his wife and children and new religious identity in a Monsey split-level? When he gets close enough for me to scan his features, he suddenly stops and about-faces, and hurries back, away from us.

Rachel starts to giggle. I don't understand what happened, and I turn to her.

"He saw your hat and raincoat and thought you were a man. He's probably overcome with shame now," she says. "He's not supposed to approach an unmarried woman for any reason."

She's still giggling, and I chatter along with her, unwitting coconspirators in an inadvertent practical joke.

A half-block or so farther on, Rachel gasps again.

"What is it?" I ask.

She holds up the plastic bag she has been carrying that holds her shoes.

"I made a knot in the bag," she says, holding it up.

I look at her, puzzled.

"Tying knots is forbidden on Shabbos, but I didn't realize what I was doing. And now I can't untie it to get my shoes out."

I suggest she could slit the bag from the side and tell her of the earlier conversation I overheard about the macaroons. She shakes her head no. She is fearful about the possibility of having broken the Sabbath by tying the knot.

Before we left the Bermans', she told me the reason she was able to carry the bag at all, since carrying is prohibited on Shabbat, was that the "eruv was up." An eruv is a public space that is made "private" by the erection of a boundary line. The boundary can be as insubstantial as a string, but it must be inviolate, that is, the fence or string or whatever creates the border must be unbroken. Eruvs are checked before every Sabbath. If they are good, a flag goes up to signify that people can push baby carriages or carry food within their boundaries. If they are down, another sign is made, and people cannot carry anything— even children—beyond the confines of their homes.

Poor Rachel is beside herself about the knot until we reach our destination and she is able to ask the man of the house about the consequences of what she has done. He listens to her story carefully, then takes the bag and holds it up.

"You can untie the knot," he tells her, "because it is not a professional knot, and it was not intended to be tied for more than twenty-four hours." He waves it off as a trifle. Rachel smiles wanly and the blood returns to her face.

And what if it hadn't been OK, I wonder. Is there some kind of penance she would have to pay? Would there be a consequence in terms of her heavenly reward? Rules matter a great deal to Rachel, I have observed, and she seems to love learning the most minuscule aspects of regulations. I try to put aside my feelings that her concerns are ridiculous, even neurotic, and try to put myself in her place, try to imagine what it might be like living within a system whose every detail I believed had been dictated by God.

I can't imagine it. I don't believe that God worries about whether or not I inadvertently tie a knot in the handle of a plastic bag on the Sabbath. And I cannot imagine what would change my mind. And that is precisely what separates me from the members of this community. The Bermans take their mitzvot very seriously. Last night, one of the youngest children, a child not yet two, accidentally turned on the light in his parents' bedroom. They didn't even consider turning the light off, as initiating or stopping a flow of electricity is considered lighting or extinguishing a flame, both of which are forbidden, according to their interpretation of biblical prohibitions.

Consequently, Sarah Shira slept on the bed of one of their children, and her husband slept on the floor of their walk-in closet. When I saw his tired face today, I was startled into a moment of somber reflection. I realized, observing his fatigue, that they care, absolutely, because they believe that God does. I want to understand that faith. I want to understand why it seems impossible for my faith to take that form.

Later, I tell Rabbi Berman about the conundrum of the knot and that I had thought of slitting the bag to get the shoes out.

"You thought about slitting the bag because you remembered

hearing us say that we could slice through the side of the container of macaroons, if we hadn't opened up the can before Shabbos."

"Right," I say. "I extrapolated."

He nods, smiling. And so begins my learning about halachah.

That afternoon, nearly everyone takes a nap because we will be up very late with the seder. I crawl under the covers, and I have a dream, from which I awake sweating.

In the dream, I invite Rabbi Berman to a party that my parents are throwing at a hotel. I am looking forward to my father and Rabbi Berman talking, but they are sitting in different rooms. My father is in a room with his students, but distracted, looking off into space, waiting for Rabbi Berman to come see him. Rabbi Berman is on the telephone in another room, talking to his own students.

I then go to look for my mother to find out what the rabbi can eat. I go upstairs and find her very tastefully dressed, with some kind of crocheted vest and lacy jewelry—probably a gift from my father. And I see food that is nicely chosen and prepared. I ask her if the meat is kosher and she glares at me. She doesn't answer, though I imagine she says, "Our family has struggled for generations to climb away from that life. Don't you dare ask me to look back." Then she descends the staircase to the party.

I run down behind her and catch Rabbi Berman just as he is bringing a finger to his mouth after dipping it in the juice surrounding a plate of brisket and carrots and potatoes. I cry out, "No, it's not kosher!"

His eyes fill up with tears and he stares at me as he recites a fervent blessing. I awake frightened.

WE CANNOT BEGIN TO PREPARE for the seder in the afternoon, when there is a lull of activity, because Shabbat does not end until sundown. "You're supposed to stay in the moment of this day and enjoy it until it's over," says Malka. "You can't focus on the next day until it is here already." This is the kind of charming thought that draws me further into Yiddishkeit: at once wildly optimistic, almost childlike, yet deeply wise.

The seder begins after Rabbi Berman and his sons and yeshivah bochers return from synagogue. They remove their hats and place them in the study. As I pass through the living room while setting the table, I look through the French doors, and I see hats on the desk, hats on hooks on the walls, hats on the windowsill. It looks like a stable, the hats like horses in their stalls, waiting to be called for their next outing, which will be during the Kiddush.

"Why do the men wear hats for the Kiddush?" I ask Sarah Shira. "Isn't a yarmulke good enough?"

"It's a little extra respect that's shown when praying," she says to me.

I wonder how these customs were elaborated over the years. Was there a group of men praying one day in a little ghetto somewhere, and one of them looked over the group and thought: "Gee, we look like a bunch of schleppers standing here with our bald pates and raggy clothes and yarmulkes. Let's wear our hats while we're praying to God." And they did, and soon everyone else in the village did as well and eventually the custom spread, backed up by a rabbinic interpretation.

Why do the Chassidim wear long, curly peyot, while Rabbi Berman wears none, and some of his students wear sidecurls pushed behind their ears? Is it a fashion statement or a religious position? Or both? If a particular supplier of silk to the town of Belz died, and the only other supplier came with a very different cloth, could this have led, over the ages, to the change of a custom in men's cassocks that, years or maybe centuries later, developed religious significance? Of course, that line of thinking is not the way people here think.

It is now close to nine o'clock, and it is time to begin. The men and boys sit to the right of Rabbi Berman. Sarah Shira and the female guests sit to his left. Malka, the eldest girl, sits at the very end of the table, and I wonder why she has removed herself so far from the action—the talk that takes place at the head of the table. Rabbi Berman wears a kittel, the traditional white coat a Jewish man first dons at his wedding, and thereafter when presiding over the seder. Beside him is a pillow on which he leans, as is customary for the leader. I understand the custom was one shared by Babylonian kings as well as the Greeks when they conducted the Symposia.

The table is long, and there are about twenty-five people here, about as many guests as family members. Shaul, Chaim, and Shlomo pour the wine. Rabbi Berman says the brachah, leans to his left on his pillow, and drinks his cup of wine. And so we all lean as we drink. Then he pulls out a small silver pitcher with a bowl, and pours water over his fingers into the bowl. He passes it to the student to his right, but I notice it doesn't reach the women. He points to the pieces of lettuce in front of us on small plates. We dip the lettuce in the bowl of salt water that passes, and eat it. The familiar taste of the salt water over the greens opens up my memory to the seders I attended as a child at my grandparents' house in Brookline. I think of the beautiful table my grandmother set with her fine china, linen, and silver. We each had our own cup of salted water, in which we dipped pieces of bright green parsley. She was a fine cook, and the meals she prepared were far more elegant than any I encountered in the Orthodox world, though they included traditional fare: sublime chopped chicken liver for appetizers, matzoh ball soup, gefilte fish, roast chicken and potatoes, and green beans. My grandmother's table was the center of religion in our family. Her table provided us with our Jewish memories, tastes, and smells. I learned years later that not far from the table, in the basement of that house, was a complete set of blue glass Passover dishes, the vestige of an earlier time when my grandmother changed all her plates for the holiday.

Rabbi Berman pulls out the middle matzoh, breaks it, and places one half into a napkin that he folds and tucks into his kittel. That is the afikomen, which the children will try to slip out of his pocket during the meal. I think of my grandfather reaching into the navy blue velvet matzoh cover in which he placed the matzoh we used for the seder. I once peeked inside the bag and was surprised to see that a white cotton sleeve separated the middle matzoh from top and bottom. Our custom was that he hid the afikomen for the grandchildren to find. We learned every inch of that house hunting for the afikomen. No matter who found it, my grandfather would generously and happily peel a fresh $10 bill from a stack for each of us.

Here the Bermans do not use the familiar square matzoh. Rather, their matzoh is round and very thin. Shlomo tells me this is schmurah matzoh, which means, literally, "guarded." Its ingredients were watched very carefully from the time the wheat was harvested to make sure it didn't get wet for long enough to make it chometz. It is very expensive and comes in heavy cardboard cake boxes.

Rabbi Berman lifts the plate, puts it back down on the table, then recites a prayer, and I read along in English. "This is the bread of affliction which our forefathers ate in the land of Egypt. Let all those who are hungry come and eat with us. . . ."

He explains that this is the traditional beginning of the Passover story and is read in Aramaic, the secular language of the Jews at the time. Before families sat down to the seder, someone would go to the door and call out this invitation in the local tongue to all who might be passing by.

One of the students offers another intepretation of why this opening is recited in Aramaic rather than Hebrew.

"God liked to listen to the Jews recite the Passover story from their own mouths, rather then through the usual intermediaries, the angels. We are told He liked to hear this in Aramaic, a language the angels don't understand."

It is then that the click happens, that moment when I seem to fall quietly through Alice's hole into a chamber in which I am lost in a collection of illuminated esoterica. The next thing I realize is that Simcha is singing the four questions. He has a big smile on his face and he does an excellent job. Then Dovid, who is three, begins to sing, holding in front of him a children's book with large letters. I think he has memorized the questions, but he holds up the book to pretend that he is reading. I can't believe that this three-year-old has memorized the four questions, a paragraph's worth of text, in Hebrew no less. Both Dovid and Simcha sing the questions, in a lovely melody that I have never heard before, and I realize that the melody is the key to learning the questions, for then the prayer becomes a song. Why didn't we ever learn the tune? Why do the Reform squeeze all the juice from the rituals?

Rabbi Berman encourages the children, particularly the youngest ones, to participate. The text explains that the very word "haggadah" comes from the verse in Exodus, "And you shall tell (vehigaditah) your child on that day, for this sake did God act for me when I left Mitzrayim." He explains that the entire seder is built to teach and maintain the interest of the children. The seder is important, it makes clear, not only because it tells the story of the miracle of the deliverance from Egypt, but also because it encourages the children to ask questions, the basis of Jewish learning.

Later, as we prepare to make another Kiddush over wine, one of the children covers up the matzoh and says, "So the matzoh isn't insulted." It reminds me that in synagogue, when the rabbi is speaking, or when there is an interruption of the Torah reading, the scroll is covered in the same way. It seems touching to me, the honor bestowed on the book, as if it had feelings itself, or self-consciousness.

Although I have been to many seders, the give-and-take between Rabbi Berman and his children and students opens up the story for me as no other has before. I see that the Haggadah itself is like a cryptic map that waits to be decoded. A single line refers to mountains of learning, and following its puzzles and implications takes you on a journey through Judaism itself. I am quite overwhelmed as the evening goes on; overwhelmed that the children remain well behaved throughout, though we don't begin eating until 11 P.M.; overwhelmed by how meaningful the Haggadah becomes in knowing hands. Rather than being an uninspiring act of recitation, a struggle to complete before hunger and boredom set in, the seder here is a master class, a dip in the river.

THE NEXT EVENING, we go through the entire seder a second time. I had never heard of having two seders—my family barely got through one every year. But Jews in the diaspora are supposed to celebrate holidays for two days rather than the one day they are marked in Israel, because of the inaccuracy of the lunar calendar. The proper day for the start of the holiday was not always clear, hence the tradition of celebrating holidays twice to guarantee hitting the right date. Rabbi Fried from Dallas is one of the world's experts on this subject, and has written a book about it, *Yom Tov Sheini Kehilchaso.* I remind myself to read it when I get home.

The essay that I wrote for NPR passes from guest to guest over the course of the weekend and several people come up to me and offer comments. I am surprised by how heartfelt their responses seem, how easy and natural conversations are with them. I sense no awkwardness between men and women. Rather, I find the people are remarkably interested and eager to talk. Of course, we won't be able to hear the piece, because turning on the radio on the first day of Passover is forbidden. So, I won't hear it myself until next week when I receive a tape from Fred Wasser.

I watch the men carefully, and notice that most are very solicitous of their wives, and very involved in the care of the children. Husbands and wives speak to each other in pleasant, respectful voices. It seems that the traditional separation exists at the synagogue and around the table, where the men get the places of honor near the rabbi. But I don't see that separation spilling out into social interaction. I wonder if the periodic ritual separations into boys' and girls' clubs actually creates a fresher, more respectful reconnection.

This trip, I don't push my way in with the men. Rather, I hang back to see where the natural currents carry me. As the weekend goes on, I realize that the more comfortable I feel, the more frequently I retreat to the kitchen. After a period of time with the men, I begin to feel guilty about my great good luck in being accepted, and about leaving the women behind, scraping and cleaning vegetables. The more fun I have, the deeper into the texts I go, the more I feel I am betraying someone. I get up and walk into the kitchen, though I dread the idea of starting to help, because the work is endless. As soon as I sweep the floor, a dozen small children walk through, and it is dirty again. Once one meal is finished, it is almost time to begin the next. I am amazed by Sarah Shira's persistent good nature, always a smile on her face, always delight in her children and her guests, but I notice that she is helped by numerous women—both the guests and the several young women who seem to have a more formal helping role here. Sarah Shira is the project coordinator and head chef.

What is it about helping that makes me feel, as soon as I remove myself from the men's presence and move to the women's area, that I cannot leave again? I look at Rachel's red raw knuckles. If I don't help, another woman will have to. Something inside me propels me to the kitchen and into the company of women, though it makes me feel angry and despairing to be there. Am I carrying my mother along with me here? Do I hear her imaginary rebukes for breaking away and joining the men? Is that in fact what she would have liked to do?

I help clear the table between courses, and help to serve the next course. I carry in steaming bowls of chicken soup filled with squash and sweet potato. Then I help slice the gefilte fish, place it on a plate with a piece of carrot and tomato. Twenty-five plates. After that, platters of meat and chicken and vegetables and salads are readied and served.

At the far end of the table, where I sit, and which affords easier access to the kitchen, it is hard to hear the discussion around the rabbi. This irritates me, as does the noise from the many children. Although I have chosen to throw my lot in with the women, I still bristle at the division of labor. The young men are happily engaged with the rabbi at the head of the table, and the women are tending to the chores elsewhere. I find myself scrutinizing the women and ridiculing them in my own mind for submitting to these customs, for covering their hair with the sheitels. Have they lost their minds? Do they think they are living in sixteenth-century Poland?

But then I cool off and realize that the women are very attractive, more so than in your average gathering. They are elegantly dressed and shod, and more importantly, they seem tranquil and centered. I notice that the wigs have the effect, on the old women, of making them look much younger than their years. And in the younger ones, it offers an air of mystery. What is under that wig that must be hidden? I wonder why, if the quality of sheitels has improved so much that the best ones are hard to distinguish from the women's own hair, they are acceptable. Isn't the point that a married woman should no longer look attractive to men besides her husband? Why, then, allow great-looking wigs?

Later, I ask Rabbi Berman, and he tells me: "There is something very special about a wife's hair to her husband. It is a very sweet, intimate expression of her, a curl on her forehead, a dampening from the heat. Even if the sheitel is very good, it is still a covering, almost a helmet. My sister, who was just married, looks different to me now, even though she spent a lot of money on her wig. She doesn't look the same. And that's how it is supposed to be—her true beauty is only seen now by her husband."

I am touched by the idea of the exquisite and unreproducible intimacy between husband and wife, but wonder if the beautiful idea retains its power in real life. And what, if anything, is the man giving up for his bride that matches the notorious discomfort of these wigs? I feel that when I try to adopt the thinking of this crowd, a little voice in my head points out an anthropological or sociobiological explanation for Orthodox ways and their attempts to control women and subdue their impulses. I cannot erase this voice, though I know it is highly conditioned by the culture in which I was raised and which in many ways was formed in direct opposition to traditional patriarchal cultures like this one. I decide, for the time being, to set my feelings aside and observe; perhaps I will come to understand the issue in a new way.

Over the course of the weekend, I have several chances to talk to Malka Berman, who at sixteen is a very bright young woman and is as passionate about Yiddishkeit as is her father. In fact, Sarah Shira says that of all her children, Malka most resembles her father in character. I ask her how she tolerates being closed off from the learning she loves by the unending load of housework that falls on her young shoulders as the only grown female child.

She says, "Well, when I was very young, it bothered me, and I used to go over to the door and open it and yell, 'Oh, you little brats come inside and start helping.' All I did was get angry and it didn't do anything. I realized pretty quickly that it wasn't going to work.

"But I think I must have known how important the work was, because it didn't bother me that much. It drives you crazy when you're cleaning up all the time, but I remind myself that I'm doing something very, very spiritual, even though it doesn't look that way. Thinking about it that way, I feel good."

It is clearly hard on Malka, being the only grown girl in this family of boys. When she is torn between joining a discussion of Torah at the table or helping with housework, she says she asks herself: "Is the thing you have to do—will it go away, will you have another chance to do it later? Can no one else do it, and do people really need it? Then do it now and God will give you what you need later. If you need something and God knows you need it—I just read this somewhere—He will provide it. God will never take away good from those who pursue Him. Those who pursue God will never lack good. If I really need something, God knows it as much as I do. So if I really need to relax now to learn something, then I can do it. But suppose my mother needs help this minute, and someone needs to be driven somewhere, and the kitchen's a wreck—don't worry. I'll get a chance to do whatever I need later. It happens."

I am moved by her generosity and her goodness, but it seems to me that she uses a great deal of her energy not only doing the housework that her brothers don't have to do, but also, convincing herself that the restrictions that bind her are all for the best.

JUST BEFORE THE conclusion of the seder, we eat one last piece of matzoh, the afikomen. I look around the table and notice people are chewing determinedly in silence, struggling to produce enough saliva to get it chewed and swallowed. I am reminded of something my Orthodox friend Ruchama Feuerman once said to me about the afikomen: "The chometz is puffed up. It reflects our arrogance. The matzoh, it says in the Zohar, is the bread of healing. And it is amazing how humbling it can be to eat that afikomen. It's the end of the evening, you're tired and full, but you have to get through that last piece. And when you're chomping through that matzoh, you really feel what humility is. You've never tasted such plainness."

Even after this exercise in humility, and even after everything is cleaned up, I am too wired to sleep. It is 2 A.M., and the rabbi is still sitting at the table.

"I had a dream this afternoon," I tell him. "But perhaps it's too late."

"No, that's OK," he says. "I love dreams."

So I tell him my dream.

Of course, he's no Dr. Andresen. He doesn't help me probe for the meaning, but rather, he tells me what he thinks it means.

"I think it represents your own ambivalence about Yiddishkeit," he said, "particularly the fear of the primitive."

I am impressed that he realizes my mother is a stand-in for me in the dream. She doesn't want to "go back." And neither, it seems, do I.

What can he have? Can he have me? My mother says no. But he has already put his finger into the sauce. As we talk, Rabbi Berman looks quite concerned, and he breathes in a different way. I get the feeling that he takes my conflict quite seriously, and is treading very carefully.

We talk on, and I feel, suddenly, that I want to tell him something.

"I feel that I was given a message of some kind when I was in Texas," I say. "I realized that I needed to reconnect with my own past, with Jews, with learning. I do not question that. And in some ways, I understand now that all those years I was writing about Indians, I was really looking for my own story. Why else could I have become so involved? Why did I weep when I left the home of a ninety-year-old man who sat on a stump in front of his house, looking out on the most astonishingly beautiful valley, saying 'This is where I am tucked into the land. This is where I belong'? Although this man was blind, he still knew every inch of the buttes around him. The land and his tradition informed him in a way I could never imagine. Why did I weep if on some level I didn't understand his conflict in my blood and my soul? How could I have cared?"

The rabbi nods. "It's amazing," he says. "Amazing."

"The problem," I say, "is that I was looking one way when I should have been looking another. But that is my story. It has been in many ways a painful trip, and at a certain point I feared I had lost everything. But I can't look back and think it would have been better had I never begun it."

I search his face. "Do you see?" I ask. I want to let him know that I cannot abandon the education and the understanding of the world I have forged over the last thirty years. I want him to understand that after struggling to create a voice for myself, there is no way on earth that I intend to stifle it. But this is not exactly what I say.

"I look at these young women and I envy their innocence," I say. "I see in the religious women a fecundity and a tenderness that comes from being protected from hurt. And at some level, I would give anything to be back there.

"But on the other hand, I know what I have learned, and there are things I have gained that these women don't have. Having come this far, I can't go back."

Rabbi Berman says, "I don't believe there is anything inconsistent between the work you do and Yiddishkeit. You can continue to work just as you do. Perhaps some of your methods would change, but that's all. Nobody would ask you to give up your work."

We sit in silence for a few moments. It occurs to me that I wanted him to reassure me that my journey was not a waste, that sometimes one has to go very far away before realizing where home is. I feel he understands this.

I have found my way back to New York. And I have found my way to Judaism. But which Judaism is to be my Judaism? Which home is home?

As I WAIT TO RETURN to the city with Rachel, I sit in the study with Yehuda-Aryeh. Kids wander in and out. He is asking me about federal law as it applies to American Indians. Suddenly, he looks at me and says, "You're not someone who can be made fun of."

"What?" I ask.

"No one would make fun of you," he says.

I am quiet. Then I laugh, imagining the Monday-morning quarterbacking sessions that must go on in this house.

Before Rachel and I leave Monsey, we stop at the local supermarket to stock up on Passover supplies. The store is filled with religious people, men and women. Since the community has a very large Orthodox population, the store carries kosher meat and aisles and aisles of Passover food. There is "Kosher for Passover" cake mix and candy and macaroons and soap and soda pop and tuna and cheese.

I remember that when I was a child, my sister and I usually kept the Passover; that is, we refrained from eating bread, though I'm sure we ate grains and beans because we didn't know they were also forbidden. But we never made Passover cakes. It seemed to us that the purpose of Passover was deprivation so as to remember the hardships of the Israelites who left before their bread had a chance to rise. What sense did it make, then, to eat all kinds of cakes and treats that had been made with potato or matzoh meal? Even if it wasn't breaking the law, wasn't it breaking the spirit of the law?

Later, I ask Ruchama this question. She thinks for a few minutes and says, "You know there are four questions that are asked? Why do we eat matzoh, the bread of poor people, yet we dip food like rich people? Why do we eat the bitter herbs, the food of affliction, and yet recline in our seats like rich men? So the four questions really have one answer. It's because on Passover, we recall not only our bondage in Egypt, but also our deliverance. We remember our sorrow and suffering but also our joy. So, we should abstain from bread, but we should not abstain from pleasure in eating."

As Rachel and I wander through the supermarket, and look over the hundreds of products, I decide that I will not only keep the Passover ban on chometz, but I will try to keep kosher for one week. So I buy kosher milk and kosher cottage cheese. I buy a potato-pancake mix and matzoh. I buy eggs and gefilte fish and horseradish. I buy some kosher chicken and some beef bones to make soup.

For the rest of the week, I feel virtuous and clean. I don't eat milk and meat products together. I try to think of feeling plain and humble. I separate out some silverware that I designate for dairy and others for meat, and I use white china for milk and, for meat, a set of red stoneware dishes I got from Rabbi Groesberg, the fleishig dishes that he gave me when he left Dallas for California. I had taken them with the idea of making my kitchen kosher and using the stoneware as my meat dishes. I had also wanted to keep a bit of Rabbi Groesberg close to me.

But at the end of Passover, when I restock my cabinets with bread crumbs, crackers, cereal, and pasta, I gradually let go of my attempts to stay kosher. I don't do this because I didn't find satisfaction in the week's abstentions. Rather, I stop because I did. I stop because I did feel virtuous, and I am suspicious of that feeling. I do not want to believe that if I keep kashrut, God will watch out for me. I do not want to believe that if I follow Orthodoxy, I will be rewarded with good health. Job's story shows it is a transformation, a journey into the unknown, that brings him an experience of the divine, not a retreat into dogma.

However, I wonder, could it be that the journey into the unknown, for me, doesn't mean more freedom, but rather making just those commitments I resist?

Chapter Eight

∝

DESIRE

I WAS LOOKING for a story to tell.

I had been asked, as had the other six grandchildren, to offer memories of my grandmother, Lillian, at her funeral.

But hard as I thought, as many images of my grandmother as I could conjure, I couldn't find a story—neither one that she had told me, nor a story about her—something with a beginning, a middle, an end.

I could see her vividly: presiding over the table during holiday dinners, carrying out her raspberry chiffon pies in their silver pie plates and carefully setting them down on the table with a little gasp of effort. I thought of the miniature swans at each place that she filled with almonds she had roasted in butter and sprinkled with coarse salt. I thought of her white, wavy hair, which was fine and shiny and thick, and of her delicate hands. They were the only delicate hands in the family, the nails elegantly shaped into neat ovals.

Though plenty of vivid images came to mind, none would cohere into a story. I searched for images of action. I remembered her driving me to riding lessons and scaring me to death with her speed and bad peripheral vision. I remembered once going with her to Schrafft's for a lime rickey. But no stories. There were duties fulfilled, people cared for, but where were the stories of loves, of dreams, of ambitions? How did she understand her life? How did she understand her place in history, her social class, or even in her family? This was not an issue, for me, of mere curiosity.

One of my younger cousins is also a writer. Before the funeral, I asked her if she had a story about our grandmother. She confessed that she was also having trouble finding one. We talked for a while about the puzzlement of our predicament. No stories. No plot.

"Have you ever thought about what plot is?" I asked her.

She looked at me with interest.

"A friend once told me, 'Plot is desire.'"

My cousin's eyes grew wide. I brought up something Hegel said, that desire is the wish to be completely known to another. I said that I believed the only way for some of us to satisfy that deep wish to be known is to find a way to tell the story of our lives. I venture to say that writing the story of our lives—in whatever fashion that may be, from creating photo albums to sewing quilts to running a restaurant to writing music or stories—is a central human imperative.

I also struggle with plot because at a deep, almost preconscious level, I lack the sound of the stories of the women who preceded me. Although I have had more adventures than I can record, I have yet to find a voice for them. As a writer of nonfiction, I write other people's stories as a way, I have come to think, of exploring and telling my own.

None of the other grandchildren came up with a story, only fragments, memories, thanks. Back at her house after the funeral, I looked carefully at my grandmother's wedding portrait, which my mother had dug out of a box and displayed in the dining room. There was a whisper there of hopeful virtue, but no happiness. She held a bouquet of white lilies. I realized with a start that white lilies had also adorned her casket, and I asked my mother who had chosen the flowers. She said the funeral home had chosen them. On what information did they base their choice? I asked her. "I suppose they chose lilies because they had the impression she was an elegant person," my mother said, and walked away. But how would they know that? I wondered. They had had no information about her life. They chose lilies, I am convinced, because all they knew was her name: Lillian. We had left the story to be written by strangers.

My cousin rejoined me, and as we studied the wedding photograph, she told me of visiting my grandmother in the nursing home, where she had lain mute and partially paralyzed after a stroke for several months before she died.

"Her nightgown fell away once, and I saw her scar," my cousin said.

She was referring to the mastectomy that my grandmother had undergone at the age of twenty-three, an event that neither she nor anyone else in our family ever talked about. Later that day, my grandmother's sister confessed to my mother that she suspected her sister's surgery may have been unwarranted, that the tumor may have been benign, yet the doctor had recommended a radical mastectomy nonetheless. "If it were my daughter, I'd do it, just to be safe," he said. A second opinion was never sought.

Now, all of a sudden, other bits of the story came my way. My grandmother never much liked my grandfather, but her parents told her he was a good catch: a graduate of Harvard Law School, from a good and educated family. Lillian told her sister Esther that, in outline, he was all she had wanted. But, she lamented, he was fifteen years her senior. However, she also said, because he was older, she felt she could tell him about the operation, something she'd never be able to tell the young men who squired her about town.

So they were married, but they didn't get along. After a year, my grandmother, with her baby, my mother, in her arms, left her husband and went back home. But her parents told her she couldn't stay. She was damaged goods, and lucky to have a husband at all. She had no choice but to go back.

And so she did, climbing the steps of the old subway cars, riding past the areas of town where before her marriage she had been happily employed as a social worker. It was like seeing her life in reverse. Something died in her then. She shut herself down. Because no one would listen, she would not be known, even to herself. As I see it, her desires were pushed away, thereby robbing her life of shape and movement. She busied herself with women's work: cooking and sewing and entertaining. And she became increasingly distracted. My mother once bitterly referred to her as "autistic." I think that her children suffered from her distraction. Denied the concentrated attention they needed, they grew up with terrible furies, angers that could never be soothed.

It would be naive to imagine that my grandmother's withdrawal did not affect my mother as a young woman trying to craft a role for herself in the world. As a college student, my mother was very adventurous, traveling alone through Europe, and studying for a year in Paris. When she returned home, she struggled to reconcile her daring nature with the expectations of her family and marriage to my father at age twenty-three. Perhaps the agoraphobia that beset her as a young mother offered a solution of sorts to the competing pulls of her dreams and the reality of her life: as long as terrifying fears prevented her from venturing out, she couldn't test the traces of home and hearth. And who knows if she also felt obligated in her own way—as I may have tried as a child to limit my own imagination in an unconscious attempt to restore my mother—to honor her mother Lillian's lost dreams?

My grandmother's story and her parents' heavy-handed cruelty weigh on me. I believe I have felt their effects, diluted and filtered, throughout my own life. Like many others, I struggled to develop a voice, to find my way in the world, but my unusual inheritance was to have to fight through unnamed, unacknowledged fears that floated across every surface I crossed. As a child, I exhibited what I understand now to be symptoms of my mother's agoraphobia: on certain occasions—a new school, horse shows, a visit to a new friend—I became sick with nausea. However, I never let it stop me. Over time, the nausea disappeared, and I came to enjoy the thrill of the frightening and the new, sometimes perhaps a bit too much.

Because of the family legacy of abandoned dreams and unnamed fears, I am particularly resistant to attempts to silence me, send me to the kitchen, or surrender my fate to another. Although Judaism's ancient traditions appeal for many reasons, the customs that regulate the role of women in the Orthodox world feel more alarming to me than they might to someone with a different family history.

My mother and I spent two days after the funeral going through my grandmother's house, looking into closets and drawers. We found the silver pie plates with leaves and grapes around the handles, the miniature swans, her wicker sewing basket. Then there were boxes of recipes in my grandmother's hand and also some in her mother's. Stuffed in every closet and cupboard were things both important and inconsequential: wrapping paper, old photos, *Woman's Day* magazines, letters, receipts, travel brochures, recipes for her babies' infant formulas.

As I went through the boxes, I wondered what could have driven her to save all this? Did my grandmother have the vague, preconscious wish that one day, someone would take the pieces of her life and make them into a story, the story she could never construct?

I thought of this as I stood on top of a chair, peering into the highest kitchen cabinets. Tucked into a corner behind half a dozen old double boilers was a delicate glass bowl. It was covered with dust and grime. I washed it. When it dried, it sparkled in the sun, and I saw it was in fact a luminous Venetian glass dessert bowl with lilac handles and a lilac foot, and a knob on top in the shape of a rose. It was a sauce dish, with a hole cut for a spoon.

But where was the spoon? It must have been broken or lost. Instead of throwing the dish away—this flawed beautiful object—my grandmother hid it out of sight, the same way she had hidden herself. The dish is the one thing I brought home from her house. It stands next to me on my desk now, holding a piece of her story and, I've come to realize, a piece of my own as well.

Chapter Nine

Chapter Nine

❧

CONGREGATION
B'NAI JESHURUN

BACK IN MANHATTAN on a Saturday morning after the Passover holidays, 1994, I head toward the French neoclassical brick and stone Church of St. Paul and St. Andrew on the corner of West End Avenue and Eighty-sixth Street. I have heard that Congregation B'nai Jeshurun meets here, and has done so since the ceiling of its synagogue caved in the previous year. I feel a bit apprehensive about walking into a church to attend synagogue services, and I walk past the entrance a couple of times, wondering whether I should do this. I know that part of this reaction comes from my Orthodox friends, who would not step foot in a church for any reason. But I have been told that the music in the shul is wonderful, and it is just around the corner from my apartment. I watch for a few minutes from across the street, and I see men in yarmulkes and women in nice clothes walking up in solemn Sabbath demeanor.

I follow them up the sagging marble steps, and in the sanctuary I am met by a small gray-haired woman with a kind smile who hands me a prayer book and Chumash. The room is large, with pleasant cherry-stained pews and balcony. In the front is a dark, carved bimah. Behind it and up on the altar stands a wood cabinet holding the Torah. I survey the space, looking apprehensively for a cross or other Christian iconography. With relief I find none, and then I look above the Ark and see, hanging from the ceiling, a huge banner that stops me short. On a square of simple muslin, in large capital letters, is printed HOW GOOD IT IS WHEN BROTHERS AND SISTERS DWELL TOGETHER IN HARMONY. I stand fixed for a few moments, trying to control the feelings that rush to my throat. I am overwhelmed with a feeling of Dr. Andresen's presence, and a sweet sense of gratitude. I am ashamed of my hesitance to enter this church and I realize that clannishness proves its impotence in the face of human generosity. Dr. Andresen, a Christian, offered me sanctuary when I was lost, just as this church offered refuge to a homeless congregation.

I walk toward the front, find a seat, and sit down. I glance up again at the banner and in a few moments I recognize it as a variation of the first line of the prayer "Hinei Mah Tov." I am moved again when I realize it was the Jews of this novel pairing who came up with the words to support it, and it was the Jewish liturgy that offered it. But how different it is here from Beth Emunah, my little strip-mall shul with the leaking ceiling tiles, plastic chairs, and the odd hodgepodge of members. It is a grand, comfortable space, with wooden pews, filled with a great many people of all ages.

A gentle-looking young man with curly brown hair and a beard sits down at a keyboard in front. He begins to play softly and the congregants hum along with him. In a few minutes, a young rabbi named Rolando Matalon walks to the bimah. He steps up to the microphone and begins to sing in a lovely, clear tenor. I look around me at the congregation and see a roomful of Upper West Siders. They appear familiar to me. In many ways, I think, I am one of them.

But then I think of my Orthodox friends, who would not approve of the loudspeaker system, nor the playing of musical instruments. The loudspeaker violates the prohibition of turning on and off electricity on the Sabbath, and the very religious believe that music, as an expression of unmitigated joy, should not be allowed in the synagogue until the Temple in Jerusalem is rebuilt.

The cantor, or chazzan, Ari Priven, begins to sing the morning blessings, and the sound causes me to look up instantly from my siddur. I have never heard such a sweet voice. It is at once full of joy and fear, pride and humility. The chazzan's body twists and turns as he sings, as if he were making love to God, and I cannot look away from him. I think of the Kabbalistic notion that "in the high spheres there exist temples that can be opened through song only," and I am sure that this man has the keys.

I recognize bits of the melodies here and there and join in when I can. I recognize the beginning of the Amidah, where we invoke the names of the patriarchs, but then I have to stop almost immediately, as I hear something unfamiliar. I realize the congregation has added the names of the matriarchs to the prayer. I am stunned. It never even occurred to me that the women's names were missing, but hearing the names Sarah, Rebekah, Rachel, and Leah included beside the names of Abraham, Isaac, and Jacob opens up my heart in a way I never imagined. I glance over the prayer book and see the matriarchs' names are not included there. The decision to include the names was made by the congregation itself.

I realize I have graduated from Beth Emunah to a much more urbane world. I look at the weekly bulletin, the Kol Jeshurun, which was handed to me as I entered. I see announcements about engagements, weddings, bar and bat mitzvahs, births and deaths, but also many social activities: groups to help the elderly get to synagogue, to help the ill or the grieving, an employment bank, a support group for the infertile, a homeless shelter, and calls for fund-raising for people in countries from South Africa to Bosnia. Upcoming speakers include the Israeli ambassador, Colette Avital, and a member of the Israeli Knesset.

It appears that the congregation is strongly leftist in its politics. There is a call to action for a protest over the killing in Bosnia, which is preceded by words from the Talmud: "Whoever is able to protest against the transgressions of his own family and does not do so is punished for the transgressions of his family. Whoever is able to protest against the transgressions of the people of his community and does not do so is punished for the transgressions of his community. Whoever is able to protest against the transgressions of the entire world and does not do so is punished for the transgressions of the entire world."

I know that the congregation, though the second-oldest in Manhattan, was moribund only a few years ago, until it was reinvigorated by Marshall Meyer, onetime secretary to Abraham Joshua Heschel at the Jewish Theological Seminary. Meyer lived in Argentina for twenty years, where he brought the Jewish community back to life and was a vocal opponent of the country's repressive military juntas. He returned to the United States and in 1985 took over the pulpit of B'nai Jeshurun, where he led the congregation's renaissance until his recent, unexpected death from cancer.

It seems from the bulletin that Meyer's vision of human rights informs this place. And it seems as well that the theology of Abraham Joshua Heschel plays center stage. Before the Torah reading begins, the rabbi asks us to turn to some photocopied pages of Heschel's *Man's Quest for God*.

"This chapter deals with the place of symbols in the Jewish tradition," the rabbi says. "Humans are the symbol of God." I see that the page of the book actually reads, "Man is the symbol of God," but the rabbi has made the word gender-neutral. He continues to do this throughout his speaking, alternating between the words God and Adonai, never saying "Him." Sometimes, rather than use a third-person pronoun, he addresses God directly, saying "You." The distant patriarchal God has been brought face-to-face with us, in the fashion of Martin Buber.

"Nothing can symbolize the infinite, the Creator of the universe," Rabbi Matalon says, "and yet there is something in the world that the Bible does regard as a symbol of God. "It is not a temple nor a tree, it is not a statue nor a star."

He leaves the text and says, "In certain civilizations the highest point in their midst was the construction of the Temple. It was the fulfillment of creation. As you will see in today's Torah portion, the fulfillment of creation is not the construction of the Tabernacle; it is Shabbat, the celebration of the holiness of time."

He turns and points up to the banner, "How good it is when brothers and sisters dwell together in harmony."

"That is why," he adds, "the sign says 'when' and not 'where.' It is not the space that is holy, but it is the way we use time, how time is sanctified." How modern this idea sounds, compared with a place-centered concept of sanctity. Conceiving of time as holy opens up the idea in a new way.

I look around me. The balcony is almost full. There must be six hundred people here, and this is a Saturday morning, when most of Manhattan is in Central Park or eating or shopping. The simple presence of so many bodies here moves me.

I BUY A TAPE of B'nai Jeshurun's Saturday service, and I listen to it at home while reading along in the Conservative prayer book. I quickly learn the prayers and after a few months am able to sing through the entire service. Every Friday night and Saturday morning, I enter the sanctuary, sit in the same spot, and talk to very few people. Compared with tiny Beth Emunah or the Orthodox shuls I have visited, the congregation feels somewhat unfriendly and cliquish. I rather like the freedom this allows, however. I read and listen and pray, losing myself in the liturgy and the Torah portion without distractions.

The B'nai Jeshurun services have a rhythm and structure that I understand better every week. We are brought through an ancient formula that has moments of quiet contemplation, resounding declaration, searching, repetition, beauty, and magnificent delicacy. When the Ark is first opened, I feel connected to very early childhood memories of the library. The book created and saved the Jew, as it saved me. At the end of the service, the prayer that accompanies the placement of the Torah back in the Ark is so mournful that, as at Beth Emunah, I cannot sing it without fighting through a lump in my throat. Although I know a beautiful harmony for the tune, most of the time I cannot get it out, as my throat is too tight to produce the high notes. We Jews miss our Book when she is gone.

THIS WEEK, the bar mitzvah boy is very small and very cute, and when he approaches the Ark to lift out the Torah, he is accompanied by his little sister. As he holds the Torah, his new suit large on his shoulders, the Torah heavy in his arms, he leans slightly toward her to see the words of the prayer book she holds for him. I am struck by the absolute honesty of the children's body language. I can see the boy's obvious closeness to his sister, and the posture of deferential protectiveness he has already assumed toward her. Further, I know that the sister will soon take her place here too. She will not be excluded, relegated to an inferior celebration. She will read from the Torah, just as he is doing today.

The boy's parents present him with his own prayer shawl, which reaches almost to the floor. But this is one suit that he will never outgrow. The parents explain that the prayer shawl belonged to the boy's grandfather, whose presence is suddenly writ large here, and it occurs to me that Judaism is particularly concerned with weaving together the fabric of generations. It is a religion that keeps all its members with us. It honors the living as it remembers the dead, and celebrates the connections that persist between us all in blood and memory. The woman's voice breaks at one point as she speaks of her father. Everyone here understands the influence of our forebears and is moved by the invocation of the faithful who preceded us. We Jews understand particularly the weight of inherited values. The midrash says that Joseph was able to reject the advances of Potiphar's wife in part because the image of his father flashed before him. Even the ancients understood how profoundly we are influenced by the morality of our forebears.

I feel a great happiness for this young man and his little sister, who are not entering the world alone, but are welcomed by a community enriched with customs and teachings that can guide them in finding their own relationship with the past, each other, and the divine.

ON OCCASION AT B'NAI JESHURUN, a baby girl is named. During the reading of the Torah, the parents approach the bimah for an aliyah with the infant, and the rabbi says, "May the one who blessed our ancestors Abraham, Isaac, Jacob, Sarah, Rebecca, Rachel, and Leah bless this mother in Israel and this father, as well as the daughter born to them. Her name among the people Israel shall be," and then he intones her name.

The rabbi continues with his blessing: "Merciful God, grant that this child grow to maturity in good health and mind. May she be a sensitive human being, a caring daughter, woman, wife, and mother. May she be spared the ravages of war and violence, the bitterness of hatred and prejudice. May she be a blessing to all who love her, to the people Israel and to all humanity. May she be blessed with long life surrounded by her beloved family and may her parents find wisdom and length of days to raise their daughter to the study and practice of Torah, deeds of compassion and righteousness, and to witness her achievement of love fulfilled. May she be capable of loving deeply, and may she be loved deeply, and let us say Amen." He kisses the baby, and the congregation sings a sweet song.

Not long after I begin attending services at B'nai Jeshurun, I return to Boston for a visit. While at home, my mother shows me the old record book in which she kept notes about my sister and me. I open the maroon leather journal and read the first entry, in which my father describes my arrival. He calls me Nachas, a Hebrew word meaning "joy," which, he writes, he picked up from the rabbi at the synagogue.

The synagogue! If he had been in a synagogue with me and a rabbi, that could have been for only one reason, a baby-naming. As I drive in the car with my parents one evening, I ask them whether they can remember my Hebrew name. They both utter a name each. One says "Hannah," the other "Rochel."

"Hannah Rochel," my mother says. They both seem surprised that this name has popped out of their mouths.

It takes me a few moments to realize what they had said, and then, I am shaken, thinking this is the first time in my life I have heard my proper name. It sounds perfect, fits me perfectly, the sound, the way it rolls over the tongue, like an introduction and a conclusion: Hannah Rochel.

I resist the temptation to read some kind of cosmic significance into my recollection that it was Hannah who taught the Jews how to pray, because since I started going to shul, the members of my own family, each in his or her own way, have turned a bit toward Judaism as well. Although I secretly rejoice in the finding of this name and its significance to me, I also feel a nagging doubt. I'm not sure my parents' recollection is correct. The name is too perfect. It fits too well.

I continue the search for my name a couple of months later, when, back in New York City after the death of my grandmother, the name of my grandfather's shul suddenly comes to mind. If I had been given a name, it was surely there. I call directory assistance, learn that Kehillath Israel is still in existence, and dial the number. I reach a secretary and tell her that I am trying to find the record of my baby-naming. She asks me for my birth date and I tell her. She sighs and says she's afraid those records have all been destroyed, but says she'll check in an old storage area to be sure.

A couple of days later, she calls me back.

"Well, you are very lucky," she says. "We had those records in a box. I found the cards the rabbi wrote, for both you and your sister. Tell me your address and I'll send them to you."

A week later, a simple white envelope arrives in my box. Inside, I find three pieces of paper, each containing photocopies of three-by-five-inch cards, handwritten in English and Hebrew. The cards are hard to read, as the rabbi's script is crabbed, and English and Hebrew lines are intertwined. I find my date of birth, April 26, and the date of my naming: May 3. I see the name of the hospital, Beth Israel, in which I was born, and the names of my parents in Hebrew and En glish, my grandparents, and great-grandfathers. I pore over the card, sounding out the Hebrew letters.

My mother's Hebrew name is rendered as "Josepha," daughter of Kalman (Coleman) and Lillian. I find my father's Hebrew name, Saul, and his father's Hebrew name, Solomon, the son of Jacob. My father's mother's Hebrew name was Hannah, also the daughter of a Solomon. I stop. That's the first clue. If my grandmother's name was Hannah, I was not likely given the same name, as Jews do not name children after living relatives.

I slowly identify which word must be my name, and then begin to pick out the letters.

I read the letters mem, yud, and nun, and sound it out as "Minnie." "Minnie!" That's my Hebrew name. It is also the name of my cat! There is a second name, and I see resh, chet, lamed, or "Rochel." Further down the card, my name is spelled "Minna." I remember that my mother's maternal grandmother was Minnie Rosenberg, and her paternal grandmother was also Minnie—Clara Minnie. Although their husbands' names are on the cards, the names of my great-grandmothers are not. The only forebears not mentioned are the two women after whom I am named.

My name is Minna Rochel. I burst out laughing. It is a Yiddish name, Minna, rather than a Hebrew name. I was named after two of my great-grandmothers in my grandfather's synagogue, most likely with a rabbi wearing a black hat. My sister's name, which in English is Karen Ruth, is hard to decipher. After many tries, I determine it must be Carmiel Rivka.

I have discovered one piece of the puzzle of my Jewish life: my name. I think of the many trips I made to the bimah in Texas with a borrowed name, Ilana. At B'nai Jeshurun, congregants are called to the Torah by the number of the aliyah, not by name, unless they are called for a special occasion like a birthday. I have not yet been called to the Torah by my real name.

I ATTEND A COMPLETE High Holiday service for the first time in my life in the fall of 1994. Congregation B'nai Jeshurun, which, for High Holiday attendance, has now outgrown not only its own synagogue but also its adopted meeting place of the Church of St. Paul and St. Andrew, has decided to hold services in the grand sanctum of the Christian Science Church on Ninety-sixth Street and Central Park West. As at the Eighty-sixth Street sanctuary, there is very little Christian iconography here, and the one stained-glass window that might offend is covered with a sheet.

I am surprised that the prospect of entering a church irks me again, but the presence of several elderly members of the congregation, especially one Yiddish-speaking couple, Holocaust survivors both, elegant, mannered, fiercely devoted to one another as well as to the congregation, reassures me. If they can accept praying in a church, then so can I.

The chamber is elegant and imposing, and I look up to the marvelous chandeliers and towering pipe organ and feel awed, but I then remember a peroration given to us by the rabbi a couple of weeks ago in anticipation of this service: he reminded us that these Yamim Noraim—"Days of Awe"—are about a most intimate connection between each one of us and God, and that we should concentrate our thoughts and prayers at all times toward that end and not be distracted by the beauty or grandeur of our surroundings. So I try to become very quiet, open myself to the prayer book and what Rabbi Matalon will say to us. I have noticed that he has a remarkably intimate relationship with this congregation, and everyone calls him by his nickname, Roly. He has an air of gravitas about him, and appears to take his job very seriously.

The opening prayer, he tells us, was composed by Marshall Meyer, the man who asked the congregation to hire him as his assistant rabbi as soon as he graduated from the Jewish Theological Seminary in 1986.

"O God, Creator of time and the universe, sovereign of all being, as we gather in prayer to greet another new year, our hearts and souls tremble before the uncertainty of time and the mystery of life." Rabbi Matalon's voice is big in this big place, but there is a small flicker, a catch in his voice with what I imagine to be thoughts of the friend and teacher who tragically is not with him here.

"On this evening," he continues, "the symbolic anniversary of Your creation, we stand here in Your presence in all humility, very much aware of our failings and our falseness, of our attempts to escape from Your challenges and the powers You have bestowed on us. We are more sensitive than ever to the ephemeral quality of our lives, to our multiple rationalizations and indifference."

As he reads the words composed by his friend and rabbi, he seems to speak to Meyer directly, transforming his painful absence into a presence. Sometimes he looks small and lonely up on the bima by himself, but then he leads us on with the words of the deeply mourned Meyer, urging God to "grant us the wisdom to distinguish between right and wrong, between the good and the better, between the creative and the destructive, so that we may achieve that which endures. During the forthcoming days of scrutiny and repentance, help us to concentrate, O God, on our tattered souls and our atomized personalities. Quicken our tired and insensitive hearts so that we may genuinely pray and thus ennoble our being."

The holidays prove to be an exhausting, exhilarating passage, almost two weeks of intense observance, beginning a week before Rosh Hashanah with Selichot, the preparation for repentance, during which time we hear the first strains of the special holiday melodies, and continuing through Rosh Hashanah and Yom Kippur. The rabbi and the chazzan lead us on what can only be called a journey, at times demanding and physically difficult, at other times joyful. It is not for a moment mundane or without intense surprises. It rolls through valleys of introspection and up over peaks of heartfelt joy and communal exhilaration, confounding us, cheering us, sometimes offering us glimpses of immense beauty. Much of the service I am encountering for the first time. The pattern of the tunes slowly becomes clear, though I am scrambling to keep up.

Rabbi Matalon has chosen to interweave the prayer book service with several stories written by Rabbi Nachman of Bratzlav, a great-grandson of the Ba'al Shem Tov, the founder of Chassidism. Nachman, we learn, was a mystic who lived a mysterious life. He was wracked with internal doubt and crippling mood swings. He wanted to create a new ideal Jew, and through his fantastical stories, his teachings, poetry, and meditations, he influenced his followers in a new direction.

"Through his tales," says the rabbi, "Nachman shares the deepest longings, fantasies, doubts and fears of his own soul. But Nachman's tales are the tales of every human soul in its journey through life."

He pauses, then continues: "I invite you to join me in this journey. Where each one of us will end up I do not know. We too are alone, we too experience pain and longing and search for language and self-expression in our inner silence. We seek to unlock the profundities of our soul and celebrate living as we seek—what is it that we seek? Perhaps we will see. I just know that the Yamim Noraim are totally irrelevant without a serious committed search. You are all invited to the search."

I like his words, and I am moved to follow him. He launches into a long and complicated tale of two children lost in the forest and rescued by a group of beggars, each of whom is afflicted with a deformity of one kind or another. Many years later, when the children marry each other, they invite their old friends the beggars to celebrate with them, and so, one by one, the blind and the halt and the mute appear and offer gifts to the couple.

One of the beggars is a stutterer. But he explains to the bride and groom that he does not really stammer, rather, he chooses not to speak because words not uttered in praise of God are basically meaningless. The beggar goes on to say that he is able to tell wonderful stories. "In fact, I am extraordinarily eloquent," he says. "I am a master of poetry and speech. I can recite such marvelous parables, poems, and songs that when I speak there isn't a creature on earth that does not desire to listen, and in my words there is all wisdom."

I am seized by the thought that it was only through my own deformity—my temporary blindness—that I was offered the understanding to appreciate these tales. At that time, I was vulnerable in a way I had never been before, and it led me into an entirely new realm of insight. It amazes me how simple humility has the power to open us up to the world with a heightened perceptual awareness, while success and ego pinches us closed.

The stutterer says that he gathers together the best stories and poems and songs in the world, and he presents them to "the person of true grace." The person of true grace accepts all the stories and poems and songs, and out of them, he creates time.

"The Kabbalah interprets the creation of the world as a spontaneous act of grace," says the rabbi. "The world's continued existence

depends on our raising up and returning some of the divine abundance through mitzvot. . . . The stutterer offers back to God the
sparks of holiness he finds in the world. Without his action, the
world cannot continue to exist and time stops."

I am surprised by the parallels between what I am hearing here
and what I learned from Dr. Andresen. Nachman teaches that God
heals the world in response to the gifts of the stutterer's stories. And
Dr. Andresen believes that cure can come when he receives his
patient's stories as gifts, as offerings that have the power to change
him. Without stories, time stops, according to Nachman. By offering
their stories, patients have the chance of a new start, creating time.
Our primal structuring of meaning is narrative in structure. Stories
make us time.

THE NEXT DAY, ANOTHER STORY: "At one end of the world there
is a mountain," says Rabbi Matalon in his clear, sure voice. "On the
mountain is a rock, and from the rock flows a spring. At the other
end of the world is the heart of the world. Everything has a heart,
even the world itself. The heart of the world is the perfect form of a
human being, with a face, hands, and feet, but even its toenails possess more heart than the actual heart of any other being."

I think how touching is the way the Chassidim transform stories of
the divine into human tales. I remember a story from the midrash
about Moshe once catching a glimpse of the back of God's head, and
what he saw was God's gray hair bound with the leather straps of his
tefillin. How vulnerable and touching an image—the back of God's
head, old man's hair tousled under the tefillin as He walks away from
His prayer.

"The spring and the heart face each other from the two ends of the world," the rabbi says. "The heart yearns greatly for the spring and wishes to come to it. Its desire is so great that it cries out with yearning. The spring too longs for the heart. This heart suffers in two ways. The first is the burning heat of the sun. The second is its terrible yearning for the spring, which it eternally faces from afar, longing for it with all its soul and crying out to reach it."

When the heart needs some respite, a great bird comes to offer shade from the sun. This, the rabbi tells us, is divine grace. "But even in these moments of rest, the heart gazes at the spring and never ceases to yearn for it." The heart cannot move to the spring because were it to do so, the mountaintop would vanish from its sight, and were the heart unable to see the spring, it would die. Thus, the heart can never come to the spring and stands forever facing it, yearning and crying for it from the depths of its soul.

"The spring has not time of its own," he continues, "for it is above time and does not exist within time.

"How then, can the spring continue to exist in the world? It receives time as a gift from the heart, day by day. When each day draws to a close, no time is left for the spring, and it is on the verge of disappearing. Were the spring to disappear, the heart too would cease to exist. And so, as the day draws to a close, the heart and the spring bid each other farewell with wondrous parables, poems, and songs, with words full of love and yearning."

I smile. What a wonderful story. The heart is forever separated from the object of its desire. The heart and the spring constantly yearn for each other, desire reunion and restoration, but are forever held apart by a truth of creation: the mountain is in the way. So the heart yearns, and as the two exchange stories, they create a text of their longing. It is an endless story, the ebb and flow of desire, the exchange of divine sparks. Each depends on the other. The Torah, or spring, needs the yearning heart. And the heart, the Jews, needs the spring. Creation persists through the return of the divine abundance, through the mitzvot.

"This is a story about faith," the rabbi says. "Yearning for closeness in spite of existential loneliness. Longing for greater meaning in spite of anxiety, suffering, and doubt. The longing is greater than ourselves."

He looks up from his notebook at us, adjusts the tallit on his shoulders. "The most authentic manifestation of our faith is in our longing for God."

I AM IN A BLUR for most of the rest of the holidays. The rabbi blows the shofar. The chazzan's voice fills up the tremendous space with its pure, strong sweetness. We sing, we pray, we shift in our seats. We walk home, we return to synagogue, we fast. It feels like we are all on a trek through the forest.

There are more moments that astonish me. When Rabbi Matalon falls onto the floor before the Ark and prostrates himself in a re-creation of the moment when the high priests entered the Holy of Holies, I am stunned by the simple humility of the act. Once again during this amazing service, tears rush to my eyes as I see the soles of his shoes, so intimate and private an image, like the back of God's head. As he is helped to his feet, his hand still gripping the microphone into which he continues to chant, still on key, I glance at the woman sitting to my left and I see a vein raised on her forehead and her cheeks wet with tears as well.

The pages go by, song after song, prayers we recite standing and sitting. The image of the heavenly gates swinging closed. Then the service to commemorate the 6 million dead in the Holocaust. The words of the Kaddish read by the rabbi, one by one, interspersed with our responses: the names of the concentration camps. "Yitgadal," the familiar first word of the prayer. "Auschwitz," we read.

"ve'yitkadash"

Lodz

"Sm'mei raba"

Ponary

"b'alma di v'ra khir'utei"

Babi Yar.

And on it goes through Majdanek and Birkenau, Bergen-Belsen and Dachau, Minsk and Theresienstadt, the terrible words, so cold and frightening, yet which are special spots for us, the resting places of so many of our dead, the bulk of our Torah scholars and sages, millions of others, now ashes.

And then, as if we were not already spent, a moment during Yizkor, when we mourn the rest of our dearly departed. I have the most remarkable and vivid vision of my three dead grandparents. They are standing beside many others lining the walls of the sanctuary, but in a momentary vision, they step out so that I can see them more clearly. They seem quite unaware of me, having the distracted air one imagines of the dead—preoccupied, other worldly. But they stand there, insistent, in my sight, larger than life.

And then the vision disappears, and Yamim Noraim, the Days of Awe, are over.

SOON AFTER THE HOLIDAYS, I begin to attend a class the rabbi is offering on the prayer book. I want to understand the origin of each of the prayers, and find the story behind the story that makes each one stand out. Why do prayers have different tunes, I wonder, and where did the tunes come from, and which prayers have biblical sources? I want to understand the architecture of the siddur, to appreciate not only the pergolas and the capstones, but also to understand everything belowground, the plumbing and structural supports, the basement and later additions. Why were certain bits of ancient material inserted here? How do I understand the numerous, arcane rituals?

I enter the church on a cool autumn evening and enter a parlor room on the first floor. Almost fifty people, some of whom I recognize from services, sit in wooden chairs. At first, the rabbi sits in our midst, but eventually, and apologetically, he moves to the front of the class, to stand on a platform that is slightly raised, saying he isn't moving so as to stand above us, but so that he can see everyone.

"I think we should sit in a circle," he says in his warm voice, but no one moves to shift their chairs. It seems no one minds that the rabbi sits at the front of the room, facing us, teaching us.

He asks us to open the prayer book to the sixth page, to the blessing in which we praise God for giving us the Torah.

"It is the responsibility of a Jew to study every day," he begins. "Now, we do not all have that opportunity, so a selection of texts is incorporated into the liturgy to make sure that everyone fulfills that obligation, not just to discharge a responsibility but to realize that we can't live without study."

As he speaks, it is as if he were savoring a fine wine as he forms the syllables with his lips. He seems devoted to the seriousness of words, seems to feel it in his body. He pronounces the word "God" with exquisite delicacy, making the final consonant soft, as if he were holding it on his tongue.

"It was once too expensive to have handwritten manuscripts," he continues, looking around the room. "So people used to memorize entire sections of the Torah. As we memorize it, it becomes a part of us, and we carry it wherever we go. That's why the Nazis could not destroy the spirit of the Jewish people, because we carry our knowledge and our texts inside us. Torah is not an external thing, though unfortunately it can become an external thing. But it is not meant to be. If you take it away and burn it, we still have it within us."

He returns to the prayer book.

"Now let's take a look at the beautiful blessing. The study of the Torah is a mitzvah, a religious obligation, but also one of the ways we seek proximity with God. It is an act of worship. We don't study for the sake of knowledge alone, we study so that we are exposed to God's presence. As with any other mitzvah, we recite a blessing before we fulfill it. So we say, 'Praised are you Adonai our God, sovereign of the universe, who has sanctified us with your scroll'"—I see that the rabbi translates on his own here—"'or,'" he continues, "'who adds holiness to our lives, and who gave us the mitzvah and commanded us to study Torah.'"

This, it occurs to me, was the blessing that Rabbi Groesberg recited before beginning his class on Kabbalah at the Dallas Jewish Community Center, the gesture that had seemed to me, lost in that meaningless city, so pure, so sacred, so full of sweetness and respect.

Rabbi Matalon continues by saying that God wants us not just to study, but also to savor the Torah: "'Cause that the words of your Torah may be sweet and blessed in our mouths,'" he recites. "'Be sweet in our mouths and sweet in the mouths of the people Israel so that we and our children and our children's children, all of us will be knowledgeable of your name and study Torah on its own merit. Praised are you Adonai who teaches Torah to your people Israel.'"

He looks up at us and smiles. "Do you know the traditional way for teaching kids the letters of the alphabet?" he asks.

"The letters of the alphabet are written in honey on a board," he answers, "and the child learns the alphabet by licking the honey from that board, so that the first experience of the letters from which the Torah will be studied will be sweet."

He explains that the Jews involve all their senses in their worship. "We are used to having a sense of hearing," he says. "We say 'Shemah Yisroel.' 'Hear O Israel.' And we read, 'and You shall look at the tzitzit.' And there are many things we do with touching—we touch the mezuzah, the Torah. So, our senses are involved. And here it is explained that the Torah should be sweet-tasting. And the Hebrew word in the phrase 'so that we will be knowledgeable of you' is 'llada'at,' knowledge in the sense of physical love. In the Bible, the verb 'to know' has a connotation of sexual love, and the subject here is very physical.

"By getting in touch with Torah, we're getting in touch with the giver of Torah. You read it again and again, and through the letters, you are in touch with the lover."

He continues with the blessing over the reading of the Torah. The siddur reads, "Praised are you, Lord, who teaches His people Israel. Praised are You, Lord our God, King of the Universe, who has chosen us from among all people by giving us His Torah. Praised are You, Lord, who gives the Torah." But the rabbi leaves out "Lord" and "King" and "Him" and edits the sentence so that he addresses God directly as "You." This is also what he does during services, altering the words written in the prayer book to eliminate the masculine pronoun.

A man raises his hand and says, "I have a problem with the idea that Jews are the chosen people, that we are set apart from others."

"I do too," says Rabbi Matalon.

I look up in surprise. The rabbi feels uncomfortable with the idea that the Jews were chosen? As he explores his feelings about this subject, I see a different side from the man who so confidently leads the services. He lays out his questions to us, seems to search for answers as he speaks.

"'Who has chosen us, by giving us Your Torah,'" he reads. "There are a number of different ways that this can be understood," he says, shifting in his seat. "One way it is taken is that God selected us because we are better or wiser or whatever.

"Another prevalent interpretation is that God went around and offered the Torah to all the peoples of the world, and everyone refused to accept it." This, I remember, is the interpretation I heard from the Lubavitcher rabbi in Dallas. "And then it was offered to the Jewish people, and God said, 'You have no choice. Either accept it or this place will be your grave.'

"But there's another way of looking at this. God has selected us, we don't know why, in order to make us partners in some mission in the world. Through us, God wants to give this gift of Torah to the world—which inspires us to holiness and all sorts of wonderful things. Others say, 'We have also chosen God. We are stuck with our mission, in spite of the difficulties. And in spite of the challenge, we have chosen God.' Maybe God called others and Abraham was the one who responded, or Moses was the one who responded."

He continues by saying that he read a drash by Rabbi Lawrence Kushner that pointed out that when Moses was walking in the wilderness and saw the burning bush, the miracle was not so much that the bush was not consumed. The miracle was that Moses noticed, and watched long enough to see the bush was not being consumed. Kushner pointed out that when one watches wood burning in the fireplace, it's not obvious that the wood is burning. It only becomes clear that the wood is being consumed after one stays for a while.

"Most of us would have passed by the bush without realizing it wasn't being consumed," Rabbi Matalon says. "But Moses took the time to take in the experience, to stop and look. Moses made the miracle possible.

"So, regarding the issue of the Jews as the chosen people," he continues, "I believe that we are not better, we are not worse, we are not wiser, we are not less wise. I think that the historical reality is that we have this book, this Torah. We don't know what happened at Mount Sinai exactly, if anything, because it is surrounded by mystery. But we do know that this book landed in our laps somehow, several generations later. So the question is, what do we do with it? Do we use it as a mark of superiority, or are we going to say, 'We don't know exactly how this happened, but I want to believe my ancestors had a say in accepting this, and were open to the challenge. What a privilege that I am part of the people who accepted this challenge. Am I up to the challenge? Are we up to the challenge? What am I going to do with this challenge?'

"I like to live with the tension," he says. "I don't want to resolve all the problems, because I want to live with the tension and remind myself of it."

I was very interested to hear the rabbi's thoughts on Sinai, a subject that separates Orthodox Jews from the rest. As far as Rabbi Berman is concerned, God gave the entire Torah to Moses, both the written and oral Torahs, even though they wouldn't be composed by the rabbis whose names are attached to them for hundreds and hundreds of years. And every repetition and elision in the Bible is significant and encloses a message from God.

I find this view difficult to accept at face value, and I am interested that a rabbi can still be devout and as dedicated to the search for God as Rabbi Matalon appears to be without holding the fundamentalist belief. It also jibes with the commentary of the Chumash that we use at B'nai Jeshurun, which was produced by the Conservative movement, and which seems to take note of more modern methods of textual analyses.

I attend the class for several more weeks. I am interested in what the rabbi has to say, but I gradually become disillusioned by the discussion it generates. Most members of the community, including myself, don't have a solid Jewish education. Few people make references to texts or other religious learning, yet they want to participate in class, so they talk about how they feel. The low point takes place one evening when the entire discussion is derailed, toward the end of the session, by a woman who asks that the doors be closed, and, when the gathering is appropriately hushed, she confesses, "I am an alcoholic. And although no one likes to talk about alcoholism in the Jewish community, it exists." I have to stifle a groan. I have come here to learn about the prayer book, not to listen to an AA testimonial.

Soon I stop going to the class, and instead enroll in a course on the weekly Torah portion with a Chassidic rabbi named Ben Cherney, which has been offered by the Jewish Renaissance Center, an Orthodox outreach program. I am transported by Rabbi Cherney, a gentle soul, who tells stories and parables without stopping, without ever repeating the same tale. His weekly lectures are prose poems of the most delicate intricacy, in which he develops a few themes from each Torah portion and illustrates them with stories, drashes, and a detailed analysis of the text. By the end of class, he has pulled every loose end of the story into the bouquet of his theme, which many times concerns the idea of midot, a person's (God-given) character traits, and how those characteristics play into the dialectic between the Divine plan and free will. Every week, I am sad to leave class at its conclusion. The poems he creates are perfectly formed, but as soon as I walk into the light of day with them, they fade into gossamer.

I appreciate the respect the students offer the teacher, and I am happy to listen to him. It's not that the women—for it is a class of women, mostly unmarried girls in long skirts and long-sleeved shirts—don't ask questions; they do. But they ask questions informed by previous study, questions that relate to an understanding of the text.

Of course, the philosophical basis of all the questions and answers in this class is that the Torah reflects the word of God as recorded by Moses. Every word, every oddity of language or order is meaningful, and a puzzle placed by God for us to understand. This orientation, though I'm not sure I share it, doesn't interfere with my learning. The only way for me to learn about Judaism is to know what Jewish scholars have said and written over the centuries about our sacred texts. And so I seek out classes that bring me there, into the Book.

MY APPRECIATION FOR STUDY with the Orthodox does not lead me to worship with them, however. I cannot get past the separation of men and women, in geography, roles, and expectation. I continue to attend services at B'nai Jeshurun because they move and stimulate me. Every Saturday morning, I dress and carry my blue velvet tallit bag to the shul, walk in, say the blessing to put on the tallit, and drape my shoulders in the white wool shawl. Rabbi Berman would find this silly, because to his mind, women have no business in tallitot. But I like being draped in the shawl. It encourages the feeling that I am indeed in a different space on Shabbat, one in part of my own making, one in part hereditary and historical.

The character of the services at B'nai Jeshurun is influenced not only by the rabbi and the chazzan, but also by the congregants themselves. Sometimes it is obvious that a bar mitzvah boy or bat mitzvah girl are just going through the motions, and that the family is unfamiliar with and uncomfortable in the synagogue. But at other times, there are girls and boys who are from families engaged in the Jewish world, and who, it is immediately clear, are at home here: children who run the whole service themselves, who learn their portions with vigor and appreciation, who write a D'var Torah that shows they have related to the Book with their hearts and their intellects. I feel happy and exuberant when I see girls and boys like this, and the entire congregation murmurs a collective kvell for them.

If I ever imagine I know what is coming, however, I am thrown a curve, and return to the only proper and genuine condition in the synagogue: radical amazement. One Saturday, a pretty bat mitzvah girl walks up with her parents to remove the Torah from the bimah, and when it is time for her to begin to read, nothing comes out of her mouth. After a few beats, the rabbi steps in. We have just had a long string of bar and bat mitzvot in the shul, and I am feeling a bit snippy. By this time I have made friends, and I turn to one beside me and crack, under my breath, "Don't they have any non-speaking roles for these kids?"

In a moment, my face burns red from shame when it becomes apparent that this girl has special gifts. Not the gifts we are used to looking for in the bar and bat mitzvot, but qualities far more subtle and unusual. In another time, one might have called this girl a simple soul. There is not a shred of sadness, disappointment, or "what ifs" in the people who surround this child. It is clear that she has been surrounded all her life by the best teachers and a loving family who have helped her use her abilities to their fullest. What she cannot do becomes instantly irrelevant. What one sees is an otherworldly sweetness and pureness of heart. And in the end, I feel I have been in the presence of an illuminating dignity. Odd that a child who has trouble beginning her Haftorah portion leaves me with such an elevation of spirit, but I am reminded of something Rabbi Matalon said about Shabbat: "We speak differently on Shabbat than we do on the other six days. It is not just a shmittah, a strike of work. We have to rediscover Shabbat every time we reenter it." And this child embodies the spirit of Shabbat, of rest and peace and of kindness.

In her talk, she tells us that she very much enjoys the lighting of the Sabbath candles, and she adds wistfully that she wishes her family did it more often, and in a flash, a picture of modern life comes to me: the professional couple with demanding careers, mothers whose frantic schedules make it difficult to be home at sunset on Fridays, who can rarely prepare a traditional Shabbos meal. This reminds me of a story I heard about the old Talmudists, who disapproved of running, whatever the day of the week. They said if you ran about, your eyes would go bad, because rushing around keeps you from seeing clearly. There was, however, a remedy for the effects of this needless movement: watch the Shabbos candles, and the strength would return to your eyes.

When the girl finishes her D'var Torah, the rabbi points to a statue of an angel near the rafters (we are in a church, after all) and tells the girl that the word for "angel" in Hebrew is "moloch," and that molochim are sent to earth to deliver messages. The rabbi tells her that she is an angel, and she has been sent to earth to deliver her own message. She looks at him, self-possessed, hopeful, patient, and I feel we have all received this message. On this day, we were all touched by the Shabbos queen, in Heschel's words, her "majesty tempered with mercy and delicate innocence that is waiting for affection."

MY MOTHER COMES TO VISIT one weekend, and I ask her if she will attend services with me on Friday night. She agrees. The sanctuary is packed to the rafters, and once again, I am struck by how moving is the simple sight of Jews gathered together to pray. Just after singing "L'cha Dodi," the song that welcomes the arrival of the Shabbos bride, the congregants dance around the chamber, a practice initiated by Marshall Meyer. My mother watches quietly and I sing along. I notice my mother opening up her handbag at one point. I see out of the corner of my eye that she is dabbing at her nose with a tissue. To keep away my own tears, I try to look elsewhere and concentrate on the prayers. At the conclusion of the service, after the final blessing, I turn to her and I see her face is wet. I reach out my arms to her and we stand there in the pews, crying together over a longing we cannot express, a gulf that seems too large to cross, a connection that, as a matter of heredity and family history, seems to be forbidden us.

B'NAI JESHURUN is a grand emporium for the soul, stocked with a wide selection of fare. Everyone can find something here—it is a congregation of social action and responsibility, with a homeless shelter, a lunch program, and a number of national and international initiatives going on at any time. There are parleys for gay members of the congregation, groups for single parents and infertile couples. It is a place to worship, to learn, to commemorate, mourn, and celebrate.

The effect of B'nai Jeshurun on the uninitiated is profound. One day, a prosperous-looking man in his forties sitting next to me turns to his companion, a member of the congregation, and says, "I am overwhelmed. I was brought up Orthodox, and I haven't seen anything like this." He straightens his posture, throws back his shoulders, shakes his head. "I haven't seen anything like this."

On another day, I noticed a woman and her daughter, guests at a bar mitzvah and clearly not Jewish, sitting in front of me. As I was

standing during the parading of the Torah through the sanctuary, I
saw tears running down the woman's face. After the service, I walked
up to her and told her I couldn't help notice her reaction, and was
very interested in knowing, if she could tell me, why she had been so
moved by the service. She started right away to tear up again, and she
said, "I can't tell you. I'm not Jewish, but I found the weight of tradition so terribly strong in here."

Once, during the summer, I was standing in the back of the sanctuary and observed a couple in their sixties, dressed in tourist clothing, walking out after having dropped in for a few minutes. The
man was beaming, and he asked me several questions about the congregation.

"You know," he said to me, "the Reform movement just killed
Judaism. There was nothing left of it when they were through. But
this is amazing. Look at all the people sitting here on a beautiful day
in the summer. They have all chosen to be here—not outside, or
elsewhere, but right here, under prayer shawls and yarmulkes, men
and women, side by side. I feel so moved," he said.

Every service, we tighten the weave of the fabric we are making.
We celebrate births, deaths, marriages. We stand and remember the
dead and recite the ancient Kaddish prayer, which says nothing
about mourning, but rather praises God. What a beautiful way to
honor the memory of someone we love, I think, to reaffirm our faith.
We offer special prayers for the sick, and the sick among us recite
prayers for themselves before the open Torah scroll. Here, at our
best, we are all family, and there are no social divisions. When a family of mourners is led back into the synagogue by a special escort following the shivah period, we all take note, and we grieve for them.
The established ritual tells us what we should do to relieve others.
We look around to see who stands to recite the Kaddish prayer and
we remind ourselves to offer them a kind word. The religion is a

great leveler. We are just Jews here. We celebrate and mourn the same way. We all depend on each other for support. When Yitzhak Rabin was assassinated by a Jew, this was the place we came to grieve and rage together. This is where we do not have to explain as much.

MUSIC, AS I LEARNED from Rabbi Fried, occupies a central place in Jewish life and worship. The Chassidim in fact believe that the world is itself a song. "The realm of heaven sings; the Throne of God breathes music; even the tetragrammaton YHVH is composed of four musical notes."

Singing has its own particular sweetness for me. Although I have a deep speaking voice, my singing voice is mysteriously high, and hearing elevated, clear sounds emerge from my throat is like gaining access to secret rooms in a well-known house. Music and the memories it stirred played a role in every step of my path back to Yiddishkeit, from my first visit to Beth Emunah, to the recollections of childhood visits to synagogue services with my father that were stimulated by Dr. Andresen's talk of a string quartet.

So, I am thrilled in the summer of 1995 when I am asked to join the B'nai Jeshurun choir. Preparations for the next High Holiday services deepen by a hundredfold my understanding of the liturgy and my connection with the service.

The longest piece of the two dozen or so we learn is called "Unetane Tokef." Though we don't have time during rehearsals to probe the meaning of the piece, I have the feeling it is central to the service, and I try to learn as much as I can about it myself. First, I find out that the title means, simply, "You give us."

The song appears in a section called Musaf, literally, "additional." I pull out some books and read that Musaf is an extra Amidah prayer that is recited on Shabbat and on holidays after the Torah service. The Musaf Amidah differs from the regular Amidah in that it makes specific reference to the former Temple sacrifices. On Rosh Hashanah, it is different still, emphasizing God's role as a judge who is "compassionate and merciful."

I see from the order of the service that "Unetane Tokef" is sung right after the Musaf Amidah and just before the Kedushah. Because every detail of the liturgy is soaked in religious and historical significance, I imagine that its proximity to the mention of sacrifices is significant, as well as its emphasis on God as a merciful judge. The Kedushah following the Musaf Amidah, I read, includes the first verse and last few words of the Shemah, additions made in the fifth century of the common era, after the Persians prohibited Jews from reciting the Shemah in their services. The Persian government inspectors, sent to the synagogue to enforce the ban, routinely left after the recitation of the Amidah, convinced that the Shemah had been skipped, so the pieces of the Shemah that had been woven into the following prayer remained unnoticed. The altered prayer has been retained since then as a reminder of those persecutions.

I am puzzled by the references to sacrifice and defiance here on the occasion of Rosh Hoshanah, and wonder what they herald. One day, during choir rehearsal, Rabbi Matalon and Rabbi Marcelo Bronstein, also a former student of Marshall Meyer's in Argentina, who has just arrived to join Rabbi Matalon in the B'nai Jeshurun pulpit, enter the sanctuary. Rabbi Matalon asks the choir if we know the story behind the "Unetane Tokef." Most of us shake our heads no. He tells us that in his mind the prayer sums up all of the themes and agonies of the High Holiday service. He tells us that the prayer appears in Or Zaru'ah, a thirteenth-century text, and recounts an episode in the life of Rabbi Ammon of Mainz, who is asked by the local archbishop to convert to Christianity. The rabbi, who has been bothered by the local lords and clergy for a long time on this question, asks for three days to consider the question. He hopes the request will put them off. However, when he gets home, he is overwhelmed by the realization that his tactic of delay could be interpreted to suggest that an expression of doubt had passed from his lips. He becomes terribly distraught and fails to return to the archbishop with his answer. Upon being approached again by the church authorities, Amnon proposes his own punishment: cutting out his tongue. The archbishop demurs, saying it is not his tongue that is guilty, but his feet, by not returning to answer in time. And so, he informs Amnon of the punishment: he will have his feet cut off.

But first, Amnon is tortured, his fingers chopped off one by one, as he is repeatedly asked if he will convert. He refuses. After his mutilation, Amnon is placed on a shield and sent home. The Days of Awe are approaching, and Rabbi Amnon makes a final wish: that his relatives bear him to the synagogue, where he wants to sanctify the name of God before the Kedushah. He passes on as soon as he utters the last word of his prayer.

Three days later, Rabbi Amnon appeared in the dream of another rabbi, Kalonymus ben Meshullam, to whom he repeated his poem. And so it was recorded and handed down through the generations in the form of this prayer and song.

When I return home, I look back over the music and try to understand how it fits with that terrible story. The song is at once mournful and energetic, intimate yet with grand choral effects. It is written in A minor and contains flourishes and ornaments that conjure images of worlds from Spain through Jerusalem. The opening section contains two recitative sections sung by Amnon—and now, the chazzan. The notes indicate a free rhythm, something like speech. It is followed by another, shorter section, with the same basic outline of notes, except it is embellished, with a more active rhythm, as if the singer is getting more agitated, worked up.

I turn the page and see the meter changes to 4/4. The chazzan sings four systems alone, with the chorus entering to repeat and embellish the last words of each, making up an ancient song pattern, I discover, recorded by Rabbi Akiba in the Temple of the first century. "The great shofar is sounded," sings the chazzan, which the chorus answers with a ringing declaration: "Great!" I see that the Musaf Amidah is punctuated by the blowing of the shofar after each of the three middle blessings, just as in "Unetane Tokef" the chazzan's words are punctuated by their repetition by the chorus.

Then, the meter changes again, to 6/8, introducing some uncertainty, some hesitation. The musical notation indicates this line must be sung quietly. The words are "and a still small voice is heard." The music is becoming more dramatic, more complex, and the words are a reference to I Kings, when Elijah climbs up Mount Horeb to hear the words of God and says: "And behold, the Lord passed by, and a great and strong wind rent the mountains, and broke in pieces the rocks before the Lord, but the Lord was not in the wind; and after the wind, an earthquake, but the Lord was not in the earthquake, and after the earthquake there was a fire, but the Lord was not in the fire; and after the fire a still, small voice."

How complex and frightening is this passage, saturated as it is with the power of the unspoken. The chorus joins the chazzan for the first time in the next section. The words read, "The angelic hosts, seized with fear and trembling, declare." Then suddenly, a solo instrumental part interrupts, and it is answered verbatim by the chazzan. It's a true answer, an echo, emphasizing its importance. The line reads, "Behold it is the Day of Judgment." A melodic section follows. Now the chorus is functioning differently. The bass is operating like an organ point at the bottom, emphasizing the point, and the alto and soprano have melodies that are very close in range, and for the first time in the piece, in dotted rhythm, creating a sense of heightened emotion or agitation.

An instrumental passage follows that introduces, through accidentals—A-sharps in this case—a different key, and it does so by the use of augmented seconds. The passage has an exotic quality that suggests a Middle Eastern bazaar. The chazzan sings, "And, as a shepherd causes the flock to pass under a staff." The chorus, now divided into a traditional Baroque-style four-part harmony, repeats the line, the sopranos reaching up higher and the basses lower than before.

The chazzan finishes the sentence in a variation of the opening melody that creates the effect of vacillation or movement. "You will bring everything that lives before You for review, determining the life and decreeing the destiny of all." The passage ends with a formal, four-part harmony that the sopranos conclude with a shining high repetition of the word "destiny." I can imagine Amnon, torn between the knowledge of his own faith and the guilt of his hesitation, hoping that God will see him fairly.

A refrain then repeats: "On Rosh Hashanah it is written. And on Yom Kippur it is sealed." The refrain is interspersed with additional verses sung by the chazzan, lines that carry us back into Jewish history: "How many shall pass away and how many shall be born, who shall live and who shall die, who shall live out their years and who shall not, who shall perish by fire and who by water, who by sword and who by beast, who by hunger and who by thirst, who by earthquake and who by plague, who by strangling and who by stoning, who shall rest and who shall wander, who shall be at peace and who shall be tormented, who shall be poor and who rich, who shall be humbled and who exalted."

The section concludes with a rousing passage in which the chazzan and the chorus join together. The sopranos reach their highest, the inner voices are more active, creating the feeling of an anthem. It introduces the central message of the piece: "But penitence, prayer, and good deeds can annul the severity of the decree."

The prayer ends with the chazzan singing one last passage of declamation, a poignant, graceful statement derived from the thirteen attributes of God. Rabbi Amnon is true to his God, yet even as he declares his faith, he knows he has erred with his hesitation, making his torture more poignant and his thoughts about destiny more fraught. I feel I now understand the significance of the references to sacrifices in the Temple, and the appropriateness of Rabbi Amnon's choice to sing before the special Kedushah that recollects the persecution of the Jews by the Persians. Rabbi Amnon offers an affirmation of God's power and truth as he confronts the painful facts of his own hesitation and sacrifice. Although the prayer insists that God knows everything, even what we have forgotten, the climax of the prayer is in the soaring declaration "But penitence, prayer, and good deeds can annul the severity of the decree." Although God sees all, His judgment can be softened if we examine ourselves and our actions with honor and scrupulousness and perform the deeds that make up the center of Judaism, honest atonement, meaningful prayer, and dedication to justice and good deeds: teshuvah, tefillah, and tzedakah. It is a startlingly simple entreaty, the bedrock truth that shines behind the bombast: God asks us simply to turn to Him.

ARI PRIVEN'S RENDERING of the piece is mesmerizing, so elevated in feeling, so rich in implication, one can close one's eyes and imagine Priven as Rabbi Amnon himself atop the shield upon which he was borne into the Temple by his disciples. Helping the chazzan and the rabbis lead this service as part of the choir has placed me in a line of descent, connecting me with forebears I never knew, who were also singers in the synagogue. It seems almost impossible that four years ago I had not known the first thing about a synagogue service, not known more than two Jewish songs, had been unaware that I was descended from a long line of cantors.

It seems a true fulfillment of years of accumulated desire and silent longing to be connected with a system, a world, a family of learning whose accumulated knowledge and wisdom beckons to me. The purpose of humans on earth is to connect the physical with the heavenly. It is the unique work of humans, something that no other creatures, heavenly or earthbound, can accomplish. We do so by sanctifying the ordinary and making it holy. We do so by elevating the basic acts of eating, or awakening, into revelations of the divine by blessing them, making them holy: by taking note of our own gratitude.

In singing in the choir, in using my voice to communicate the heavenly sounds of the prayers, I feel the extraordinary satisfaction of fulfilling a purpose, no matter how fleeting. I have a feeling of a great, calm sureness of knowing I have done something right.

A FEW DAYS BEFORE YOM KIPPUR, Rabbi Matalon calls to ask me if I would like to give a D'var Torah during the afternoon service. He says I can speak about anything I like—personal reflection, a commentary—but the speech would precede the reading of the book of Jonah. I tell him I am very grateful to be asked, and I hope I will be worthy of the task.

All I know about Jonah is that he was swallowed by a big fish.

I call my Orthodox friend Ruchama. She suggests I look over the sefer and see what interests me about it. She mentions a few thoughts that came to her mind right away. Isn't the idea of repentance troublesome, she asks me. You do something wrong, you should pay for it, right? How does one explain the concept of mercy, of getting out, as it were, of your rightful punishment?

She also mentions that at one point in the story Jonah becomes furious and yells at God, criticizing him for his attributes—kind, slow to anger. Is this, Ruchama asks, supposed to be funny?

I walk over that afternoon to West Side Judaica, a wonderful store filled to the rafters with books and religious articles. It is run by a family of Chassidic Jews who belong to the Sanz dynasty, originally from Poland. Carla is known far and wide as the book expert; and she can be counted on to know just about any title of a Jewish nature both in and out of print. More astonishing, she knows in exactly which of the store's myriad piles it can be found.

The book of Jonah is not hard to find. Neither is what I want to write about. When I climb to the podium before 2,000 people three days later, I am not the slightest bit nervous. I can't wait to speak. The title of my speech is: "Jonah and the Whale: 'Return to Me and I'll Return to You.'"

"Yom Kippur. The Day of Atonement," I begin.

"Every Jew learns this phrase as a child, and repeats it over and over until it becomes a metaword—so important, yet so often said, that its meaning disappears within it. But what is atonement? For what should I atone? When do I know when I am finished?

"During these Yamim Noraim, these Days of Awe, I have learned different words for this holy time, more subtle words that provide a richer opening to understanding. But the same question remains, and must remain: what does God want of me?

"This year, I looked for clues in the book of Jonah. It is read in its entirety every year on this day, and is clearly a story about repentance and mercy. But it too has been obscured by familiarity. We read that Yonah is a prophet who is dispatched by God to warn the citizens of the Assyrian city of Ninevah to repent of their evil ways or be destroyed. But Yonah does not want to carry out his mission, and attempts to flee from God's sight by escaping to sea. When a storm threatens to capsize the boat on which Yonah has caught a ride, his shipmates realize Yonah is the cause. They toss him overboard and the storm subsides immediately. Yonah himself is saved from death by the fortuitous arrival of a great fish, who swallows him.

"After three days and nights suffering in the fish's belly, Yonah repents and tells God he will indeed fulfill his mission. The fish then spits him up on dry land, and Yonah reluctantly performs his duties. In fact, he does his job so well, and the Ninevites repent so thoroughly, that God spares them. This throws Yonah into a deep despair and he rails against God for displaying his mercy.

"As I studied commentaries and sources, I realized this was quite a complicated tale, clearly about rebirth and redemption, but resistant to easy interpretation. I felt that one key to the story could be found in a conflict within Yonah's character. Once I had probed that split, I not only better understood the story, but I was led directly into the center of the idea of teshuvah itself—and there, to hints about the answer to my own question: what is Yom Kippur?

"Yonah is identified as Yonah ben Amitai, son of Amitai. The root of the Hebrew word 'amitai' is 'emet'—truth. Yonah is the son of truth, or man of truth. As a child, Yonah was saved from death by Elijah the Prophet, and it is written in the Talmud that Elijah was sent to Tzorfas just to raise Yonah from the dead. The boy Yonah had a purpose: he lived as proof that Elijah was the prophet of truth, and that the word of God was truth.

"Truth seems to be an important element in Yonah's life, yet he seems to have an ambivalent relationship with it. After the Ninevites repent and God spares them, Yonah berates God for His mercy: 'I knew that you are a gracious and compassionate God, slow to anger, abounding in kindness, and relentful of punishment,' he says. The scene is odd, almost comic. Yonah rails at God's goodness, and the words he chooses bring to mind the Thirteen Attributes that Hashem revealed to Moshe in Exodus: 'Hashem, Hashem, compassionate and gracious, slow to anger, abounding in kindness and truth, storing up mercy for thousands of generations . . .' The two descriptions are almost the same, except Yonah forgets to mention Hashem's central midah, or attribute: emet—truth.

"Yonah, the son of Amitai, the man of truth, has trouble with the truth. What else do we know about him? His first name, Yonah, means 'dove'—the universal symbol of peace, shalom—the bird sent off by Noah to find firm land. Yonah was born to reveal the truth, yet he is named for peace. The sages tell us that shalom and emet are not only opposing midot in Yonah, but form a central conflict in the soul of every Jew: what is our responsibility: to stand up and speak the truth as we see it, or hold our tongue for the sake of peace? There is a saying that only in the future, 'Emet v'shalom noshoku'—'Truth and peace will meet (or kiss).'

"A central question of the story is this: why did Yonah refuse to deliver the prophecy? It is said he knew the Ninevites would repent, and he was afraid for Israel, afraid that Israel's own sins and obduracy would then be starkly revealed. It is written, 'He loved Israel too much.' Though faced with the truth—God's order to deliver the prophecy and the Ninevites' sinful ways—Yonah was pulled by his desire for peace, that Israel remain unmolested.

"Yonah's conflict over truth leads us to the heart of teshuvah. For isn't there something untruthful about the idea of repentance? Once a person sins—in theory, that should be the end of it. He or she is guilty, has betrayed him- or herself and God. How can one undo a sin with words? Repentance defies the logic of Prophecy, Wisdom, and Torah. But Hashem insisted that repentance be a part of the world. It is written, 'Seven things were created before the universe,' and they include Torah and repentance. The sages explain that without repentance, creation could not endure.

"Teshuvah is an exception, a tremendous act of chesed, or loving kindness, on Hashem's part. It reflects God's personal relation to humans and God's desire that we be recharged every year with the possibility of bettering ourselves, the chance to reach for purity of heart and mind.

"We all share Yonah's conflict between peace and truth when we ask ourselves: what does God want of me? Wouldn't it be better not to look toward God, better to avoid a painful self-examination, better to turn away from truth to maintain the illusion of internal peace? We may think so, but then we have missed the meaning of teshuvah, which means literally 'to turn toward God,' to be in God's presence. One does not turn toward something he or she fears. To turn toward is a gesture of love. To turn toward God is to be granted the privilege of seeing our potential, our perfectibility. When we turn away, God calls us back. God beseeches us, as God beseeched Adam and Chava in Gan Eden, after they turned away in fear. 'Where are you?' God asked, 'Aiekah?'

"On Yom Kippur, God offers us a unique gift—the opportunity to return to God the gifts we possess—strength, intelligence, mercy, kindness—and recommit them for a higher purpose. In preparation, we, like Yonah, must battle with ourselves, perhaps battle with our deepest conflicts. But what is important to keep in mind is that Hashem wants to see us, whatever our progress along the path. We are told that on Yom Kippur a sincere effort is greatly rewarded: Says Hashem, 'Shuvoo elai veashuvah aleichem amar Adonai—Return to Me and I shall return to you.'"

ONE SATURDAY in March of 1996, as we begin the Torah reading, I realize we are reading the same Parashah (Torah portion) as we did when I first stepped into B'nai Jeshurun two years ago. I think how much has changed. Today there are two rabbis, and during our discussion of the Torah text, Rabbis Matalon and Bronstein debate with each other, rather than Rabbi Matalon discussing the portion with congregants holding hand microphones. It is also a different experience for me: when I first came here, I slipped in and out of the synagogue week after week, unknown, no one saying anything to me or greeting me. Now I feel I am a member. I am known. I have become part of the fabric.

I see from the Kol Jeshurun that there will be a bar mitzvah today. And I am surprised to see that the mother of the bar mitzvah boy is Kate Wenner, the sister of Jann Wenner, publisher of *Rolling Stone* magazine. Kate Wenner gave me my start in journalism. During a year off from college in 1980, I walked into her office at *Rolling Stone*, where she was editing a magazine called *College Papers* that later became a yearly insert in *Rolling Stone*. She asked me to write a piece about "What I learned during my year off," and she directed me to work with a young man named Adam Moss, now editor of the *New York Times Magazine*. He was very encouraging to me, and leaving his office, I thought, maybe, maybe, I could be a writer! It was the most unlikely eventuality I could have conceived, but it was my dream.

I think back to what I wanted to say in that essay for Kate Wenner.

My goal was to explain that I was trying not to control my world, endeavoring not to clear too narrow a path between point A and point B, so that I had a chance of experiencing the unexpected. I wanted to let life happen to me and in so doing find out who I was. It occurs to me I was trying to shake the fears with which I had grown up, and see the world for myself. In many ways, I have followed the journey I was attempting to map out for Kate Wenner. I wanted to move through the world in a new way, hear it in a new way, feel it in a different way. I wanted to grow up. Thank God for me, that journey, in its very roundabout way, led me back to a tradition that seeks perfection: not a static ideal state, but an ever-changing one, one that inspires deeper understanding, greater feeling, greater wisdom.

I look around the congregation, and suddenly I realize that Jann Wenner is sitting a few rows away from me, his arm around his wife, and his youngest son is climbing over them both. The first piece I wrote for a national magazine was a cover story for *Rolling Stone*, and Wenner has long been a symbol for me, first, of my dream of becoming a writer, and then of my first success. How strange it is that on this day, the anniversary of my first Shabbat service here, I should see not only the woman who gave me my first chance, but also the man in whose magazine I enjoyed my first success. It has been a long, unexpected journey home, and had I not taken a detour to the Southwest, I might never even have made it back. I might never have been able to recognize home when I got here.

Kate Wenner and her husband place the tallit over their son's shoulders, and Kate tells him that the tallit belonged to his grandfather, whose first Yartzheit took place only a week earlier. "The tallit offers you roots. It attaches you to your roots, and to a place. And through the roots, you get nourishment. 'Etz Chaim He'—Torah is a tree of life for all who seek it." She describes her father then as a kind man, dedicated to his Jewishness. "When you wear this," she says, her voice quavering, "may you feel the arms of your grandfather around you."

And I see again how much Judaism values the embrace of our forebears, particularly the faithful ones, many of whom burned with the hope that their descendants would revere the tradition that had defined their own lives. It occurs to me that that embrace is made so much more solid when the values of those ancestors are clear, their desire freed. And even if aspects of our inheritance are lost in any particular family by circumstances or choice, there remains for all Jews a guide. And it is the Torah, the book of all books. It is not a human being, and never dies. Even if we never find a congregation that exactly fits our needs, or a rabbi who is perfectly understanding or available the moment we think we need him or her, we all have the Book. It stimulates, confuses perhaps, maddens, and soothes. But it is there always, like a good foundation, to hold us together and help us learn who we are.

"Where is God?" the Kotzker rebbe asked.

And he answered: "Wherever you let Him in."

I don't know if Jake felt the arms of his grandfather around him on that day. But I felt arms around me. When it is time to put the Torah away, when we sing "Etz Chaim He," the heavy-hearted farewell, this time, my throat does not tighten, I do not feel the tears rise. Rather, I sing a high, soaring harmony, which lifts the sad tune to a note of exhilarating anticipation. Good does return, of that I am now sure.

Chapter Ten

❧

IF NOT NOW, WHEN?

"I LIKE YOU AND I LIKE TO TALK TO YOU," Rabbi Berman says to me on the telephone one warm spring evening. "But the truth is, at some point, I want to engage the entire person, no holds barred. And I got signals from you that you did not want to be pushed, deeply questioned about your beliefs in the basic truths."

It is April 1997. Since my return to New York, I have studied with Rabbi Berman for two years, taken a yearlong class on the Parashah of the week from Rabbi Ben Cherney and taken classes with Rabbi Meir Fund on subjects ranging from the works of Rabbi Moshe Chaim Luzzatto, a medieval Kabbalist, to the Talmud. For a year, I learned with Ruchama Feuerman, who, along with her husband Yis-roel, has become a great friend. Over those four years, I also availed myself of the great number of lectures and teachings offered by rabbis and scholars in the Jewish community in New York. For a year, I was studying four nights a week, all with Orthodox teachers.

Yet, still, I continue to worship at B'nai Jeshurun. I do not keep kosher, nor do I observe the Sabbath as the Bermans do. Over the last six months or so, I feel that Rabbi Berman has distanced himself from me. We no longer speak as much on the telephone, and although I know he is troubled by a pinched nerve in his neck and concerned about his responsibilities at home, I feel it may be more, and finally, I ask him about it.

"You are still interested in watching, like a tourist, in observing the life, appreciating its poetry, the learning," he says, hesitantly at first. "You are happy to have an ethnic attachment. But I sense you are not encouraging me to engage you in debates that get right to the very bottom of your questions."

"Rabbi Zalman Schacter-Shalomi once asked," I reply, not entirely surprised by what he is saying, "'Does God really care whether or not I tear a piece of toilet paper on Shabbat?' The truth is, it is hard for me to believe that He does."

"I think this question gets to the very heart of Yiddishkeit," says Rabbi Berman. "How does he know the details don't count? In science, we can measure the minutest changes in levels of hormones. In matters of spirituality, we are not prepared to believe that details count. These days, the search is not perceived as a search for God's will, rather it is a search for self-improvement or gratification. Man remains firmly planted within himself. Gan Eden then becomes a worldly idea. But what is missed is the idea of a process that turns a person from a mortal into an immortal. It is a very subtle process, a transformation of the spirit.

"Torah says Judaism is morashah, an inheritance for all," he continues. "Then some rabbis said, making a play on the word, it is a m'orassah—the betrothed. Judaism is like a woman, you don't understand her until you've lived with her for a while. The rabbis then say 'If there is a betrothal, then the inheritance is possible.'"

"Must one have faith before committing?" I ask.

"I don't believe you have to have faith before moving forward. You can suspend belief if you're prepared to suspend disbelief. Listen to it in its own voice, and when the journey's over, tell me what you heard."

"I am still listening. But you are saying you want me to make a decision that will radically change my life."

"The question is," he continues with great energy, "if it's all true, are you prepared to live this way? If not, then there may be no reason to continue the journey. I asked you about eight months ago: What does your Conservative rabbi really believe? You said he commented about a bar mitzvah girl that it was a shame she didn't keep kosher. How about everything else in the Torah? How about a Cohein marrying a grushah? How about driving to shul on Shabbos? How about using the mikveh, which ninety-nine percent of Conservative Jews know nothing about. What are his beliefs? What are the consequences of his beliefs? What are the logical implications of his beliefs?"

I reply that I would find it awkward to ask him these questions point-blank.

"I couldn't worship the way you do," says Rabbi Berman. "I couldn't. I'm not made up that way. The problem is, you don't tap into the critical thinking part of your personality when it comes to Judaism."

I disagree, but I don't say so to him. Rather, I say I feel that if presented with an all-or-nothing choice, become Orthodox or leave the premises, I am afraid I will lose my tie with him and the other Orthodox whose company and teaching I value highly.

"And I'm afraid of other things should I decide in the other direction."

"What other things?" asks Rabbi Berman.

"Estrangement from family and separation from the world that I know."

"Yeah. But the fact that you have this comfortable other place to go to, the fact you can go in there and have an aliyah, sing in the choir, tell stories, gives you an out. You can go there and be comfortable not asking the questions," he says. "But what does it all add up to? Is there an afterlife or isn't there an afterlife? Is there reward and punishment or isn't there reward and punishment? Is there something called the soul and what happens to the soul? These are basic, basic beliefs in Judaism."

"Even before I try to answer those questions," I say, "there's still so much to learn—there's Chumash, there's ritual. I still feel like I know only the tiniest part of it."

"That's true," he says. "I'm not arguing with that. I'm not trying to accelerate your process. I was just commenting on the overall issues."

What I do not tell him is that the questions he asks don't really concern me. I don't need to know their answers right now. I do not believe in God because I believe in an afterlife. I do not believe in God because of the reward I may earn. I believe in God because of a series of ineffable experiences I had in Dallas.

In fact, I think the answers to Rabbi Berman's questions are unknowable, and should I gain some insight into them—the questions, not the answers—over my lifetime, I would feel gratified. I do not expect answers, don't need them as he does. At least not now.

Rabbi Fund, an exhilarating teacher with whom I studied for three years and at whose home I celebrated a most astounding Passover, a veritable tour through Judaism and over five millennia, gives me a similar lecture. I am not insulted or hurt. I knew this day would also come. In spite of my differences with both rabbis, I find the life of the Orthodox that they exemplify to be both elegant and inspiring.

Am I sacrificing an afterlife if I do not follow the commandments? I won't know that until I am dead. Having had the experience of the dream of a trip through my brain, the dream that Dr. Andresen likened to a near-death experience, it is impossible for me to perceive death as judgment. It seems much more likely to me to be something like absorption into the vast energy of the universe.

The truth is, I tell Rabbi Berman, were I a man, I might just make the jump into Orthodoxy. But the role of women, which is defined and enforced by social pressure, is insupportable for me, even though secular life offers women its own rough ride. I am moved by modesty, but such virtues can be expressed in the way one solves intellectual problems or in the way one runs one's life in the world, not only by covering the head and body, which has other more unpleasant implications.

"The woman's world requires incredible binah, or understanding" Rabbi Berman says. "Almost a dialectical capacity to hold two opposing ideas together in mind at the same time, and then to harmonize them. Should not women be equal to men? Yes. Are they equal in Yiddishkeit? No. It's not easy. Only through acute and subtle understanding can you see how both can be true at the same time.

"If you look at all the things that women did over the centuries," he continues, "they're trivial. They're menial and trivial. You could hire someone to wash the dishes, do the laundry, you could hire someone to cook, nannies to take care of the babies, at least on a certain level. So much of what takes up a woman's time is menial and what kind of a position is that? What kind of people end up as hospital orderlies, you know what I mean? It's not the most honorable, dignified role to be in.

"If it's expressed through the guf," he says, "the body, it's going to be one reality. If it's through the neshomah, the soul, it's going to be another reality, diametrically opposed realities. I want to make this point a little more clearly because I consider it a very important one.

"The Alter of Kelm," he says, "in explicating a portion of the Gemorrah, says the best of doctors will not escape from going to Gehennah, or hell. There have been all kinds of explanations why the rabbi has said that. Is it because they're arrogant? Because they don't ask questions?

"He had a tremendous insight," says Rabbi Berman. "He said the doctor is caught up in the contradiction between what he does and the spirit of what he does. What does a doctor do? He has to hurt, to inflict pain. So he has to desensitize himself, distance himself. It's natural to do that. So what happens? The sforim explain that there's chomer and there's tzurah—the act and the essence of the act.

"If the doctors are spiritually developed enough to go beyond their senses," he explains, "beyond the guf, the physical, limited reality of what they're doing, they are promoting a living, caring, development of their personalities. Because they're relating to the tzurah rather than the chomer."

Rabbi Berman continues with thoughts on the holy act of serving. "There's a story in the Gemorrah about how Rabbi Gamliel, the leader of the supreme court, the leader of the generation, was going around serving people at the table. So somebody said to him, 'How can you do that? You're the leader of the generations. This is not befitting of you to do this.'

"And he said, 'Am I any better than Avram Avinu who ran to the Arabs and served them?'

"So another rabbi said, why go to Avram Avinu, why not go to

Hashem—doesn't He make the rain fall and the earth give forth its fruits? He's also taking care of us—that's what God does. So, when you're serving, what you're doing is godly.

"Again, if we look at it only through the guf, then it loses its meaning and as a result it's repudiated. And that's a problem society has. There are things in life where the chomer and tzurah line up naturally, and there are things where they are literally at different ends of the spectrum. And it takes a certain amount of spiritual sophistication to know the difference. And society has to have this kind of sensitivity to foster these kinds of values. I'm not saying it's majestic to be a servant. I'm saying it's majestic to be noble, to be a king, a queen, a prince."

He goes on: "I think that our society's difficulties in knowing the difference is one of the things that feminists are reacting against. I'm not blaming the women. I think if anything, it's a male problem. It's also a cultural problem that serving became associated with menial labor."

At this point I interrupt. "I understand what you are saying, and it's moving and puts the idea of service in a whole new light. But what about the fact that housework is mostly drudgery that's physically tiring and repetitive and nerve-fraying?"

"And it's different when you're a lawyer or a doctor?" he asks.

I smile and acknowledge he probably has a point. Except of course, the woman who is a doctor or a lawyer has power, money, prestige, and the experience of acting in the world, with all the associated satisfactions as well as frustrations that entails.

"If the person feels that in running a home," he explains, "they are shaping lives, shaping society, then they're emulating Hashem in this act. That perspective makes it seem very much different from that of a maid.

"My mother raised twelve kids, and how many thousands of diapers did she do?" he asks.

"But there's no question about it—as strange as it sounds, and I don't want to resort to clichés or stupid, simplistic ideas, but at the end of the day, there's something ennobling and something highly creative about what she did."

Privately, I maintain my doubts.

MALKA BERMAN is back from Israel. She is much more talkative than she was a few years ago and seems to have a newfound confidence. One Shabbat afternoon, I sit with her in her father's study, and as the children play in the backyard and most of the adults catch some sleep, she begins to talk, and the words pour out of her at breakneck speed. She wants to tell me all that she has learned during her studies in Israel, and she speaks fast and often in partial sentences. For the most part, I nod and make encouraging noises, and she continues. In time, I understand the shape of her thoughts, though not all the specifics.

But then she surprises me. "I realize that I am not made primarily for Torah study," she says to me. "Not like a man. The strongest impulse in me is to help other people, and I would like to become a psychologist." At nineteen, she already has earned from the seminary the equivalent of a B.A. degree. She tells me she could now either get a masters in social work and become a licensed counselor, or she could get a Ph.D. in psychology.

"If I were going to care for people's souls and minds," I say, "I'd want to be as educated as possible."

"But I'm not sure how much I'll learn studying psychology," she says. "I believe the most psychology I know is actually what I understand instinctively and what I know from Torah."

"Education is never a waste," I say. "Learning is not a handicap."

"A hundred percent," she says.

But then she lets me know there are a few other things on her mind. She is at the prime marriageable age, and people around her are already beginning the complicated negotiations that are part of matchmaking. Her parents are sending out queries about certain boys, and boys are looking at certain girls. The general rule is that the top yeshivah boys are the most desired. Malka says her parents have their eyes on one boy whose representative said he was getting fifty calls a week and it looked like he was hoping for full support for three years.

I am puzzled. What does full support mean? Malka tells me it means that the boy wants to continue to learn in yeshivah for another three years without working, so either the girl has to work or her parents have to help out—or both.

"If I got a teaching job," she says, "I could earn a good part of what we'd need, and my father said he'd help out with the rest."

"But what about your plans to go to school?" I ask. "And your desire to become a psychologist?"

"Well, I can go back to school later, possibly," she says.

"And babies?" I ask. "Can you put them off for a couple of years? You already have a great advantage, having your B.A. at nineteen. Three or four years and you'd have your Ph.D., and you'd only be twenty-three, time for plenty of babies."

"It's not done. Birth control isn't used."

As I hear her, I am filled with all the modern-world arguments about how this system thwarts women's ambition. Malka has explained to me that she really doesn't have a chance to go to school, that she, like most of the women in her community, will get a low-paying job, support her husband for three years, have two babies, and then, just as she is about to give birth to her third, he will get a job and begin to support them. By then, her hopes of school will probably have disappeared.

"There are more good girls than good boys," she says. "And the boys are easy to spot. They graduate at the tops of the yeshivahs. The girls are harder to see. You have to look more closely at their characters, their personalities." She can't afford to put off marriage, or she may lose out on the best boys.

Although I feel disappointed for her, I can't say a word. Her parents supported her desire to continue her studies, but, in the end, she chose not to enter a secular Ph.D. program and to limit her contact with the outside world. She made this decision herself, with the advice of rabbis. She wants to take her place in the system in which she was raised and that informs her every thought. She knows it involves sacrifices, but it also may bring the highest rewards. Not only is she choosing a meaningful life, but she believes she is doing no less than participating in the redemption of the world.

I admire Malka's devotion, and appreciate the great and constant effort she exerts in her life to understand her proper place. I hope the jewels of a religious life offer her charms far richer than those available in the world she turns away from. She is a bright young woman who, had she been a boy, would likely have been a rabbi. But I am not in a position to know the sum of what she has gained for what she has given up.

Of course, neither is she.

"I REMEMBER ONCE when I was living in Israel," Ruchama Feuerman, says, her speech coming fast, as it does when she is excited by an idea. "I went to Shabbos at the home of a family in Meah Shearim, a very traditional religious area of Jerusalem. They had many daughters, and I remember everyone sat down, from the wife to the youngest daughter, and the husband stood up and he served everything. He served the cholent, he served the salad. It was very regal, it was very sexy the way he did it. It was just amazing. He made it seem like the most male thing to do in the world. I'll never forget that."

This story reminds me of something Rabbi Berman once told me. He said he was talking to some of his yeshivah bochers about masculinity. Most of the young men felt masculinity definitely had something to do with *Rocky* or the Marlboro Man.

"I told them about an episode that I witnessed when I was a child, eleven or twelve years old," says Rabbi Berman. "We were delivering mishloach manos, Purim packages, for Rav Moshe Feinstein, and I was with a friend of mine. The rabbi's wife gave us the mishloach manos, and we would go out with them over the Lower East Side; and she'd give us a quarter, a lot of money in those days. And at one point, we were waiting around to get more mishloach manos, and Reb Moshe comes over to us and he sits us down at the table and cuts a big piece of cake for us and puts it on a plate and ten minutes later comes by to help us say the after-blessing, and it made an indelible impression on me. Here is the person, mamash, the light of the generation, who's taking time to make sure we can say a blessing over the cake. To me, that's an indication of Jewish masculinity. There's something big enough, rich enough, developed enough, strong enough that a person like that can be preoccupied with someone else."

I tell this story to Ruchama, and she makes a long exhalation.

"You know," she says, her eyes getting bright, "there is one image I have of Yisroel that I think of whenever I am aggravated with him, because whenever I think of it, I fall in love with him all over again." She explains that the night before her son's brit milah, or circumcision, a few young neighborhood children came over to recite the Shemah as part of Leil Shimurim, or "Night of Guarding," a vigil to ward off any evil that may interfere with the upcoming ceremony. After the children say the prayer, they are given sweets or a little cake. "So, the children came over," says Ruchama, "and they did their thing and Yisroel took them into the other room and gave them cake and explained how to make the blessing. And he was speaking to them as if they were adults. He was taking them very seriously. And they were transported at the way they were being treated like grown-ups. And my love for Yisroel just swelled when I saw that."

I nod, smiling at the similarity of these tales, the masculinity expressed in kindness, the empathic identification with the children, the devotion to a system larger than ourselves.

I AM A GROWN WOMAN, with a fully developed personality, experience in the world, and a few accomplishments of which I am proud. Yet I am hesitant about making certain commitments to Yiddishkeit that at some level I would like to make. I wonder, why am I so concerned about losing myself in Judaism?

Yisroel Feuerman comes from a religious family that can trace its roots back to the Ba'al Shem Tov and whose members include illustrious rabbis and educators. He and Ruchama live a thoroughly Torah-observant life, but they read widely and are engaged in the world. They do not exclude foreign ideas from their house, nor from their interior quests. Ruchama writes fiction and Yisroel was trained as a psychoanalyst. Their lives seem heavily weighted by arcane religious obligations, but their inner lives are rich. I believe they are enlivened by a never-ending and ever-deepening dialogue with Judaism.

"You cannot underestimate the fear of faith," Yisroel says one day. "Faith makes fools of us all. After all, perhaps there is no God."

I am surprised to hear him say this.

"When I was a kid of eight or so," Yisroel continues, "I read the Great Pumpkin story from *Peanuts*, and I said to myself, 'This is just like the story of the Messiah: it's just another Great Pumpkin story.'"

Yisroel goes on to tell me that he often wonders what life would be like without the restrictions of Orthodoxy. In fact, he says, he believes that one day he will see for himself: one Shabbos he'll roar off on a jet to a remote destination with his family and live for a time on the other side. As he continues to talk, I think that even if he feels this is a rebellion he may make one day, his experiment, in the end, would not lead him away from Yiddishkeit, but rather, back with renewed commitment.

Yisroel tells me he believes that the path to Yiddishkeit is nothing less than a search for the self. Even among those born into religious families, he says, the end is the same: self-discovery. This seems very different from the model one expects from a frum person, but then, Yisroel is an iconoclast who likes provocative ideas.

"I believe that the Messiah will come," he says, surprising me again. I wonder how he means this, whether he believes that the Temple will be rebuilt and sacrifice reinstituted. I ask him.

"I think that everyone has a Messiah," he says. "Perhaps it is growth or change or salvation. It's your job to discover it, but the Talmud does say that your own life comes first."

"Who is your Messiah?" I ask.

"For me," says Yisroel, "the Messiah is the other. In a relationship with a mate or a rabbi or friend, one can find oneself and one's beliefs. And even God."

"All you need," adds Yisroel, "is desire."

Chapter Eleven

✺

LETTERS FROM ISRAEL

I AWAKEN TO THE SUN streaming in the window of my bedroom. It is November 1994, and my gaze follows its customary morning route to the window boxes of blue and yellow violas, over the ailanthus tree and up to a gargoyle that sits atop a nearby apartment building. It was many mornings before I realized that the ornamental fixture on the corner of the building was a rooster, tail plumed, facing the rising sun. Now, it has become my touchstone, the charm I seek every time I look out the window.

I fix on the rooster for a few sleepy seconds, then my eyes fall to my desk, to the ivory box, the computer that pulses at me, humming with its readiness to connect to the world. In the last month, this machine has been completely transformed for me, from a passive recipient of my thoughts and words, to a connection to the world. I throw off the covers, step to the computer, and turn it on.

A few months ago, in the course of reporting a magazine story about computer hackers, I was told that the best hacker in the world lives in Israel. This was not, I was told, a hacker who searched for credit card numbers or telephone codes. He traveled through computers around the world to learn how they worked. He is mysterious, quiet, different from the other hackers, and far more sophisticated. He leaves no prints in the sand. I was intrigued, and immediately thought I might like to write about him. I was given the young man's handle and the address of an American Internet access provider through which I could contact him. After a few weeks, I sent off a note, introducing myself and asking the hacker if he'd be interested in having someone write a story about him. I promised I would conceal his identity if that were necessary.

His first note to me was formal, cordial, and noncommittal, in almost perfect English, and signed "Jonathan." I was surprised to get a reply at all, as I had been warned that this fellow was quite reclusive. Further, I didn't expect to receive a reply in such fluent English, nor did I think I would receive a note signed with a name. I saw from Jonathan's return address that he wrote from a computer at an Israeli university.

It was a few days before I heard from him again. His tone was personal; engaging but reserved. I liked his modesty, or was it false modesty that caused him to refuse the title of best hacker in the world? He replied again enigmatically, never answering my question, but nevertheless advancing our conversation. In a week or so, we were exchanging letters daily. Jonathan told me that he was born in the former Soviet Union, in Latvia. When he was eleven or twelve, his family moved from the Baltics to a southern republic, Azerbaijan, where his father ran the first factory in the USSR to manufacture Marlboro cigarettes. In 1989, just before the fall of Communism, they left for Israel. Jonathan's mother is a mathematician, and when they first arrived in Israel, they lived in Herzliyah. He worked on a computer degree and then served in the Army in the paratroopers. Now he is biding his time taking classes in ancient Greek history and languages.

Our computer conversations wander here and there. He tells me he is looking forward to an exhibition of van Gogh paintings that is scheduled to open in Jerusalem, and says he very much likes *Night Café*. He seems to have an active social life, which is unusual for a hacker, and he tells me that he has a horse.

How is it possible that I have stumbled upon a character who seems to have popped from my own skull? He is a soldier-scholar, like my fantasy of Israelis: brave, clever, disciplined. I admire their derring-do, not only in building a nation from the desert, but also for the cleverness with which they continue to outsmart their hostile neighbors. My childhood dream was to be a surgeon in the Israeli Army, to connect myself with a world of people of mind as well as action.

But further, Jonathan likes van Gogh and Greek myths and literature. He has a horse. But then again, he is a hacker. Could he be making himself up? Could he somehow be inside my computer, prowling around through my life and my thoughts, constructing a character with the use of my own notes?

Our writing becomes affectionate, flirtatious. Once, when I begin a note "Jonathan, dear," he replies: "I wonder why did I turn all red when I read only this line!" Not long after, he asks, "Am I of interest to you only as a story?"

At the Metropolitan Museum of Art, I buy a postcard of the Jean-León Gérôme painting *Pygmalion and Galatea*, based on the Greek myth of a Cypriot king who falls in love with his ivory sculpture of a woman that Aphrodite brings to life. I set it before my computer.

* * *

IN A FEW WEEKS, it becomes clear that Jonathan does not want an article written about him. By then, I don't really care. The intensity of our correspondence is heady and absorbing. Perhaps the combination of almost instantaneous responses with the complete lack of physical or sensual information about the person on the other end of the line has the effect of engaging the imagination so vividly. Everything I don't know about him I invent, and invent, I do, until I have indeed constructed my own (male) Galatea.

Finally, I decide I want to see who Jonathan really is and I decide to go to Israel. I have been wanting for a long time to visit the country, and Jonathan offers a good excuse. When I write him a note to say I am thinking of visiting during the winter holidays, he says he'd love to meet me, but he also mentions that he will be busy in school. Over the following weeks, however, his letters become more and more ambiguous, until, the day before I am to depart, he lets me know that he will not see me, that in spite of everything, he doesn't really know for sure who I am, can't really assure himself that I am not an FBI agent.

At first, I am stunned. For reasons I do not understand, our communications that last day are disrupted by computer failures and odd disconnections. I don't know if it is colossal bad luck or perhaps Jonathan's powerful hand behind the scenes. I am disappointed, but I remind myself that he is a hacker, that he spends his time getting into places he doesn't belong. I wonder if he is dangerously paranoid, until my sister suggests it is probably not uncommon for FBI agents to pose as journalists. How could he know who I was, really? she asks.

But still, our messages had become so intimate, it is hard to understand his decision. I feel that I have in a sense been hacked by him. And as I prepare for my trip, I come up with an idea about how to hack him back. I will take the few facts he told me about himself—facts that may or not be true, but which are checkable—and I will track them down, and try to find out whether a person actually exists at the end of the trail. Conceivably, he could be several people writing to me, or a girl, or an old man.

It's an adventure, a mystery, made all the sexier, in my mind, because it is going to take place in Israel.

RUCHAMA SAYS TO ME: "Whatever happens with the guy, he got you to Israel. You've said for a long time that you wanted to go, but I wasn't sure it would ever happen. Then along he comes, and you're going."

ON THE AIRPLANE, I sit beside a barrel-chested man of about fifty years with handsome, even features, wearing a knitted yarmulke, the sign of a modern Orthodox, or observant Zionist. I am intrigued by him; his very bearing symbolizes all that excites me about Israel—the promise of a fruitful embrace of the contemporary and the ancient, the active and the thoughtful, the body and the mind.

I am tongue-tied, however, and can't speak to him. He gets up from his seat just before the meal is served, and a half hour later, when the airline attendant threatens to take his food away, I ask her to leave it for him. When he returns to his seat, he says, "So, you were looking out for me."

I smile. He asks me why I am visiting Israel. I tell him I have long wanted to visit and am going to see some relatives I have never met. After a while, I tell him the story of the hacker. He listens, amused. Then he tells me he is a professor of computer science at Tel Aviv University, and I burst out laughing.

"Well, you have no idea if any of what this boy told you is true," he says. "You know these characters like to make up stories about themselves, make themselves feel good by becoming someone else."

I nod.

"You know his name?"

I tell him I know only his first name and his initials. But I have a few facts, perhaps not true, but facts. For example, he says he keeps a horse at Mishmar Ha'Negev. I ask him if he has ever heard of the place.

"Of course," he says. "It is about fifteen miles north of Be'er Shevah on the way to Tel Aviv. I have a friend who lives in Tel Aviv who keeps a horse at a moshav, or farm. He rides it once a week, and they take care of it for him, and let other people ride it. That's entirely plausible, what he says."

I explain that the young man grew up in the former Soviet Union, and though he became a paratrooper, he told me he was insulted that because he was born in a hostile country he would never be accepted into Mossad. This seemed to upset him a great deal. The professor looks interested, then says, "Perhaps he is a spy, a double agent. How do you know?"

I nod. He says, "This is exciting. It's an interesting trip. I wish you the best of luck."

I thank him.

"Start with the horse," he says.

He hands me his card. "And if you get in trouble, call me."

BEFORE I BEGIN MY SEARCH for Jonathan, I settle in with Bracha and Yossef Aroch, grandparents of a friend from New York who have an extra room to rent in their Jerusalem apartment. Bracha and Yossef instantly become substitute grandparents for me. I drive Yossef around town to shop in the open-air markets, where he greets everyone by name. He knows so many people, including Knesset ministers and other officials, because before retiring he was their tailor. "I made a lot of pants," he tells me, smiling broadly. He loves food and enjoys picking the best items from mounds of displays: oranges, kiwis, herring, lamb, salami, and particularly bourekas, a Middle Eastern pastry. Bracha is sweet and kind and soft and seems still to be in love with her husband in the way a young woman would be, though they are both in their seventies.

I fall in love with Israel instantly. I feel intimate with everybody, even the crazy drivers on the roads with whom, having learned to drive in Boston, I share the habit of ignoring most traffic regulations. Because of my ties with the Bermans, I am invited for Shabbat with religious families in Har Nof and the Old City, most of whom are transplanted Americans. I stay in apartments carved out of what seem to be original structures of the Old City, and I visit large, sunny homes in the new religious communities that are sprouting all over the Jerusalem Hills. I meet young boys who, at age seven, have memorized the entire Torah in Hebrew, and I stay with ba'alei-teshuvah who spent the greater part of their lives in ashrams in Vermont and now make statements like, "We expect different things of our son and our daughter." I am struck by the observation of an Israeli that, even in Israel, the religious live in galut.

I find myself increasingly drawn to the secular men and women who fight Israel's battles in the Army and create her future in the universities, in the arts, and in the business world. It is the living Israel and the archaeological Israel—and their interaction—that speak to me.

I am in Israel on Christmas Day, and I revel in the quiet of it, in the absence of piped-in Christmas carols and the competitive, commercialized revelry that has become December in New York City. Instead, I visit the Shrine of the Book, which houses most of the

Qumran scrolls, ancient Jewish manuscripts dating from the Hellenic-Roman Period that were found by Bedouins in eleven caves near the Dead Sea. The fantastic building holding the scrolls is reminiscent of the shape of one of the pottery vessels in which the manuscripts were found. Inside, it is dark, quiet, mostly belowground. Displayed in a clear plastic case that runs around the museum hall is a two-thousand-year-old copy of the Book of the Prophet Isaiah. Its letters are small and extraordinarily neat, and the parchment pages are sewn together in perfectly even stitches. The text is almost exactly the same as that which has been handed down to us, attaching, physically, forcefully, the words with the land and the people and their belief.

I find a guide, Moshe Dan, who specializes in showing how the passages of the Bible conform precisely with the present-day geography of the Holy Land. He takes me on a walking tour in which we follow the steps of David and Saul, Jonathan and Ruth, Elimelech, Naomi, Boaz, and Samuel throughout their biblical journeys. The towns of Schem, Mamre, and Hebron are exactly as they are described, as is the spring of Gihon, where kings were anointed. In Hebron, my car breaks down and we hitchhike back to Jerusalem with a chicken farmer and his Palestinian partner, but not before we see the biblically significant sites of the city and visit the famous pistol-packing Rabbi Levinger, a radical who fervently believes the Jews should maintain a presence in the city where Abraham and Sarah are buried. We also visit the restored Avram Avinu Synagogue, built in 1540 and destroyed in 1929 during an Arab revolt, when it was desecrated and turned into a public lavatory. I open the doors of the Ark and peek at the beautifully dressed scrolls and admire the peaceful sanctity that has returned to this place. As we walk through the Israeli section of town, which is heavily guarded by Army troops in the streets and atop buildings, Moshe quietly shows me that he carries a pistol tucked into his own belt. A former American academic, he has, over the years of his life in Israel, become something of a right-winger himself.

I visit the bustling city of Efrat, whose Rabbi Riskin was once the rabbi of Lincoln Square Synagogue on the Upper West Side. I am amazed that many of the towns the media refers to as "settlements"—conjuring images of trailers and tents in the wilderness—are in fact solid, prosperous, modern towns with stylish, well-made houses. I spend the day with a well-known activist, mother of four, who is fighting Arab attempts to limit expansion of the town. I read her propaganda and try to step into her shoes. I ride up to the top of a disputed hill with her, where Israeli soldiers guard a checkpoint, and I think of the Navajo and Hopi reservations and the "bros" guarding the survival camp. I also note her friendship with the elderly Arab man who rides a donkey to his olive grove just behind her backyard, and I think of the Hopi woman who tended her garden on land just adjacent to Ella Bedonie's parents. Though the tribes were waging battles against one another, the individuals maintained their friendship. How do these paradoxes affect the movement of history, I wonder.

During the course of my visit, I meet peaceniks, and I also meet religious Israelis who don't believe Israel should relinquish a single inch of its precious land. Although some of their views on the Arabs appall me, I too share a tribal emotional pain at the thought of giving away any part of the land over which our ancestors trod, and whose stories are recorded in our holy book. But I understand, from my work with the Navajos and Hopis, that compromise is inevitable.

I meet religious women who are trying to fashion a form of Judaism that allows them to study and learn and participate in the world of Torah on an equal basis with men but still remain faithful to halachah. I enjoy Shabbat lunch in the Old City apartment of one of these women, who runs courses over the Internet, and am moved and intrigued by her faith, learning, and independence.

I am thrilled to be surrounded by Jews. It is like a constant carnival, a celebration. I feel that everyone is a relative, the kind of relatives you'd like to have: expressive, interesting, engaged. In fact, I meet real relatives on my father's side who welcome me into their homes in Tel Aviv and Jerusalem and serve me great banquets of food. Israeli homes are overflowing with the bounty of the land, and no living room is complete without a huge bowl of fresh fruit. My friend Ruchama once told me that vegetables and fruits taste better in the Holy Land, and I am hard-pressed to argue.

I meet rabbis and rogues and holy men. In a little business-reporting foray, I meet Israeli entrepreneurs engaged in the high-tech field. I also spend many days in the Old City, visiting museums and the tunnels beneath the Wall. In Bethlehem, I pray for Ruchama, who is pregnant, at the Tomb of Rochel, and I stand beside Arab peasant women wailing and keening before the crypt. I visit the Sea of Galilee and hike over the Golan Heights. I visit Masada and walk into the hills near the Dead Sea with a Haredi couple and their children. The wife never mentions her husband's name in public—refers to him instead as "my husband" because, she says, his name is so intimate to her she doesn't want to share it with anyone else. I visit an Israeli physicist in Tel Aviv who once worked with my father, and have Shabbat dinner with her family and the family of her daughter's boyfriend, who are celebrating their son's certification as a helicopter pilot in the Army. It is there I feel a deep tie. The young couple, Ayelet and Offer—both names mean "deer" in Hebrew—are beautiful, sexy, brave, and smart. They are in the Army now, and their parents, just winding up their own reserve duty, are engaged in the country and the world as teachers, scientists, intellectuals, business-men. The family, though not religious, gathers for a traditional Shab-bat meal, full of laughter, talk, jokes, stories.

I find it poignant—and painful—that as I visit the Israel Museum, and examine Torahs saved from various expulsions and upheavals, all around me I hear people speaking German. And then, at the Kotel, as I watch religious men wash their hands in the basins set up on the plaza, I hear the muezzin call Muslims to prayer at the Dome of the Rock built on the old Temple Mount, several hundred yards away, and it occurs to me that tolerance and mutual respect are the only virtues valuable here. Jerusalem is so old, and revered by so many that, as I hear time and again, every rock in it is sacred to some-body.

That same day, after I buy a silver menorah for my sister, I hear that an Arab terrorist blew himself up in a bus on Jaffo Street, the same street on which I earlier made my purchases. Some things never change. Bracha asks me, "You want I should make you a shid-duch?" She looks at me quizzically, and I see doubts pass over her face. "He's rich."

THE LANDSCAPE OUTSIDE of Jerusalem is a mix of old world and new; first the modern white apartment complexes growing like lichen over the Jerusalem Hills, and then farther on into the country, stands of sycamores bordering the roadsides that conjure Giverny more than the Middle East. It is surprisingly lush, with tranquil rolling hills and patchworks of rich black cultivated fields with skins of budding winter crops.

Mishmar Ha'Negev is exactly where the computer scientist said it would be and is marked by a large sign on the highway. I turn onto a paved road that meanders past a charming group of small houses covered with climbing red roses. I continue on into a compound with the rattletrap feel of a working family farm.

I find someone who speaks English and tell him that I am looking for whoever is in charge of the horses. The young man, a Canadian, tells me that would be Shimon Levy, who is out for a few minutes. The young man brings me into the kibbutz dining room and offers me coffee or tea. He tells me that he made aliyah a few years earlier and is now in charge of the chicken farm here.

After a few minutes, we walk back to a factory, which he tells me makes Styrofoam products, the kibbutz's main business. As we stand out front, a man rides up on a motor scooter. He has gray unruly hair and a handlebar mustache that hangs over his mouth. He parks the bike and walks into the factory. He is tall, well built, and strides with a casualness that tells me he has great confidence in his effect on his world. He looks quickly in my direction, then away, pretending he doesn't notice. His bearing is so striking that I determine privately that he is Odysseus himself, returning from his travels.

Shimon Levy, the factory chief, wears a plaid lumber shirt, whose tails hang perfectly to show off his strength, his height, his long bowed legs. The Canadian follows him into the factory and speaks with him in Hebrew for a few minutes. Levy listens gravely, shifting his pipe in his mouth. I stand aside; I can understand but a few words. Finally, when the message is over, Shimon turns.

"He'll talk to you in his office," says the Canadian, and I follow Levy back though the factory and into an office cluttered with computers, papers, posters of Israel.

We establish that our best common language is French. He grew up in Marseilles, and since I had visited Paris for ten days before arriving in Israel, my French, fortunately, is in working order.

I tell him my story about the boy I met through e-mail, the boy who decided he didn't want to see me because he feared I might be an FBI agent. I tell him the story of the horse.

"It's a bit of a strange story, I guess," I say to him, suddenly blushing, suddenly aware of how embarrassingly smitten I must seem.

He looks at me for a few moments, then says, "I will tell you what I know.

"There was a Russian man who came to me several years ago. He had a horse that was wild, unbroken, a local horse, a mixed breed. He asked me if I would break this horse to saddle for his son. I did so, and gave it back to him. They took the horse with them to Matar, a village not far from here. Then last year, the father called me and told me his son was going into the Army and would no longer be able to care for the horse—would I like to have it back? I liked the horse, so I took it. This man lives not far from here, and he has a relative who lives on the moshav." Shimon continues, "I can try to find him, see if he has the telephone number of the man who gave me the horse."

He picks up the phone, looks through a directory, dials. No answer.

"Was the man a diplomat?" I ask.

"I don't know, I don't remember," says Shimon, in his matter of fact, no-nonsense voice. "I felt there was something special about this man, because he could have sold the horse and made money from it. But he preferred to have the horse go to someone who knew it—even if it meant he would not make money on it. This suggests a soul," Shimon Levy uses the word "esprit," "that is not common, even for a Russian."

We sit in silence for a few minutes. I am thinking where to turn next, flipping through what I know, what track there is next to follow.

"I feel I have to find him. He is such a mystery to me," I say, feeling I must justify why I came all the way here, why I am using up Shimon Levy's time. "Is he the person I met, and wrote to for months? Or was it all lies, confabulations? And if so, who is the character who is such a good storyteller? Does he really love van Gogh?" I tell Levy that when I was in Paris, I purchased a couple of reproductions of van Gogh's paintings, and I hoped to leave them for Jonathan, even if I never saw him, as a sign that I had found him.

"I had a correspondence once," Levy says to me, shifting his pipe in his mouth. He inhales and I hear a rasping, as if he had asthma or emphysema.

"I once met a girl who knew a lot about music. I loved her and decided I had to learn about music so I could talk with her about it. So I bought records; I bought Debussy and Chopin, Tchaikovsky. I listened to these records until I felt I understood them, and we wrote to each other about it. I learned a lot about music from her. Your story of the paintings reminds me of this."

I look up into Shimon's face. I wonder what message he is trying to convey. We seem to have run out of things to say, so I ask him if he'll show me the horses.

"So what happened with the girl who loved music?" I ask as we walk out.

"Oh, that ended when I was twenty and made the decision to come to Israel," he says, shrugging. We go over to the stable in my car, and he walks up to a small bay mare in the second stall. "This is Livna," he says, giving her a pat on the nose.

"She's small," I say. "Barely fifteen hands." Jonathan said his horse was a long-legged black gelding.

"Yes, and she has short steps," says Shimon. "She's also three months pregnant."

"This horse would be very small for a boy who is over six feet tall," I say. "Have you ever seen the boy?"

"No, I never met him. I simply broke the horse, the father took it away, and then they brought it back." Shimon walks down the line of horses and he tells me a bit about each one.

"This is my horse," he says, pointing out a bay Arabian stallion. "I also owned his father, who died. I loved that horse, loved him more than a friend." Beyond the stalls, toward the west, I see the pasture stretching up toward more cultivated hills.

"Is this where you ride?" I ask. "Do you just go off that way?"

Shimon nods.

"This is your little piece of paradise here, isn't it?" I say. The warm breeze has blown over the smell of citrus trees.

"Do you know the story by John Steinbeck," he asks, "called *The Pastures of Heaven?*" I shake my head. I don't recognize the title.

"Well, these are mine," he says, extending his arms over the field, adjusting the pipe in his mouth, his breath labored.

We stand looking over the ancient, neat fields, marked off by field-stone walls, and I think of the phantom, Jonathan, who has brought me here and whose presence hovers over this beautiful place. And then I think perhaps I have found a perfect end to my story. In Shimon Levy, I have found a soul who conforms with my own fantasy of what Israel is all about. With his natural talent and self-taught engineering acumen, he has created the kibbutz's primary business. He quotes from American literature and has told me that he helps handicapped children to ride the horses that he loves. It is he who has an "esprit" that is unusual. We get into the car and I drive back to the factory.

"Please call me if you come to New York," I say.

"I promise you that I will," he says, and we shake hands. He climbs out and shuts the door. I watch him walk into the factory, and I drive away, back across the pastel, cultivated fields and through the great old weeping sycamore stands.

* * *

WHEN I RETURN TO JERUSALEM, I call the Russian man who bought the horse for his son. He speaks no English, so Bracha talks to him for me. After she hangs up, she says, "The boy is in an elite unit in the Army and he's eighteen years old." This makes it unlikely to be Jonathan, who has had time to e-mail me for the past few months, and who, it appears, must be older. The next day, just after I leave the house, Shimon Levy calls with another name, but by the time I return, I have already visited the university from whose computers Jonathan sent his e-mails. At the computer center, one employee says, gesturing in the air, "The man thinks like a computer. Even when he explains to us what he does, we can't understand it."

Oddly, as soon as I arrive, one of the computer center's main routers goes down, so, although I am very close to Jonathan, I cannot send a message. One of the men who works in the center decides to take me under his wing and show me around the campus, preventing me from scouting around by myself. I sense he is strangely protective of the hacker, whom he says now helps the university protect its system from intruders. Although I am given Jonathan's telephone number, I decide I will not call. Instead, I leave a note and some van Gogh prints from the Louvre—these are my own prints in the sand. I am disappointed that I will not see him, but I have come to the end of the line. I have established that he exists. I learn his full name. At that point, I have hacked him back, and I call a draw to the game.

The intense interest that drew me to seek him out and with which I conducted my search has colored my stay in Israel, made it a mesmerizing place. I meet David Bar-Ilan, executive editor of the *Jerusalem Post,* and later press spokesman for Benjamin Netanyahu.

Although I am quite sure I will never know enough to report for an Israeli paper, even one that is published in English, I wonder, however, about an American paper or magazine. I would love the chance to come back for an extended time.

In addition to the new friends I make and the vivid impressions I take back with me, I leave Israel with the paradoxical conclusion that, for the first time, I can imagine having a husband and a family. Here, marriage seems the fulfillment of a promise, not an affliction, not a giving up. It is a place where parents and children have a joint purpose, where they work side by side to build a nation, worship the same God, fight side by side in the same Army. For the first time in years, I feel very young, filled up with life, truly hopeful of the possibility of union—of spirit, life, destiny.

WHEN I RETURN TO NEW YORK, I plunge with renewed enthusiasm into my work and studies. I do not write to Jonathan, but see my rich, embracing trip to Israel as a touching conclusion to that flirtation. As Ruchama said, if the relationship had amounted to nothing else, it had got me to Israel.

One day, several months after my return, I see on television that there has been a new terrorist attack on Israelis, this one at a bus station frequented by soldiers on their way home. I see pictures of soldiers with red berets crying and holding the torn, bombed clothing of their dead comrades, and I am suddenly stirred again by thoughts of Jonathan. This was the unit to which he told me he belonged. So I write him a short note to see if he is OK.

To my surprise, he writes back promptly and berates himself for not seeing me when I was in Israel. Our correspondence resumes and quickly regains its intensity until July 1995, when Jonathan arrives in the United States with a green card. He stays with relatives in Baltimore, and after a couple of weeks comes to visit me in New York. He is tall, six feet four, handsome, brown eyes, curly hair, and the sexiest voice I have ever heard. He looks like he could be one of my father's graduate students. My mother says, when she meets him for the first time, that he looks like a relative.

In two weeks, he moves into my apartment and gets a job on Wall Street. I learn that his hesitation about seeing me in Israel was primarily a symptom of his youth. He is quite a bit younger than I am. Although obsessed by hacking, he was also deeply concerned about its illegality and conflicted about the dubious relation with authority in which it put him. When he arrives here, he renounces hacking completely and dissociates himself from the characters he knew in that world. He tells me that for the first time in his life he feels free to define himself positively rather than in opposition to something he doesn't want to be.

"I couldn't be myself in the Soviet Union," he says, "because I was a Jew. I couldn't be myself in Israel because I was a Russian. But in New York, no one sees me as anything but what I am. Here I can be myself."

One day, as I am showing him around the city, we pass the huge sculpture of an old man bent over a sewing machine, a memorial to the Jewish immigrants who labored in the garment trades. It is snowing, and as we look at the sad giant, Jonathan reaches over and brushes the slushy snow off the man's head and shoulders.

One year later, in Paris, Jonathan asks me to marry him. In September 1997, we are married in an Orthodox ceremony officiated by Rabbi Daniel Berman, Rabbi Meir Fund, and Rabbi Yerachmiel Fried of Dallas. Although Jonathan's childhood in the Soviet Union included no religious education, and he chose to undergo a brit milah at age fifteen after he arrived in Israel, the only religious denomination he knows is Orthodoxy, which dominates the scene in

Israel. He could not imagine being married by anyone but an Orthodox rabbi, and I am not opposed to an Orthodox ceremony, especially one conducted by my teachers. So we dance, men and women separately, to a klezmer band, and we eat gourmet glatt kosher food. I make a quietly feminist statement by asking my friend Ruchama to make some comments under the chuppah, and Meir Fund sings and plays his guitar. On a small table under the wedding canopy, I place old nickel Shabbos candlesticks brought over on the boat from Lithuania by my grandmother's mother, and my namesake, Minnie Rosenberg. I wear my mother's embroidered wedding veil, bought in Paris many years ago. At Jonathan's and my aufruf at B'nai Jeshurun — another nod to modernity, for in the Orthodox community, Jonathan would do this alone — the occasion of our receiving an aliyah on the Saturday before our wedding (and the occasion of my being called, for the first time, to the Torah by my real Hebrew name), my father and sister weep convulsively as the members sing and dance around us, holding a tallit over our heads.

And it is here that the stories I live and the stories I tell come together. And I begin a new work, in which I am neither the only character nor the only storyteller.

Chapter Twelve

∞

WHAT NEXT?

ELLA BEDONIE'S MOTHER BESSIE HATATHLIE, a traditional Navajo woman, was bothered by something she saw while visiting her daughter in college. "How can you have a bathroom inside your home?" she asked Ella, who then lived in married-student housing at Northern Arizona University. "The home is a sacred place and you should not go to the bathroom in it."

This remark amused me, then startled me. For Navajos, the hogan—their traditional igloo-shaped one-room house—is sacred not only because it is the place where they raise their children, but also the place into which they usher their gods. Religious ceremonies are held in the hogan, every piece of which—the entrance poles, the doorway, the ceiling—has religious significance and is built, the Navajos believe, as the gods built their own homes.

I was moved by Bessie's idea of the home as sanctuary, and I couldn't let go of the idea of a place in which the divine is expected. Although modern society has been desacralized to a great extent, there are still numerous remnants that reveal the primordial importance of the experience of the sacred. For example, the doors of synagogues or churches—whose majesty and grandeur can affect even the nonreligious—mark boundaries between the sacred and the profane. The demarcation itself is important, as in the doorways of homes or other buildings that are marked, if not by imposing architecture, then at least by gargoyles or signs (such as the mezuzah on a Jewish home) to invoke divine protection. There are also behaviors characteristic of passing across thresholds: a bow, a touch or shake of a hand, a prostration, traces of notice paid to the spirit guardians of the door. Our celebrations connected with the laying of the cornerstone of a new building are related to ancient practices of blood sacrifices made to animate new constructions.

Although Conservative Judaism, influenced by the work of Abraham Joshua Heschel, focuses on the concept of sacred time rather than sacred space, I was intrigued by the idea of a space into which the divine is welcomed. In Israel, I visited the Cave of Mochpelah in Hebron, the site, it is believed, of the graves of Abraham and Sarah. When I was there, the Squerer rebbe from New York and about twenty followers of his Chassidic sect had not gone inside the monument but rather had gathered on the outside steps. I was told this is where Jews had prayed for the hundreds of years that they had been prevented from entering the building by the Muslims, who controlled it until 1967.

"Were the stairs holy?" I asked. Yes, but by virtue of the fact that so many Jewish prayers had been uttered there. It was the whispered prayers lodged among the rocks and candle drippings that had made the steps holy.

Thinking about sacred spaces, my thoughts wandered to the strange sunken shower in my grandmother's house. Off a downstairs bathroom in this elegant Georgian home in Boston was a mikveh, or ritual bath, used by Orthodox Jewish men and women. Behind a door that at first glance appeared to be a closet, about twenty steps led into a deep, white-tiled shower stall.

As children, my sister and I dreamed of filling the mikveh with water and swimming in it; we could have done somersaults and never touched bottom. But we were not allowed. Even though my grandmother had never used this ritual bath (it had been built by the previous owners), there was a nonnegotiable rule that this room was not to be used for fun and games.

For forty years, the mikveh went unused. The green paint above the tiles faded and flaked; moisture spots grew until they were the size of balloons. The tiles on the steps became loose. But every time I visited my grandmother, from my earliest childhood until the house was sold, I opened the door and looked in. I didn't know why I was compelled to inhale the familiar mustiness, let the mysterious feelings wash over me. Sometimes I closed the door behind me and called out; I heard the echo of my own voice.

I knew that a woman dipped in the mikveh to restore ritual purity at some point after the completion of her menstrual cycle and before physically rejoining her husband. And I knew that some religious men dipped in the mikveh before the Sabbath. But it wasn't until I returned to New York that I learned more. While accompanying Ruchama to the mikveh (where she dipped some new cooking vessels in a separate chamber to make them kosher), she told me about the ritual of immersion. First, she cleaned herself thoroughly—between her toes, under every nail, behind her ears, in the holes of her pierced ears. She even removed her nail polish. In the course of this methodical cleaning, she had an opportunity to think about the last month, to take an accounting of things, to observe changes. As she inspected her hands, arms, and legs, memories of the last month's joys and pains, desires and failures, came to mind. The scrutiny of her body offered an opportunity for the examination of her soul, and the body's cleansing offered her a parallel opportunity to renew her spiritual intentions.

There was excitement and anticipation involved as well, as her trip to the mikveh marked the end of the two-week period in which Orthodox husbands and wives refrain from touching each other and sleep in separate beds. Married women say that when they return to their husbands after the mikveh, they feel like brides once again, full of hope and expectation, and that this mandated separation serves to keep excitement alive in a long marriage. Of course, it is in the time just after immersion that the woman's fertility is highest and conception most likely; it is part of the sacred marriage bond that children begin to grow after a time the mother has prepared herself for a meeting with the divine.

It also occurred to me, as I glanced into the changing rooms and saw piles of fluffy white towels, Q-tips, and other cosmetic items, that although this was a private ablution, the women here were sharing a ritual not only with their forebears—mothers and grandmothers—but also with the entire fabric of religiously observant women. Bessie Hatathlie had a puberty rite as a girl, during which time she was "molded" into a woman in the pattern that First Woman was molded at the beginning of time by Changing Woman, a Navajo god. Her daughters and granddaughters had similar rites, during which they were given instruction by one of their elder female relatives. What rituals did I have? Graduating from college? A daily run? A book tour? In my family, like many other families of modern, assimilated

Jews, ritual is considered primitive, a throwback. Further, some people find the custom of the mikveh offensive; the idea that a menstruating woman is unclean seems primitive to us. Although I had never dipped in a ritual bath at the time I last saw my grandmother's mikveh (traditionally, it is used only by married women), I rather liked the idea of it. I don't think of it as cleansing impurity, but rather as an opportunity to prepare oneself for a meeting with the divine, a meeting with oneself.

Ritual, something you do over and over, links you with those who came before; you understand it and them a bit more each time. Modern life has eliminated ritual in favor of ideas or symbols. When we were growing up, our holy place was no longer the synagogue or the mikveh, but the university. Learning was sacred for us, but I could see it lacked one great thing: the animating presence of the "other"—the divine. There is no question that people need and seek out rituals. They calm us, they gratify us, they may repeat old stories, both pleasant and unpleasant, while we indulge in the unconscious wish of altering their endings. Rituals anchor us, help us recalibrate our internal compasses. I think religious rituals serve a similar purpose. They make belief manifest in one's daily life, for isn't ritual the active repetition of our sacred stories?

I was never sure if the mikveh in my grandmother's house was real, that is, built according to the laws set forth in the Torah, as I never knew those rules until recently. I learned that the chamber could not be filled with tap water alone; the contents were required to circulate with rainwater collected in another chamber. But I remembered a shower faucet in the wall of the sunken room. Could it just have been a fancy shower?

My grandmother was ill by the time I returned to her house to examine the room closely. I opened the door and walked down the mikveh's steps, unhappily dislodging some tiles from the drying grout. At the very bottom, I peered at the wall: there was indeed a crude hole that twisted into a cement passage. Now what was behind there? I hurried up the steps and across the hall, down the stairway to the finished basement, then into the cellar and toward the laundry room, to the place I calculated to be beneath the mikveh. There I found a tall cement-block wall. I dragged over a chair, grabbed hold of the top of the wall and pulled myself over it. Inside, beneath me, like an open sarcophagus, was a concrete cistern. A network of pipes leading out the side of the house suggested that rainwater may have been collected in the backyard and piped in here, where it could then flow through the wall into the mikveh.

Hanging over the top of the raw cement-block wall, looking into the smooth, ancient lines of the cistern, I wondered why it had been blocked off. No one could go in to clean it this way or fix the pipes. Had my grandparents done it when they moved in as a sign that this was a ritual they had outgrown? Or, conversely, had their predecessors walled it up when they learned the new owners would not use it? Was there some effort made to protect the insides of this sacred chamber from uncomprehending or hostile eyes?

I climbed back upstairs, imagining the former lady of the house taking a trip down the elegant upstairs stairway, all clean from her bath, and then down the steps of the mikveh. Who was she? Did she have children who had been conceived after those trips? When I got back to my grandmother's room, I told her I had been looking at the mikveh and her eyes lit up. Though she had been quite unresponsive for days, she smiled. I wondered why that place excited her, that place she never used.

I realized what I had been searching for every time I closed that mikveh door and listened for my own echo. It wasn't myself I was trying to hear, but rather the splashes and steps of that woman making room for the sacred, performing a ritual that connected her with generations of women before her. I was waiting to hear her voice, their voices, so I could learn what they believed, and even more, what they did. I had no one who could teach me or show me.

The echoes of that place perhaps had something to do with why my grandmother protected it, kept it from frivolous use. Something important happened there, a ritual that held a piece of our imaginations, though it no longer had a place in our lives. Like Marranos—Spanish Jews who converted to Catholicism, yet hundreds of years later still observed secret customs they didn't understand, such as lighting candles on the eve of the Sabbath—my grandmother, in her own benign way, honored a tradition whose purpose she no longer understood.

My grandmother died not long afterward, and her house was sold. Even though I have mementos of her here with me, I was sad to learn that the new owners planned to demolish that mysterious chamber off the downstairs bathroom and turn it into a closet. To them it was a meaningless remnant, a puzzling mechanism of a foreign culture, as bewildering as interior plumbing was to Bessie Hatathlie. And so by all rights it should be for me too. But it is not. I feel a tender wound when I think of that primitive cement cistern, still as a sleeping baby, cracked into pieces, the pipes sold for their copper.

The mikveh is an intimate symbol of faith, the chamber where a woman goes, alone, to prepare herself for the conception of a child, the cardinal act of a small tribe. Jews have built mikvehs for two thousand years wherever they have lived, from Jerusalem to Berlin to the ancient fortress of Masada, while under Roman siege. Ritual immersion is such an important rite that in traditional communities the mikveh is built before the synagogue. Some Soviet Jews, prevented from public worship, built secret mikvehs at great personal risk, in solemn testimony to the unbroken faith that links the generations one to another.

BEFORE MY MARRIAGE TO JONATHAN, and after several weeks spent learning the rules of Taharat Hamishpachah, or the laws of family purity, from Ruchama, I take the subway to Brooklyn, and Ruchama accompanies me to the mikveh. It is plain brick on the outside, modest, indistinguishable from any other building, but inside, it is grand, inviting, spanking new, resembling a Roman bath with sandy-colored square stone walls and vaulted archways. I have already done my preparations at home, bathing for an hour, rubbing away callus and dead skin from my feet, knees, and elbows, trimming my nails. I have brushed and flossed my teeth, washed my hair and poked straight earrings with alcohol through the holes in my pierced ears. I have soaked and scrubbed and wiped every part of my body. And I have removed anything that could keep the waters from completely enveloping me — rings, earrings, dirt.

I learn from Ruchama that I am expected to cut my nails until they are flush with the ends of my fingers. I'm no nail fetishist, but cutting my nails to the quick seems excessive. Furthermore, I cannot abide the idea that the length of my fingernails would be dictated by someone else. I call Rabbi Berman and tell him this requirement bothers me. He says that if it makes the difference between whether or not I go to the mikveh, I can keep my nails a little longer. It doesn't, and if I were pushed, I'd cut them, but I accept the reprieve. I remember Ruchama telling me that the rabbis can help with interpretations of the rules to make life easier. For example, they want to get the husband and wife back together as soon as possible, and can be helpful in certain determinations regarding the duration of the "clean" days following the end of menstruation.

"Sometimes it's good to put your fate in someone else's hands," she says. I just shake my head.

"Why can't you make the decisions yourself?" I ask her. "I don't think I could bring myself to ask someone else's permission in such matters."

"It's a relief to rely on others as well as myself," she says. "It's a relief to have guides. I consider the rabbis—the ones I relate to and respect—as people I'm including in my own spiritual journey. I feel grateful and I feel connected to God's will when I ask a 'shaylah,' a question about halachah. It's a kind of dance, finding my own will within God's will."

I say, "But if the rabbis can alter rules to make life easier, or to facilitate or prevent conception, what other rules can they bend? And then why can't they bend still others? If the rabbi has the power to direct women in these most personal and most consequential of realms, what guidelines do they use? And against whom or what do they measure themselves? And how do they prevent themselves from getting too powerful?"

Ruchama tells me rabbis allow exceptions to rules only within well-established parameters, which are themselves also part of halachah.

"It's well known that the seven days of waiting are subject to extenuating circumstances," she says. "No rabbi could make that up. They make their decisions based on precedents, like in any legal issue. If there were no precedent for a solution, no rabbi would offer it."

Ruchama says she finds halachah "amazing" and regrets that I haven't studied it seriously. "It's stayed remarkably constant despite changing communities, climates, and environments," she says, "yet it's responsive to peoples' needs. Living within it is like learning to write in certain poetic forms. When you write a sonnet, you write it within strict rules. The rules create the beauty and the balance."

Hmm. I do think one finds freedom within limits. However, this discussion leads me to think about some thoughts Rabbi Matalon offered, in one of his classes, about the infallibility of texts. He was discussing the conundrum of what to do with prayers or readings that are illogical, sexist, racist, or otherwise problematical to the modern sensibility. He pointed out that some streams of Judaism have eliminated certain prayers—for example, the morning blessing that thanks God "who hast not made me a woman." Others leave the Hebrew alone and alter the English. Rabbi Matalon indicated that he was not comfortable with changing the Hebrew texts and preferred reciting the Hebrew as it was, and perhaps moderating the English, and thinking of its multiform meanings, "making it part of the dialogue, part of the tension." (For example, the Orthodox interpret the above-mentioned prayer to mean that men thank God for not excluding them from the mitzvot from which women are excused—they thank God for requiring additional responsibilities of them.)

What is ultimately important for the tradition, Rabbi Matalon believes, is maintaining respect for the texts and continuing a dialogue through the generations. He does not believe the texts are sacred by virtue of revelation, however, as does Rabbi Berman, but rather that they are sacred because Jews have died for them and sanctified them by reciting them over the millennia.

Rabbi Matalon pointed out that making mental notes of problems in the texts and mulling them over is a custom attested to by marks in the Torah itself: "In the scroll, there are words in which certain letters are much larger than the others. There are dots over certain others. These are ways in which the tradition indicates there were problems in interpreting the text. Certain legends, stories, and interpretations were attached to those dots and odd letters. At one time, everyone knew what the legends were, but no longer. The only thing that's left is the mark in the text. It's like having an asterisk, but no footnote at the bottom of the page."

In English, he noted, the problem with referring to God as He is easily resolved, referring to God as "You" or alternating between "She" and "He" when reading aloud. In Hebrew, however, it's very difficult because the word for God is masculine. He told us a story: "A little Israeli girl said to her father, 'God is a man,' and her father said, 'Why is God a man?' And the girl thought for a little while and she said, 'because God is a boy's name.'"

He mentioned a solution to this issue that he particularly liked. It took place during a Friday night service at a time when the B'nai Jeshurun congregation routinely recited Psalms in English before singing L'cha Dodi. When they came across the pronoun "He" for God in the prayer book, some people said "He," some "She," some "It," and some "You."

"There was a sort of a chorus," he said, "something that was blurred. And that was magnificent. It conveyed the right thing. It conveyed a cloud."

This, as Rabbi Matalon said, seems to be the kind of praxis that allows moderns not to abandon various problematical prayers, wordings, or ways. But here I am, at the mikveh, following arcane regulations that have been given up by all but 10 percent of the Jewish population, a practice that is not embraced by the Conservative movement. Why am I here? I like the idea of the mikveh, perhaps because of its personal connection through the mikveh in my grandmother's house. Also, in spite of my discomfort asking a rabbi to make decisions for me, I do like the idea of hewing to tradition. I respect the concept of obligation and cringe at the tendency of many to consider religion just another elixir in the quest for self-fulfilment. I realize I feel critical of Jews who don't keep kosher and who don't observe the Sabbath, yet I am one of them. I try to pursue the question "What does God want of me?" as long as the answers don't threaten to force me out of my world.

I think of the definition of "religion" that Dr. Andresen once read to me. It derives from the Latin "religare" which means "to tie back," according to Merriam-Webster's, or "bind fast," from the *Oxford English Dictionary*. Religion offers a binding to the past, to tradition, to God. It offers an avenue for belonging. Ties that bind can also restrict and chafe, yet in the struggle is the challenge, and out of the struggle comes understanding.

I AM USHERED into a beautiful bathroom with spanking tub, mirrors, and shiny stone walls. I take a quick shower just to get wet, and comb my hair until all strands are lying in the same direction. I step into a white terry robe, and after going through the checklist, I ring the buzzer to call the mikveh lady. A young religious woman in a blond sheitel comes to inspect me. She looks over my hands and feet and spots a tiny speck of clear nail polish. She rubs it off with a cotton ball and a bit of nail-polish remover. She asks if I am Sephardic and I say no. Apparently Sephardic women have different rules about nail length. She mentions the longer-than-usual fingernails, and I tell her I got permission from my rabbi. She nods. She touches me with great gentleness, gives me a tender smile, and leads me to another chamber, in which is an angular pool reached by several steps and a stainless steel railing. The woman lifts the robe off my shoulders and I step down the stairs. My body feels very light and free as I step into the water. When I reach the bottom, I turn and look at her for instructions. "Dip in the water, making sure to get your head and all your hair under, and don't cross your legs," she says. "Then stand up." I do so, and she smiles and says, "Kosher!" Then she asks me to recite the brachah written on a chart on the wall. It is printed in Hebrew and English transliteration. I read it aloud, and she motions me to dunk again. The water is pleasantly cool and clear. I come up, blowing bubbles out of my nose, tipping back my head to let the water run off. One more dip, she tells me, and I linger for a few extra seconds underwater thinking to myself a few hopes I have for my marriage. I imagine the words going straight to God through the special water. When I step out, my wet hair plastered to my skull, I am beaming like a little girl.

When I rejoin Ruchama in the waiting room, there is a party of women with baskets of food wrapped in bright cellophane. Ruchama tells me it is a Sephardic custom for family to greet the bride-to-be with nuts and fruits and other delicacies when she emerges from the mikveh. I am moved by the sweetness of this practice, and I imagine my grandmother Lillian here, giggling in childlike delight, as she often did at the sight of something new. Perhaps she would have handed me some almonds that she had roasted and salted, or some of her famous fruit compote, in celebration of the first time she had seen a woman emerge from the mikveh.

AFTER MY FIRST DIP in Brooklyn, I find my way to the mikveh on the Upper West Side of Manhattan. The building is not as grand, but the mikveh lady is Hungarian and has an accent like my father's mother, whose Hebrew name I now know was Hannah. She wears a housecoat and a blond wig and is warm and chatty. The place is homey and easygoing. In every shower is a reminder about breast self-examinations, and tucked discreetly in the corner of the mirrors are numbers for women's shelters and abuse counselors. I feel the place is eminently woman-centered, woman-embracing. Although I am not accustomed to finding myself in such places, I feel comfortable here.

In addition to counting the days for determining when I should dip in the mikveh, I am checking other signs to predict when I might be ovulating, because Jonathan and I would like to have a baby. My trip here tonight marks the intersection of the two methods, ancient and modern, religious and secular. I feel happy and calm, and I have come to love the opportunity for a luxurious bath, which I take at home. (The claw-footed tub in our turn-of-the-century apartment is outrageously long—in fact, as long as I am tall.) Lying in it, completely submerged save an oval around the top of my face, the sounds of pipes echoing in my ears full of water, I think of women in Temple times preparing for the mikveh, scrubbing the sand out of their skin and luxuriating in warm water, probably for the only time they will do so in the month. I imagine them in public baths, pouring water from large pitchers for each other. I find the process of sitting in the hot water for one whole hour an almost obscene luxury, one that affords me time for all kinds of imaginative wandering.

I know I am ovulating today. I imagine an egg inching its way down a Fallopian tube and I try to send good feelings and intentions its way. I know that the word "mikveh" means "hope." I am about to dunk in the rainwater pool, a deliberate act of purification and renewal with which I hope to set a new life off on its fabulous journey toward becoming a human. I would like the baby that might grow from that egg to be full of the knowledge of his or her mother's kavannah, or intention, that it have a successful journey sanctified by the richness of the tradition that its mother is discovering. I hope that the baby will grow to become an adult who knows the animating power of belief.

On Passover, every Jew is commanded to imagine that he or she was present at the exodus from Egypt. None of the slaves who left Egypt actually made it to the promised land, so their astonishing act of rebellion and self-determination benefited not them, but the generations to follow. One seder night, Yisroel Feuerman offered a more mystical interpretation, suggesting that we are commanded to imagine ourselves present at the exodus because we were present in the hopes of our forebears at that time. Our forefathers and foremothers wandered in the desert for forty years to secure freedom for us, souls they could only imagine. And so, I imagine a soul preparing to inhabit the tiny egg making its way through my body. I hope that that person who may emerge will one day assume his or her place among the 600,000 and come to love the remarkable tradition they offered up to the world. I hope he or she will learn to read and speak Hebrew, and therefore have full access to the mysteries of the original texts.

The mikveh lady looks at my hands and feet and turns me around and lifts up my hair to check the back of my neck. I think it's funny she should check these areas, as if I were a worker in the fields. "OK," she says, and lifts the terry robe from my shoulders and holds it in front of her eyes while I step down into the warm water. I dunk and she says "Kosher," and I recite the blessing and dunk twice more. When I am done, I feel like staying in the water and doing somersaults, swimming around slowly underwater like a fish. After hesitating for a moment, I climb back out and up the stairs to the robe the mikveh lady holds out for me. I put on my clothes (one is not supposed to wash off the mikveh water right away), dry my hair, and step out into the cold December air.

The next day, I have an intuition that I have become pregnant when I realize I have been humming "Hinei Mah Tov" all morning. "How good it is when brothers and sisters dwell together in harmony" reads the translation at B'nai Jeshurun. My hunch is correct. On September 24, 1998, between Rosh Hashanah and Yom Kippur, Hannah Shira was born, the spitting image of her father, who came up with her pretty name. He did not know that one of my grandmothers was named Hannah (it is also the name of his maternal grandmother), or that I once was led to think Hannah was my own name. He chose Shira, which means "song," because of the great kindness and generosity shown to us both by Sarah Shira Berman. When he announced to me his idea for names, I agreed right away. I thought Hannah Shira was perfect. The name literally means "gracious song."

I sing in the synagogue choir throughout the holidays, hoping the songs will work their way into the baby's psyche. And perhaps they do. Since her birth, Hannah Shira has always been happy, calm, and absorbed at synagogue.

I return to the mikveh a few months after Hannah Shira is born and tell the mikveh lady of my great good fortune in getting pregnant quickly and having an easy delivery and a beautiful healthy baby. She looks at me and smiles. "I am not surprised," she says in her charming Hungarian accent, "the water here, it is very good."

Notes

❦

One **Blinded**

17 "a syndrome that suggests" to "has been reported": Audrey Stein Goldings, M.D., et al., "Lyme borreliosis in Texas," *Texas Medicine* 87, no. 9 (September 1991): 63.

Two **What Is a Jew?**

23–29 "Ella Bedonie is a full-blooded Navajo Indian" to "I was picking my own way out as well": Parts of this chapter first appeared in slightly different form in Emily Benedek, "'Through the Unknown, Remembered Gate': Stories of a Spiritual Journey," *Southwest Review* 81, no. 1 (Winter 1996): 49–52.

25 "What we find" to "through cosmic life": Mircea Eliade, *The Sacred and the Profane* (New York: Harcourt Brace Jovanovich, 1957), p. 165.

331

Three Exile

70–71 "And I tell him about the lady" to "An angel from God": A variation of this story was broadcast on National Public Radio, *All Things Considered*, April 16, 1996.

Four Learning to See

78 "I had to fight my way" to "a thick fog of indifference": Edith Wharton, *A Backward Glance*, as quoted in Kennedy Fraser, *Ornament and Silence: Essays on Women's Lives* (New York: Alfred A. Knopf, 1996), p. 67.

106–107 "The offerers of sacrifice" to "between the deity or beloved and the offerer": Jeffry J. Andresen, M.D., "The Motif of Sacrifice and the Sacrifice Complex," *Contemporary Psychoanalysis* 20, no. 4 (1984): 526–559.

107 "simultaneously a gift" to "creator of communion": Ibid.

107 "children have the compulsion" to "load of all the others": Sandor Ferenczi, "Confusion of Tongues Between Adults and the Child" (1933), in *Final Contributions to the Problems and Methods of Psycho-Analysis* (London: Hogarth Press, 1955 [1933]), p. 166, as quoted in Andresen, ibid.

117 "ineffable" to "newfound sense of connectedness": David Raft, M.D., and Jeffry J. Andresen, M.D., "Transformations in Self-Understanding After Near-Death Experiences," *Contemporary Psychoanalysis* 22, no. 3 (July 1986): 319–346.

Five First Steps

139–142 "The Hebrew word for man," to "today resides in the bedroom of the husband and wife": This speech was reconstructed with the help of Rabbi Ezriel Tauber, *To Become One: The Torah Outlook on Marriage* (Monsey, N.Y.: Shalheves Publishers, 1990), pp. 44–45.

152–158 "There was a great Torah scholar" to "the life of the person who hears them": Parts of this conversation appeared in different form in Benedek, *Southwest Review*, loc. cit.

159 "something limitless, unbounded, as it were . . . 'oceanic.'" Sig-

mund Freud, "Civilization and Its Discontents," in the Standard Edition, vol. 21 (London: Hogarth Press, 1930), p. 64.

Six The True Lives of Stories

163 "Thou hast hid these things" to "hast revealed them unto babes": As quoted in Leo Tolstoy, *Anna Karenina* (New York: Signet Classics, 1961), p. 498.

169–170 "What we call the beginning is often the end" to "Is that which was the beginning": T. S. Eliot, *Four Quartets* (New York: Harcourt Brace Jovanovich, 1943), pp. 58–59.

Seven Home

201–203 "Last night was different from all other nights" to "I have wandered in the desert, and now I am home": NPR, *Weekend Edition*/Sunday, March 27, 1994.

Nine Congregation B'nai Jeshurun

243 "It is not a temple nor a tree, it is not a statue nor a star": Abraham Joshua Heschel, *Man's Quest for God: Studies in Prayer and Symbolism* (Santa Fe, N.M.: Aurora Press, 1998), p. 124.

265 "majesty tempered with mercy and delicate innocence that is waiting for affection": Abraham Joshua Heschel, *The Sabbath* (New York: Farrar, Straus & Giroux, 1951), p. 61.

268 "The realm of heaven sings" to "composed of four musical notes": Abraham Z. Idelsohn, *Jewish Music in Its Historical Development* (New York: Dover Publications, 1992), p. 414.

Twelve What Next?

314–321 "Ella Bedonie's mother Bessie Hatathlie" to "the unbroken faith that links the generations one to another": This section appeared in slightly different form in Benedek, *Southwest Review*, loc. cit.

Acknowledgments

℮

HEARTFELT THANKS to Susan Ralston, whose energetic interest brought this book to completion, and to Arthur Samuelson who perceived it in me. Thanks also to Dassi Zeidel for her untiring help, Ann Close for editorial advice over the years, and my agent Kris Dahl, ever on my side.

Special, deep thanks to Michael Frank and Jenny McPhee who helped me edit and shape various drafts of the manuscript, and Willard Spiegelman, who commissioned an essay for *Southwest Review* that formed the basis of this book. For twenty years, Jay Levi has inspired me in matters both Indian and Jewish. For that and our long friendship, I am most grateful. I am also grateful to Fred Wasser, who assigned me two pieces for National Public Radio that advanced my thoughts and work. Thanks as well to my parents for their insight and guidance and my sister for her unflagging support.

Many people—in Israel, Texas, Arizona, and New York—offered me their time and hearts and helped me along my way. I would like to thank them and others here: Solange Akselrod, Jeffry J. Andresen, M.D., Bracha and Yossef Aroch, Ella Bedonie, Richard C. Benedek, the Berman Family, Rabbi Menachem Bloch, the Blumenthal family, Rabbi Marcelo Bronstein, Congregation Beth Emunah, Congregation B'nai Jeshurun, Dallas Area Torah Association, Alex Faulkner, Marta Felcman, Ruchama and Yisroel

Feuerman, Rabbi Yerachmiel and Miri Fried, Rabbi Meir Fund, Esther Ginsburg, Rabbi Scholem Groesberg, Daniel Jackson, Rabbi Frank Joseph and family, Rabbi Nancy Kasten, Gary Ledet, Shimon Levy, Rabbi Rolando Matalon, Gwen Mezosi, Ari Priven, Helen Radin, Nancy Simon, Valerie Sobel, and Rabbi Sheldon Zimmerman.

About the Author

EMILY BENEDEK is a graduate of Harvard College and the author of *The Wind Won't Know Me* and *Beyond the Four Corners of the World*. Her articles and essays have appeared in the *New York Times*, the *Washington Post*, *Life*, *Rolling Stone*, *Details*, *Harper's Bazaar*, the *Utne Reader*, and have aired on National Public Radio. She lives in New York City with her husband and their two daughters.